C0-ARD-430

# AN INTEGRATED THEORY
# OF LANGUAGE TEACHING

# AN
# INTEGRATED THEORY
# OF
# LANGUAGE TEACHING
## AND ITS PRACTICAL CONSEQUENCES

HECTOR HAMMERLY
Simon Fraser University

Volume 2 of the Series in Linguistics

*Second Language Publications*
P.O. Box 1700 Blaine,WA. 98230
P.O. Box 82370, N.Burnaby,B.C. Canada V5C 5P8

© 1985 by Hector Marcel Hammerly

ISBN: 0-919950-03-5

Printed in the United States of America

To earlier and contemporary
theorists of language teaching,
in particular to:

Henry Sweet
Harold Palmer
Charles C. Fries
Robert Lado
Robert L. Politzer
Wilga M. Rivers
H. Douglas Brown

## Acknowledgements

A word of thanks to Professor D.R. John Knowles of Simon Fraser University, who read the manuscript of this book and gave me his comments. I am also grateful to my wife Ethel for her help and support. Of course, I assume responsibility for any shortcomings in the printed book.

*"To despise theory is to have the excessively vain pretension to do without knowing what one does, and to speak without knowing what one says."*

*Bernard le B. de Fontenelle*

# Table of Contents

# Preface

The discipline of second language teaching/learning[1] —which following Nelson Brooks I have decided to call simply *languistics*— is very much in need of an integrated theory, for otherwise it will continue to flounder from trend to trend and fad to fad following the "neophilia" so characteristic of North American society.

The lack of an adequate theory affects all our activities. Whole series of books on language teaching are being published, by several publishers, without theories to which the content of the books can be related. What research there is can only be haphazard without an integrated theory to guide it —almost all theories, past and present, have been partial in nature, emphasizing some facts and ignoring the rest.

The pursuit of excellence in the field of languistics is hindered by the confusion and faddism caused by this theoretical vacuum. Nothing is more destructive to stability and excellence in a discipline than frequent, rapid change largely for its own sake. A commitment to excellence means, among other things, refusing to "go with the flow" unless it happens to be flowing in the right direction. But how can people know what the "right direction" is without an adequate, explicit, comprehensive theory?

Even desirable trends suffer from the absence of a theory to anchor them. For example, the emphasis on communication of the last few years seems to be following the path of previous trends: (1) *acceptance* through the untiring zeal of a group of pioneers; (2) *distortion* by many of the "converts" (in this case taking the form "Communication is all that matters"); (3) *reaction* against the trend because of the results of the distortion (in this case linguistic incompetence); and (4) *rejection* of the trend as a whole, leading back to (5) *business as usual*. With an adequate integrated theory to guide research and innovation, balance can be maintained and new emphases need not go through the usual steps of distortion, reaction, and rejection.

Some might say: We know so little that theory building is premature. But we do know enough to build a theory based on empirical evidence to the extent possible and on logical inference for the rest. In any event, no theory is final; theories are subject to modification —even rejection— as additional empirical knowledge develops.

Languistics should benefit from the formulation of an integrated theory such as the one proposed in this book. But while it is hoped that this theory will help organize facts and ideas and guide research, linguistics should not become subservient to this or to any other theory. As I pointed out in *Synthesis in Second Language Teaching*, the applied empirical science of linguistics can only tolerate "the tyranny of what is true and truly works."[2]

This book has three parts: an introduction (chapters 1-3), the presentation of the integrated theory together with certain practical implications (chapters 4-9), and two chapters on practical consequences of the theory (chapters 10 and 11). The introduction discusses the nature of theory and of science (Chapter 1), the theories advanced so far in our field (Chapter 2), and the theoretical and practical implications of one recent approach — immersion— that applies communicationist and acquisitionist concepts (Chapter 3). The integrated theory is presented in terms of general definitions and axioms (Chapter 4), of laws, principles, and hypotheses derived from linguistics (Chapter 5), psychology (Chapter 6), teaching theory (Chapter 7), and other sources (Chapter 8), and of a model of language teaching based on the theory (Chapter 9). The two closing chapters deal with consequences of this theory for teaching (Chapter 10) and with research needs and directions (Chapter 11). There are also three appendices, a bibliography, and an index.

A theory is nothing more nor less than a complex hypothesis, and as such both a theory as a whole and its parts are subject to careful scrutiny and experimental validation. The present theory may prove inadequate in more than one respect. But all in all, I think our profession will be better off with a comprehensive theory of language teaching, even if imperfect, than without any definite theory. The latter guarantees perennial floundering; the former just may open the door to a new wisdom.

### Footnotes

[1]In all my publications **second language** means *any language other than the native language of the learner*, whether spoken right in the community or only in a distant and exotic land.

[2]Preliminary edition, 1982, page 25.

# Introduction

# Chapter 1: On Theory

## Introduction and Summary

*To the extent we can rely on our senses, we can verify many truths; otherwise it wouldn't make much sense to even talk of "knowledge" or "science." A theory, among other things, defines terms and describes, organizes, and predicts facts by means of a set of testable propositions based on empirical (inductive) and/or logical (deductive) evidence. Theories are essential, for no field of endeavor can be considered a science or even a discipline without their organizing principles and guidance. Unlike the "pure" sciences, the applied sciences deal with making things work; with instructional theories, this includes predicting what form(s) of teaching would best induce learning by given learners under given circumstances.*

*The best theory at any point in the development of a science would account for and relate all known facts explained by other theories, going beyond the latter in coverage and/or predictive power. All theories are subject to validation in the furnace of research and practice, a process from which they emerge either purified or as worthless dross.*

## 1.1: Truth, Knowledge, and Science

The "quest for certainty" urged on us by educator and philosopher John Dewey (1859-1953) and others may be an ideal, but that doesn't mean it is fruitless. A belief in the ascertainability of truth begins with reliance on the evidence of our senses. Admittedly, input from our senses can be distorted by strong emotions, sleeplessness, drugs, trickery, and a variety of other factors; but most of the time our senses operate free from distortion —so they *can* be relied upon. We can also rely on instrumental extensions of our senses, from microscopes to telescopes, provided they work properly.

Thus Popper's [1972:60-4] rejection of the "commonsense theory of knowledge," which claims that most of what we learn is ultimately learned through our senses, would leave us without any basis for the pursuit of truth. The statement *"This glass contains water"* is not only *testable*, as even Popper [1959:424] admits, but also *verifiable* in terms of a referent and socially accepted definitions of the words *"this," "glass," "contains,"* and *"water,"* the last of which is also chemically defined. Having tested the content of the glass (if need be), we *can* say that the statement is either "true" or "untrue" in terms of our definitions. (For borderline cases —as when the water is mixed with Scotch or pollutants— we would only modify the statement accordingly.) In the physical realm, truth *is* ascertainable by our senses: *We don't have to just guess; there is much we can know.* Denying this "commonsensical" truth is engaging in epistemological hairsplitting.

While all knowledge is *ultimately* based on the undistorted use of our senses, most knowledge goes far beyond physical facts. In so doing, much "knowledge" loses its factual foundation and ceases to be knowledge, for the original facts (if ever accurately determined) are filtered through interpretations and reinterpretations based largely on the individual experience of the person considering them. Perhaps this is the best reason for not looking upon science as a body of knowledge but as a system of hypotheses [Popper 1959:317, although that is not his reason]: there are verified facts —there is truth— at the bottom, but the superstructure isn't quite solid, for the scientific method is far from perfect.

Science is, therefore, a somewhat uncertain endeavor; but then, certainty would empty science of its meaning, as it would make the sometimes frustrating but always exciting pursuit of knowledge unnecessary. In established sciences, this pursuit of knowledge occurs at the frontiers of the discipline, a basic body of knowledge having been established earlier through trial and error. New disciplines typically show much trial and error, with different investigators describing and interpreting essentially the same facts in different ways [Kuhn 1962:17]. For example, behaviorists and cognitivists refer to essentially the same phenomena as "linguistic habits" or "linguistic rules," respectively. Another example is the analysis of language learners' errors, interpreted as mostly due to interference, overgeneralization, insufficient learning, etc. by researchers with different orientations.

Kuhn [1962:160] says that a field does not become a science until its practitioners "achieve consensus about their past and present accomplishments." This seems to be overstating the case. A science must have a basic body of agreed-upon knowledge; but beyond that, the presence of competing theories makes it no less scientific. Competing theories may even be healthy for the development of a science, provided *free* competition (access to journals, etc.) lets the best theory or synthesis emerge victorious.

A science is not just a collection of statements; it must have points of view and theoretical problems to solve [Popper 1959:106]. A science needs to (1) accumulate accurate data, (2) go beyond the available data to formulate falsifiable theories whose claims *can* be challenged, (3) make inferences and predictions based on those theories, (4) test the theories to verify or reject their hypotheses, and (5) formulate better theories —all of this (6) while using correct methodology. By these criteria, linguistics, with its pell-mell of untested, largely untestable half-theories and permutations of half-theories, is not yet a science but a very confused discipline. (It is hoped the testable, integrated theory presented herein will allow linguistics to become a solid discipline, or even a young science.)

# 1.2: Toward a Definition of Theory

In everyday speech people often refer to the facts they disbelieve as "just theories," when in fact theories are the highest level of knowledge reachable by an empirical science. A theory is far more than a collection of facts, for theories relate facts and put them in perspective. A **theory** may be defined as *a set of propositions that explain and predict observable phenomena*; it is also *an extended definition of a field of knowledge or endeavor.*

A theory should include certain basic assumptions, as definitions and axioms, and a few general principles or laws; these are higher-level propositions which can serve as premises for deriving lower-level propositions, that is, specific principles and hypotheses. The four types of propositions of the theory presented in this book are therefore *definitions/ axioms, laws, principles,* and *hypotheses* (see Figure 1.1).

An **axiom** is *a statement that needs no proof because its truth is obvious and universally accepted,* such as *"Murder is a crime"* or *"First things first."* Axioms are also called "primitive propositions" and "postulates." **Laws** *state highly dependable relationships between variables, relationships considered invariable under specified conditions*; examples are the laws of gravity and of cause and effect. Laws are *higher-level propositions that have passed every test.* **Principles** are *empirically or logically supported statements either less fundamental or dependable than laws; they are lower-level propositions but often provide a basis for further reasoning or a guide to conduct.* Examples of principles are "Teach the three R's" in education and "Specialization increases efficiency" in industrial management. As generally used in science, the term **hypothesis** refers to *any statement about a suspected relationship between variables, whether high or low in level, almost certain or very tentative.* Thus, all propositions that make up a theory, even its axioms and laws are, in that sense, hypotheses. However, *in this book the term* **hypothesis** *will refer only to lowest-level propositions that are tentative and should be the basis for further experimentation.*

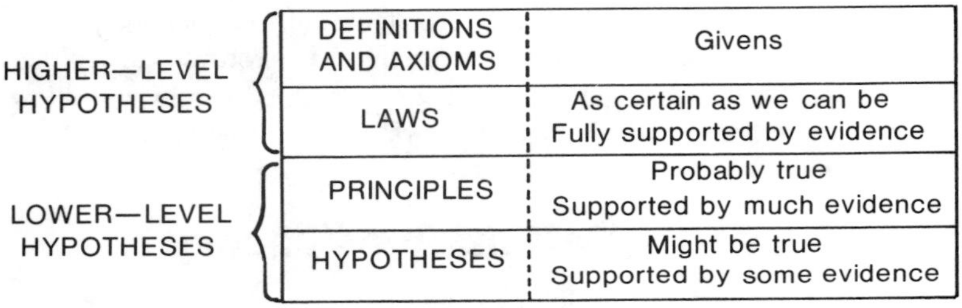

| | | |
|---|---|---|
| HIGHER—LEVEL HYPOTHESES | DEFINITIONS AND AXIOMS | Givens |
| | LAWS | As certain as we can be<br>Fully supported by evidence |
| LOWER—LEVEL HYPOTHESES | PRINCIPLES | Probably true<br>Supported by much evidence |
| | HYPOTHESES | Might be true<br>Supported by some evidence |

Figure 1.1

A good theory defines its concepts precisely, is internally consistent, experimentally testable, and as simple as possible. Unfortunately some theories, for example in linguistics and psychology, are formulated so that many of their fundamental propositions cannot be tested. Making theories impervious to empirical testing is a pernicious practice languists must reject. Untestable hypotheses are nothing but idle speculation. Simplicity in theory formulation is a rather vague but desirable concept; however, so much is still unknown in languistics that we will probably not have very simple theories anytime soon. One criterion for good theories touted in recent years, "elegance," is an extra-logical aesthetic consideration of little epistemological interest [Popper 1959:137].

A theory should (1) define concepts and parameters; (2) explain and relate existing data, harmonizing apparently contradictory results; (3) go beyond the data and predict outcomes by formulating falsifiable hypotheses; (4) guide and shape the direction of research, i.e. the observation, collection, description, and interpretation of further data (of course a *poor* theory can lead to much useless research); and (5) reformulate principles and hypotheses —and thereby the theory— based on the results of research. A languistic theory performing these functions would rescue us from the seemingly endless merry-go-round of fleeting fads and trends and help us build a solid foundation of knowledge.

# 1.3: Approaches to Theory Construction

Theories can originate inductively (on the basis of available empirical data), deductively (in the absence of such data), or through a combination of both approaches. Inductive, *a posteriori* theories are summaries of known facts. Their advantage is that contact is not lost with the facts; their disadvantages are (1) the lack of integration at a high level and (2) inefficiency as lower-level overlapping theories proliferate, asking basically the same questions over and over. Deductive, *a priori* theories precede and/or go beyond empirical observation and lead to corroborative research in a self-correcting process whereby the original educated "guesses" are either confirmed or rejected. The serious disadvantage of deductive theory construction is that, if the theory is largely incorrect, it will lead to much needless research.

Francis Bacon (1561-1626), sometimes referred to as the father of empirical science, favored induction. As inductivists see it, no theory occurs in a vacuum, for there must be at least one sensory observation (usually there is quite a number of such observations) before any theoretical propositions can be made. In their view, theories and empirical observation are inseparable. A theory that disregards empirical observation is meaningless, as only empirical observation can show the strengths and weaknesses of the theory. However, empirical observation unrelated to any theory is *ad hoc* and would seem to be fruitless.

Popper [1959:52-3] rejects the principle of induction as neither necessary nor helpful. He favors the deductive approach where theory is formulated first, then tested empirically. According to him [*Ibid.*:98], in the method of trial and error the trial must come before the error, and theories, which are part of the trial, are weeded out through observation and experimentation showing their errors. For deductivists, even the earliest observations are guided by assumptions, i.e. theories, so that science develops at all times within a "horizon of expectations" provided by theory [Popper 1972:344-7]. Observation is usually focused, so that we can't even observe "in general" but must observe something in particular [*Ibid.*:259]. The logical conclusion of this position is that no science can start free from initial assumptions [*Ibid.*:346].

Sometimes certain facts are predicted by a theory even before there are any observations to corroborate them. This is true, for example, of Einstein's theory of relativity, which he proposed without any awareness of whatever limited evidence existed. Perhaps we should not accept — maybe not even consider— isolated, *ad hoc* statements unrelated to theories; empirical work is significant only in relation to theories. Only theories can open up new domains of observations [*Ibid.*:355], but in order to do that, theories must be reasonably bold, transcend the empirical evidence, and risk being at least partly wrong.

It seems clear that theory construction need not wait until all the facts are in. There is no critical point at which sufficient knowledge has accumulated and which must be reached before theory formulation becomes possible or desirable. The many unresolved questions in our field should not preclude us from proposing theories that account for what we do know and tentatively account for what we do not yet know. If we *do not* propose integrated theories of language teaching/learning, we will continue to see fragmentary, circular, and largely useless linguistic research.

Induction and deduction represent extremes in theory construction. All theorists —whether they want to admit it or not— combine these two approaches by inductively using the "givens" of their sciences and deductively going beyond them to build bolder, more comprehensive theories. It is largely irrelevant whether a theory or hypothesis is proposed before or after empirical evidence becomes available; all that matters is that the theory or hypothesis agree with the evidence. One or a few sensory observations may get the process going, but from then on knowledge increases in terms of a mutual feedback loop involving theoretical insights, more observations, better theories, and so on.

## 1.4: Theories in Various Fields

Loosely speaking, theories in the physical sciences account only for how things are or may be; those in the humanities and social sciences are also concerned with how things may have been, might be, or should be; and theories in the applied sciences concentrate on how to do things, i.e. on ways that *work* under specified conditions. Thus, while statements about what "ought to be" lie outside of "pure" science, applied theories may include recommendations based on what is known to work and what the theories predict will work.

Instructional theories such as the one presented herein should be, to the extent possible, descriptive rather than prescriptive. There is a fine but crucial distinction between the prescriptions of methodologists and the tentative recommendations of instructional theorists: the latter, instead of generating idiosyncratic methodological prescriptions, rely on empirical evidence and logical inference based on such evidence.

Instructional theories differ from learning and linguistic theories in several ways. Perhaps the most significant difference is that learning and linguistic theories must be comprehensive as to the *whys* of learning and language but may be incomplete in their applications, while instructional theories must be comprehensive in their applications but may be incomplete as to why given procedures are effective [Snelbecker 1974:17].

It is more important for language teachers to ensure that something works than to determine why it works, as much as the latter may interest theorists. Consequently, an adequate linguistic theory must be directly concerned with its applications; it should not just explain phenomena but also describe what works and predict what else might work. In other words, linguistic theories must concentrate on the optimization of induced learning under the given conditions of language, teacher, student, and context.

It would seem obvious that, to be relevant and valid, an instructional theory must be developed within the field to which it applies. Yet in our field, language teaching, we have repeatedly been asked to apply theories from other fields such as linguistics, psychology, general education, psycholinguistics, sociolinguistics, and most recently natural language acquisition!

# 1.5: Eclecticism

Eclecticism carries negative connotations, largely because in the past it has been practiced in an unprincipled way, i.e. by haphazardly putting together disparate or even contradictory elements from any and all theories and methodologies. However, it *is* possible to have, both in the development and formulation of theories and in their application, what I have called "enlightened" eclecticism. This is the principled gathering, into a harmonious whole, of the best empirically supported elements from any relevant theories, present or past. Naturally, a new theory —whether eclectic or not— should significantly transcend the findings of existing theories.

The theory of language teaching/learning presented in this book is eclectic in the positive sense of the word. It incorporates the best relevant features from several theories in fields such as education, psychology, and linguistics, integrating them with many original ideas into a comprehensive combination that constitutes a new theory. It would take several pages to list just the names of the theorists, researchers, methodologists, and practitioners whose contributions have helped me elaborate this theory. This is indeed an eclectic theory.[1]

## 1.6: Validation and Application of Theories

No theory is definitive; all are subject to modification or replacement by a better theory on the basis of empirical tests. Only empirically confirmed theories should find widespread application. Chapter 11 discusses research and theory validation.

## 1.7: For Discussion

1. *Is the "quest for certainty" a worthwhile endeavor? Can we rely on our senses in the "quest for certainty"? Can objective truth be determined or is all truth at least partly subjective?*
2. *To what extent is "common-sense" knowledge based on social conventions? In what areas of "knowledge" are we forced to just guess, and why?*
3. *Is science a body of knowledge, a system of hypotheses, or both?*
4. *To what degree is trial and error desirable in linguistics?*
5. *How do you account for very different theories developing from essentially the same facts?*
6. *Is consensus about theory desirable in a science? Is it desirable and is it possible in linguistics?*
7. *What is a science and what does it do? Is linguistics presently a science? If not, why not?*
8. *Explain why theory is important to science. Why aren't facts enough?*
9. *Give your own examples of axioms, laws, principles, and (tentative) hypotheses from any field, including linguistics.*
10. *Give examples of untestable hypotheses from any field, including linguistics. What do you think of such hypotheses?*
11. *Do you side with Bacon or Popper on the best approach to theory construction? State the reasons for your choice.*
12. *What are the advantages and disadvantages of inductive theorizing in linguistics? Should we limit ourselves to that? At what point in the development of a science can or should theories be proposed? Have we reached that point in linguistics? Should we use both induction and deduction? If so, in what combination?*
13. *What differentiates "pure" science from applied science? How do*

*these differences affect the formulation of theories?*
14. *Are recommendations based on an instructional theory really different from those of most methodologists? If so, in what ways?*
15. *How does a languistic theory differ from a linguistic theory? From a psychological theory? From a general educational theory?*
16. *Is eclecticism in linguistic theory possible? Is it intellectually honest? Is it desirable?*
17. *Why is no theory final? Can a law be final (given overwhelming statistical evidence)?*
18. *What is the relationship between the "best" theory and empirical validation? Can theories be evaluated in the absence of formal testing?*

### Footnote

[1]For a list of most of the works that have helped shape this theory, please refer to the bibliography in my book *Synthesis in Second Language Teaching —An Introduction to Languistics*. (All references to *Synthesis* in this book are to the preliminary edition [Blaine, Washington: Second Language Publications, 1982].) Additional publications that have been influential in the development of this theory are listed, starred, in the bibliography of the present volume.

# Chapter 2: Theories of Language Teaching

## Introduction and Summary

*The history of language teaching is largely one of methods based on implicit partial theories that either follow wrong premises or emphasize only certain aspects of the process. The Logico-Literary, Naturalistic, Structural-Behaviorist, Generative-Cognitivist, Sociopsychological, Sociolinguistic (Communicationist), and Acquisitionist (Neo-Naturalistic) theories have in turn been important in our field during the last hundred years. All are still in evidence.*

*Best results in language teaching, however, cannot be obtained when incorrect or partial theories are applied. In recent times several comprehensive theories have appeared, but they have lacked explicitness and/or adequacy. A crucial distinction for both theory and practice is that between "centrifugal" language teaching (first learning, then using) and "centripetal" language teaching (learning by using).*

It is only in very recent years that comprehensive theories of language teaching have begun to appear, though not in explicit form. Other than that, for the last hundred years or so our profession has followed partial theories, which account for some facts and ignore the rest, or theories based on incorrect assumptions, usually because they originate in another discipline. (Part of the problem is that language teaching scholars have been trained in narrow disciplines —typically linguistics *or* psychology *or* education— rather than being given the interdisciplinary training that languistics demands.)

Theories have seldom been formulated as such, having instead been manifested in methods based on largely unwritten assumptions, thus making it necessary to infer the theories from the methods. As of the 1880s, the dominant methodology followed an implicit deductive theory. Thus, although naturalism has a much longer history, we shall begin our survey of theories with the one reaching its zenith during the nineteenth century.

## 2.1: The Logico-Literary Theory

Although it never seems to have been explicitly stated, this theory —to judge by language teaching practices— holds that learning a language is a matter of applying one's logic to the manipulation of written texts. Deduction is used particularly for dealing with the *grammar* of the language and is applied to words and texts in the form of *translation* — hence the "Grammar-Translation Method."[1] Apparently a surprisingly large number of schools and universities in North America still use one or another variety of the Grammar-Translation Method.

The Logico-Literary Theory is incomplete and incorrect in important ways. While in classical languages like Latin and Greek the written form is all that's available, it is quite incorrect to assume that the written form of *modern* languages is generally more important, prevalent, or useful than the spoken form. Deduction seems necessary for certain difficult grammatical rules, but certainly many rules can be internalized inductively or through guided discovery. Perhaps there is nothing objectionable in translation *per se*, but it seems clear that the Grammar-Translation Method overuses and misuses this procedure.

The Logico-Literary Theory has tended to yield language program graduates who, not unexpectedly, have a good theoretical (though pre-linguistic) knowledge about the grammar of the language and can, with some difficulty, decode written texts. However, graduates of Grammar-Translation programs simply lack the ability to understand fluent spoken language or to produce anything but very slow, word-by-word speech "cranked out" via translation —in brief, they cannot communicate in the language. It was in reaction to this reality that the reform movement of the late nineteenth century took place.

## 2.2: The Naturalistic Theory

Perhaps the oldest assumption in our profession states that, to be successful, language teaching must imitate as closely as possible the process of natural language acquisition in nurseries and streets. This is probably what members of the ruling classes in antiquity had in mind when they used foreign slaves as language tutors. The Naturalistic Theory, usually implicit and seldom proposed in terms of testable hypotheses, has remained popular to this day. Its latest manifestation is the

Acquisitionist Theory, a form of neo-naturalism actively advocated today and discussed near the end of this chapter.

The three best-known nineteenth century reactions against the Grammar-Translation Method with its Logico-Literary underpinnings were naturalistic —the Natural Method, the Series Method, and the Direct Method. The reform movement which emerged victorious in the early twentieth century was essentially naturalistic. (Not that all nineteenth century reformers in our field were naturalistic: Viëtor and Sweet, for example, had other views.)

In more recent times we find, in addition to the Direct Method and its successor the Audio-Visual Method, several other methods that try to imitate one or more key features of natural language acquisition. One variety of the Audio -Lingual Method (the "Direct" one, although not called thus) was naturalistic. So are, in one way or another, situational methods, the Immersion Approach [cf. Lambert and Tucker 1972; Shapson *et al.* 1982], the Total Physical Response [Asher 1977], the Comprehension Approach [Winitz 1981], and the Natural Approach [Terrell 1977; Krashen and Terrell 1983]. Certain versions of the Communicative Approach (which will be discussed below) are also naturalistic in orientation.

The main problem with the Naturalistic Theory is that the conditions that make natural language acquisition possible *cannot* be recreated in the second language classroom. There may be differences in the learner, his knowledge, cognitive and emotional maturity, learning strategies, etc.[2] One condition absolutely essential to natural language acquisition, being surrounded by, and constantly interacting with, native speakers, will never exist in second language classrooms. The impossibility of recreating natural language acquisition conditions in the classroom means that any claims to success by naturalistic methods should be viewed with great caution. Even if it were possible to treat classroom language learning as natural language acquisition, this would be inefficient, as it would fail to fully use the learners' knowledge and cognitive skills.

One of the most important things that needs to be realized in our discipline is that there's nothing "natural" about learning a second language within four classroom walls. Once we accept this, we are freed to consider the validity of any procedure *for the classroom situation* without having to arbitrarily accept it or reject it on the basis of its "naturalness."

## 2.3: The Structural-Behaviorist Theory

In the 1940s structural linguists who had been influenced by behaviorist psychology implemented a "Linguistic Approach" to language instruction whose principles came the closest yet to constituting an integrated theory of language teaching. There have been many descriptions of this approach and several published statements of its principles, but as with the two previous theories, the Structural-Behaviorist Theory underlying this approach was only partially stated by its proponents, so we have to infer it mostly from what they did.

This approach emphasized development of habitual (that is, internalized) control of language structure, but in the more enlightened programs communication was not neglected. The Linguistic Approach concentrated on speech, but reading was also taught, as well as some simple writing. Perhaps this was the first instance of team teaching in our field: classes were taught by (1) a native informant, who served as drillmaster and conversation leader under the supervision of (2) a linguist, who visited several classes each day to clarify points of structure.

The first manifestation of the Linguistic Approach was the so-called Army Method (from 1941 on), which had very long dialogues, little variety in grammatical drills, and no pronunciation drills; this was also known as the "Mim-Mem" or "Aural-Oral" Method. By the late fifties the Linguistic Approach, as used for example at the Foreign Service Institute (FSI), had reached a new phase that can be labeled the "Structural Method": much shorter dialogues, a great variety of grammatical and pronunciation drills, and considerable emphasis on situations and conversation.[3]

The last form of the Linguistic Approach based on the Structural-Behaviorist Theory was its adaptation to schools and colleges in what became known as the Audio-Lingual Method. Only one version of the Audio-Lingual Method was more or less close to the Structural Method that was its source.[4] But even this version was doomed to failure —not because of large classes or because school programs were not intensive, but simply because most language teachers could act as neither native informant nor linguist. This led to a distortion of the Linguistic Approach into mindless mechanical drudgery without serious attempts at communication. The result was graduates who could rattle off dialogues and do drills but could not converse. The reaction of our profession to this distortion and its inevitable bad results, when it finally came, was not to correct the situation but to reject the Linguistic Approach wholesale, throwing out the baby with the bathwater, as has happened repeatedly with various procedures, trends, and methods.

The Structural-Behaviorist Theory is also partial. Even its most elaborate formulations, those of Fries [1945] and Lado [1964], were not comprehensive enough, as they overlooked, for instance, numerous psychological considerations —which is understandable, since these scholars were trained in linguistics rather than psychology. All formulations of this theory lacked any serious consideration of the nature and importance of communication acts, an emphasis that was to come much later. However, the Structural-Behaviorist Theory is still the basis of much language teaching around the world.

## 2.4: The Generative-Cognitivist Theory

With the revolution in linguistics and psychology of the early sixties, it seemed a new paradigm would emerge in language teaching. Those of Chomsky's disciples interested in language teaching condemned past practices as based on unsound theory and urged that language teaching be based on generative grammar and cognitive psychology. Although the new linguistic and psychological theories were quite explicit, the Generative-Cognitivist Theory of language teaching derived from them was not. The closest it came to being explicitly formulated was in the work of Jakobovits [1970].

This new theory of language teaching was also partial, as it emphasized syntax to the neglect of almost everything else. Furthermore, transformational-generative grammar and cognitive psychology are inherently unsuitable for application to language teaching, since they are concerned with hypotheses about abstract mental processes rather than facts about concrete performance which so interest languists. Their rejection of the concept of linguistic habit (and therefore of interference theory) and their tendency to emphasize written language are two more obstacles to the general application of these theories to language teaching.

The nearest the Generative-Cognitivist Theory has come to yielding a method of language teaching is the "Cognitive Approach." The Cognitive Approach, to judge by teaching materials claiming to use it, is logico-communicative. It relies, like the Grammar-Translation Method, on deduction, although of course all rules are described in modern linguistic terms. Materials are structurally graded. Practice emphasizes the application of syntactic knowledge in communication-like exercises; mechanical drills —along with all other forms of habit-formation practice— are rejected, although transformation exercises are used extensively. There is however no evidence that the Cognitive Approach, which emphasizes syntax and linguistic "creativity," produces better results than the previously discussed approaches, which are also partial.

Transformational-generative grammar and cognitive psychology are too abstract and one-sided to ever produce an integrated, practical, balanced theory of language teaching. However, those few of their many hypotheses that have been empirically validated should be incorporated into any comprehensive, eclectic theory in our field. If kept at arm's length (as *all* disciplines outside linguistics should be), transformational-generative grammar and cognitive psychology can offer important insights and even some applicable ideas. It is, however, a mistake to look to them for guidance, since their concerns and orientation are very different from ours.

## 2.5: The Sociopsychological Theory

The sixties and early seventies saw the emergence of several methods of language teaching stressing the learner's feelings in the social context of the classroom. For lack of a better term, I shall call the theoretical position underlying such methods the "Sociopsychological Theory."

Three methods with this orientation are the Silent Way [Gattegno 1972], Community Language Learning [Curran 1976], and Suggestopedia [Lozanov 1978].[5]

The Silent Way offers careful but largely silent direction by the teacher; the learners are expected to rely largely on their own devices and on help from each other. In Community Language Learning, the learner is made responsible for his own learning, including its sequence and content, while the teacher limits himself to the role of unobtrusive "counselor." The Silent Way, and especially Community Language Learning seem to fit well with the philosophy of the late sixties and the seventies, when young people wanted to do "their own thing" and to relegate anyone in authority —parents and teachers in particular— to a secondary role. By contrast Suggestopedia, which originated in Bulgaria, is an authoritarian method in which the teacher is very much in charge; its claim to being psychologically based lies in its attempts to break down psychological barriers to learning through the use of music, yoga, and other relaxation-inducing techniques.[6]

Although the social climate favorable to the Sociopsychological Theory no longer exists (students nowadays not only accept guidance but *want* it), certain of the principles associated with this theory retain their validity. To a considerable extent, students *should* be responsible for their own learning, although they would not be the best judges of its progression and content. There is much students can do to help each other learn. Few would now be in favor of the teacher monopolizing classroom talk. If the right kind of music helps plants grow and chickens produce more eggs, perhaps it would be possible to determine empirically that a certain type of music, used in a certain way, facilitates language learning. But as a theory, the Sociopsychological Theory underlying these and other procedures is a very incomplete account of the second language learning process.

## 2.6: The Sociolinguistic Theory

You will recall that the Structural Method attended to communication but its distorted descendant, the Audio-Lingual Method, did not, with unfortunate results. In Great Britain, and later in other parts of Europe, the reaction against mechanical, communicationless language teaching took the form of relying on sociolinguistics as the key to understanding and imparting communication skills. Sociolinguists have in fact shed much light on the nature of communication and on that part of second language competence called "communicative competence."

The Communicative Approach developed from this orientation is mostly a matter of *greater* emphasis on communication, for there were numerous communicative activities in previous methods and approaches such as the Structural Method (when properly applied), the "Situational" variety of the Audio-Lingual Method, and situational methods. However, the Communicative Approach —at least in its "notional-functional" version— introduced for the first time precision in describing communication acts.

The emphasis on communication of the Sociolinguistic Theory was long overdue in the language classroom. Unfortunately, as has often happened in the past, a good thing has been taken by many to its undesirable extreme: Many have adopted the position that "Communication is all that matters" and that structural control is unimportant and will be a natural outcome of communication in any case. However, a premature emphasis on communication produces far more errors than can be effectively corrected, so they are soon "fossilized" as faulty internalized rules or linguistic habits. As a result, it seems many students graduate from communicative programs with the ability to fluently convey many of their ideas, yes, but in atrocious classroom "pidgins." The fact that error-laden speech interferes with communication and offends native speakers[7] doesn't seem to bother communicationists very much.

It is once again a case of a partial theory "biting off more than it can chew." Certain communicationist theorists would even subordinate grammar to communicative competence in their models of the language learning process. A more balanced view can be maintained by considering (1) linguistic competence the core of second language competence which is (2) used to communicate within (3) a cultural context (see Figure 2.1).

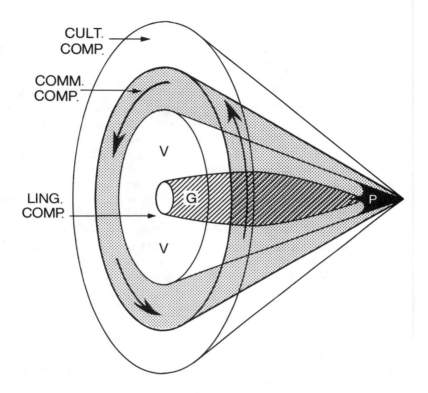

Figure 2.1

Some versions of the Communicative Approach are strongly naturalistic. We see the marriage of communicationism and naturalism especially in the Immersion Approach. If an emphasis on communication from the start and on natural language acquisition is valid, then immersion programs, where children are exposed to communication in a second language, under naturalistic principles, for twelve or thirteen years, should yield excellent results.

# 2.7: The Acquisitionist Theory

This latest theory, which claims to be coherent and comprehensive, at least in book advertisements, has been proposed in several publications by Stephen Krashen and his associates.[8] This theory is an updated version of naturalism based on the extensive research in natural language acquisition carried out in earnest since the late sixties. The theory claims that efficient and effective natural second language acquisition can take place in the classroom. Unfortunately this is not so, as we shall see in Chapter 3.

Krashen's theory of second language acquisition is indeed a coherent and comprehensive, carefully documented and probably very valid account of what happens *when a second language is "picked up" naturally in the field*. But the Acquisitionist Theory is unsuitable for the second language classroom. This should not surprise anyone, as this theory is another attempt to apply to second language programs findings and principles from a very different situation and from what is, essentially, another discipline.

The Acquisitionist Theory consists primarily of five major hypotheses, which are discussed briefly below:

(1) *The acquisition/learning hypothesis*: This claims that there are two distinct language learning processes, unconscious acquisition and conscious learning. The theory minimizes the value of conscious learning, as it asserts that only unconscious acquisition can lead to "creative" sentence generation. This can be refuted by any experienced language teacher who has led students, countless times, from the conscious learning of a rule or element to its use in rapid speech.

(2) *The natural order hypothesis*: This claims that there is a natural order of acquisition of second language structures. If there is a natural order of acquisition in the street (which some doubt), it would be determined by communication needs *in the street*. Why should this have anything to do with the order of presentation in the largely secluded environment of the language classroom? Shouldn't the order of instruction in the classroom be based primarily on linguistic, psychological, and pedagogical principles, and only as an eventual goal on what goes on beyond its walls? (Of course, if the second language is spoken in the community, this would have to be taken into account.)

Furthermore, what seems to be "picked up" early or late in the field has little relationship with what has to be taught early or late in the classroom. For example, a "late-acquired" morpheme such as the -*s* of the English third person singular cannot be *taught* late, as it is needed very early; ignoring its early omission, as suggested by acquisitionists, would tend to result in the early fossilization of the error.

(3) *The monitor hypothesis*: According to this hypothesis, we monitor our linguistic production only when there is considerable time available to focus on rules we have learned consciously. But it seems we monitor to some extent even our rapid speech, which contains much that is largely unconscious. The second language student may initially do a great deal of conscious monitoring, but through graded meaningful practice the rules eventually become unconscious ("automatic") for him.

(4) *The input hypothesis*: This states that the only thing a second language learner needs in order to develop competence in the language is "comprehensible input" at a level of difficulty slightly higher than his present competence ("i + 1"). Again, while this may be true of natural language acquisition, it doesn't apply to the second language classroom. In the latter, rather than simply *exposing* students to imprecise input of subjectively determined difficulty, the teacher would do well to *teach* a specific new rule and *then* use it in conjunction with everything else learned to that point.

Furthermore, comprehensible input is not all that's needed to develop competence in speaking and writing. Unless students are guided into producing *manageable (graded) output* and given corrective feedback on it, they will develop very faulty speech and writing. In the classroom, second language speaking in particular should not just "emerge" in some mysterious, unconscious way —it should be *taught*.

The assertion by Krashen and others that linguistic errors need not be corrected, for they will gradually disappear, is once again true (up to a point) of the natural language acquisition situation, where the acquirer is constantly surrounded by a very rich linguistic environment. But the language classroom offers an impoverished linguistic environment where the students, instead of interacting frequently with native speakers, interact mostly with other learners who misuse the language as badly as they do. In such a situation, if linguistic errors are not corrected they quickly become fossilized (habitual) as students find they can satisfy their limited classroom communication needs without self-correction.

(5) *The affective filter hypothesis*: This seems to be the only one of Krashen's five hypotheses that is applicable to the second language teaching situation. That emotions can block learning and therefore teachers must make every reasonable effort to "lower the affective filter" may be true of all classroom teaching/learning.

Still, this "lowering of the affective filter" should not be accomplished by creating false confidence through the noncorrection of errors. There *are* ways of correcting most errors without creating emotional blocks.

As we have seen, only certain implications of *one* of the five hypotheses of the Acquisitionist Theory seem valid for the classroom second language learning situation. The methods Krashen [1982] identifies as being in harmony with his theory are the Total Physical Response, Suggestopedia (of all things), the Natural Approach, and the Immersion Approach. He claims all of these methods are successful. Anyone who went to the trouble of analyzing the sound track of one of Asher's demonstration films (as I have) would find that when speech finally "emerges" in the Total Physical Response it is very defective; while this is demonstrably a very effective way of teaching listening comprehension, it is very unlikely to result in accurate speech and writing. We have already said that there is no reliable evidence of the "great success" of Suggestopedia. The Natural Approach [Krashen and Terrell 1983] should, again, result in very good comprehension but very faulty speech and writing; in this approach, errors in free classroom communication are not corrected, thus counteracting the positive effect of structural practice outside the classroom. The Immersion Approach is discussed in detail in Chapter 3.

## 2.8: What Successful Language Teaching Is *Not*

From the above discussion of language teaching theories it seems clear that successful language teaching is *not*

an intellectual exercise involving the comprehension and memorization of rule statements;

mostly translation;

the reading of literature;

having the learners acquire the language naturally the way it's done in the nursery or the street (*evidence forthcoming*);

the memorization of sentences;

a matter of mechanical conditioning;

mostly transforming sentences on the basis of abstract rules;

engaging in unbridled linguistic "creativity";

letting the learners decide what to learn and when and how to learn it; nor

just communicating.

Second language teaching/learning *is* several of the things listed above (and many others), *but it isn't any one exclusively or even primarily.* The time has come to accept that, for best results, language teaching should be based not on partial theories but on comprehensive theories.

# 2.9: Attempts at Comprehensive Language Teaching Theory Construction

Many theories of language teaching have been proposed over the years; but as noted earlier, most have been quite partial in nature. In recent years several authors have presented what in effect are comprehensive theories of language teaching, although they may not have proposed them as such; however, even these theories tend to emphasize either linguistics or psychology. Wilga Rivers' more theoretical publications, taken as a whole, amount to the first comprehensive eclectic theory in our field, although she hasn't formulated it in terms of a discrete set of explicit, integrated principles; Rivers' theory leans toward an emphasis on psychology rather than linguistics.

Two recent volumes presenting extended definitions of our field and qualifying therefore as comprehensive theories of sorts are H. Douglas Brown's *Principles of Language Learning and Teaching* [1980] and my *Synthesis* [1982]. Both tend to emphasize linguistics, although they do present many psychological principles. Brown's is a book that can be read to great advantage. Unfortunately it suffers, like much being published nowadays, from an insufficient distinction between natural language acquisition and formal language learning. The book's concluding chapter lists the main principles of the theory. While Brown makes no claim that his theory is comprehensive, it certainly seems to be. It is furthermore, as the author states, an eclectic theory.

*Synthesis in Second Language Teaching* was never meant to be a theoretical book but rather a critical summary of ideas in linguistics, a presentation of several new ideas, and a guide to research and practice. Of course a detailed discussion, with a point of view, of all the important aspects of our field amounts to an implicit comprehensive theory. The present book makes the theory explicit. This theory is, like Rivers' and Brown's, an "enlightened" eclectic theory —"enlightened" because it takes all important factors into account and involves principled rather than haphazard eclecticism, not because of any claim to superior mental illumination on the part of the author.

(Very recently Stern [1983] published a comprehensive book presenting background information important to anyone interested in formulating a multifactor theory of language teaching.)

We see then that several comprehensive theories have been advanced without sufficient explicitness, and that the one (Krashen's) making the greatest claims so far to explicitness, coherence, and comprehensiveness is based on data from natural language acquisition, a situation largely irreproducible in the second language classroom. It is time for an explicit, integrated, and comprehensive theory of language teaching dealing specifically with what has happened, is happening, and can or should happen in the classroom, a theory that spells out all its principles and that clearly states their practical implications. It is hoped this is such a theory.

## 2.10: An Important Distinction: Centrifugal vs. Centripetal Language Teaching/Learning

"Centrifugal," as you probably remember from elementary physics, means "involving movement from the center to the periphery." Centrifugal language teaching involves movement from the linguistic core to its use in communication, by a process which Rivers [1976:23] made known as (I'm paraphrasing her words) "first *skill-getting*, then *skill-using*." It seems only logical that a language form should come under some degree of control before it is used. To illustrate this principle in another field, no technician would (or should?) attempt a job without first learning how to use the required tools. *Control before use* is a general principle valid in many spheres of life, including learning to play the piano or to type, learning to drive a car, *and* learning a second language in the classroom.

This is quite different from the natural acquisition situation, where movement goes in the opposite direction —that is, "centripetally"— by deriving the core, structural knowledge of the language, unconsciously from the communicative use of the language. This works quite well in the home and the community, where the acquirer can interact almost constantly with native speakers who serve as "linguistic floaters" keeping him from "sinking" and "drowning" linguistically. However, by encouraging *classroom students* to use rules and elements in communication before they control them, the centripetal (or communicationist) approach results in far more errors than can effectively be corrected or self - corrected; in the absence of linguistic floaters these errors become habitual and the students do sink and drown linguistically by internalizing a very faulty classroom pidgin.

We cannot demand perfection from our students (although there's nothing wrong with it as an ideal), but neither should we settle for graduates who speak in classroom pidgins. Almost any language teacher with a little imagination can produce graduates who chatter away in something vaguely resembling a second language if free communication is emphasized from the start and accuracy is thrown out the window —but is this a valid educational goal? The value of a language teaching theory and of its derived methodology depends on whether it can produce fluency *with* accuracy or communicative competence *with* linguistic competence.

Language teaching theories and methods have to make, and have made, a choice on the centrifugal/centripetal question. The Logico-Literary, Structural-Behaviorist, and Generative-Cognitivist theories have been centrifugal. Most Naturalistic, Sociopsychological, and Sociolinguistic methods have been largely centripetal. The currently popular Communicative Approach, which is based on sociolinguistics, is strongly centripetal in orientation. The Immersion Approach is also centripetal. Krashen's Acquisitionist Theory is nothing but centripetal, as it considers the teaching of structure unnecessary. Of the comprehensive theories of language teaching that have emerged so far, Rivers' is centrifugal, Brown's is noncommital on this issue, and mine is definitely centrifugal, although it recognizes the great importance of communicative activities.

If naturalistic-communicative-acquisitionist (centripetal) approaches to second language learning in the classroom are valid, then the Immersion Approach should be *very* successful. Immersion programs represent the best chance such approaches will ever have: What more can naturalists, communicationists or acquisitionists ask for than the opportunity to expose children to a second language for twelve or thirteen years? Proponents of these three theories (Naturalistic, Sociolinguistic, and Acquisitionist) refer to the "success" of immersion programs as evidence supporting the validity of their theories. In Chapter 3 we will therefore consider the Immersion Approach and its implications, in an effort to separate fact from myth.

## 2.11: For Discussion

1. *Why have there been mostly partial theories in our field? What has kept them from becoming comprehensive?*
2. *What is the relationship between theory and methodology? Is it valid to infer theories from methods? Has it been necessary to do so?*
3. *Describe any experience you may have had with logico-literary approaches to language teaching/learning. Did emphasis on deduction and the translation of written texts lead to linguistic and communicative competence?*
4. *What features of natural language acquisition could/couldn't be*

*recreated in the second language classroom? What use do naturalistic methods make of the knowledge and skills of language students? Are the claims of greater effectiveness in being "natural" justified? Are they sufficiently proven to justify the loss in efficiency? Are naturalistic assumptions easily testable?*

5. *In what ways is structural linguistics a more suitable basis for language teaching than generative linguistics? In what ways is it less so?*

6. *Explain how the history and fate of the Linguistic Approach illustrate what happens to many ideas in our profession.*

7. *Why do many say that the Structural Method neglects communication? Are they justified in saying it?*

8. *In what direct and indirect ways have generative linguistics and cognitive psychology influenced language teaching? Which have been positive? Which negative?*

9. *Can one consider the Sociopsychological Theory a curiosity of the late sixties and the seventies or have the methods based on it left a permanent legacy of useful procedures? How can some of these procedures be incorporated into an "enlightened" eclectic method?*

10. *Explain why, while communication is the purpose of language, it isn't enough just to communicate. What are the effects of linguistic errors?*

11. *List the plusses and minuses of Krashen's theory in terms of its applicability to the second language classroom.*

12. *Section 2.8 of this chapter lists ten things second language teaching is **not** (at least not exclusively or primarily). Can you think of others? Which of these procedures or activities should be part of an enlightened eclectic method?*

13. *Which theories of language teaching have the best chance of being adequate? What disciplines and learning conditions would they be based on? How would they achieve and maintain balance?*

14. *List the strong and weak points of the three comprehensive theories of language teaching published so far (this may require considerable extra reading).*

15. *What difference does it make whether language teaching is centrifugal or centripetal? Which is more likely to lead to good control of form? Once basic control of a rule or form is established centrifugally, can it be improved centripetally? Is communication necessary for the full internalization of rules?*

16. *Do errors disappear in the classroom through the use of the language for communication? Can there be any improvement by that means? What would it require?*

**17.** *Explain why the results of immersion programs constitute decisive evidence for or against Naturalistic, Sociolinguistic (Communicative), and Acquisitionist theories of second language teaching.*

## Footnotes

[1]The term "Traditional" has also been used to refer to the Grammar-Translation Method. "Traditional," however, has become an ambiguous word, as everyone seems to use it to designate whatever preceded their particular emphasis. For example, at one point (the late 1960s and the '70s) "traditional" was used to refer to anything not individualized; lately, whatever is not part of the Communicative Approach is also stigmatized with the label "traditional."

[2]See *Synthesis*, Chapter 5.

[3]As an instructor in Spanish at FSI from 1958 to 1961 I was so impressed by the results of their programs that I decided to make language teaching my career.

[4]This was the "Structural" version; there were at least two others. To add to the confusion, all claimed to be *the*"Audio-Lingual Method".

[5]Others, such as John Rassias, also use one or two psychology-based procedures, but the inclusion of one or two unusual procedures or techniques does not qualify something as a method.

[6]Despite voluminous publications "proving" the superiority of Suggestopedia, its claims of great success are questionable.

[7]Politzer 1978, Guntermann 1978, Chastain 1980, Galloway 1980, Piazza 1980, Delisle 1982, Ensz 1982, Ludwig 1982.

[8]Krashen 1981; Dulay, Burt, and Krashen 1982; Krashen 1982; Krashen and Terrell 1983.

# Chapter 3: Excursus: The Immersion Approach and Its Implications

## Introduction and Summary

*Immersion programs, which expose children to a second language for many years, enjoy considerable popularity, especially in Canada. However, while children exposed for many years to the Immersion Approach develop good comprehension and can somehow communicate in most situations, much data shows their speech and writing are linguistically very faulty —they internalize a terminal classroom pidgin. The Immersion Approach is based on five myths about second language learning, myths which should be exploded, not exploited by educators to promote their views. As the Immersion Approach lacks the advantages inherent to both natural language acquisition and formal language learning, it* cannot *produce linguistic competence. Thus immersion is fundamentally flawed.*

*The failure of the Immersion Approach to produce linguistic competence has certain implications for linguistic theory and especially for languistic theory, implications on the nature of linguistic competence and its relationship to communicative competence, the role of interference, the differences between natural language acquisition and formal language learning, the desirability of linguistic correction, the best age to start learning a second language, and the validity of the Naturalistic, Sociolinguistic (Communicationist), and Acquisitionist theories of second language teaching/learning. A better way to develop bilingualism in children is proposed.*

## 3.1: A Few Terms Defined

We may define the **Immersion Approach** as *a classroom approach in which children are exposed to a second language in a "natural" way by* *concentrating on communicative activities (especially via school subject instruction) in the language.* We already have two problems: the term "immersion" and the word "natural." When we talk about an object being *immersed* in a liquid, for example, we think of it as completely surrounded by the liquid. This is not the case with "immersion" programs, in which the child, far from being surrounded by the language, has exposure to only one speaker of the language, the teacher, and is surrounded by numerous other children who misuse the language just as badly as the child does. We must conclude that "immersion" in this case is a misnomer. As to this being "natural," how natural can it be to take 20 or 30 monolingual five- or six-year-olds and thrust them inside four walls where everybody is supposed to speak another language?

*Early immersion* refers to starting this process in kindergarten or grade one, which gives the Immersion Approach fully twelve or thirteen years to accomplish its goals. *Late immersion* starts the process much later, usually in grade seven. Usually early immersion programs start with *total immersion*, meaning that nothing but the second language is used until the second or third grade, when instruction in the native language begins; from then on native language instruction gradually increases and second language exposure decreases into *partial immersion*, that is, only certain subjects taught in the second language.

An alternative favored by many but possible only in second language communities is *submersion*, which means placing an individual in a second language milieu, such as a classroom where the other students are native speakers of the second language. Of course, only the few privileged children experiencing submersion ever get a chance to be really immersed in the second language.

*Core* language programs such as "Core French" refer to the formal study of a language for a few (usually no more than three to five) hours a week. This may begin at any point, but it generally starts in grade seven or later.

## 3.2: Misplaced Praise

No doubt if a French-speaking student, after many years of *English* immersion, said things like

*He promenades the dog* from *Il promène le chien;*
*He them want* from *Il les veut;*
*I am mounted to the attic* from *Je suis monté au grenier;*
*An house white* from *Une maison blanche;*
or *The table? She's there* from *La table? Elle est là,*

one would conclude there's something very wrong either with the learner or with the learning process to which he or she was exposed. And yet, although errors equivalent to the ones just given are produced by English-speaking pupils after thousands of hours of immersion, many people, particularly educators, have high praise for the Immersion Approach!

Most language educators have praised the Immersion Approach highly. H.H. Stern, for example, has repeatedly referred to it as "highly successful." Krashen [1984:61] gushes with praise for it; for him, "it may be the most successful programme ever recorded in the professional language-teaching literature." He adds that "...no programme, to my knowledge, has done as well."

Immersion programs enjoy great popularity, especially in Canada, where many English-speaking parents have come to believe that putting their children through French immersion is their patriotic duty and that their children will thus gain a clear competitive edge in life. Immersion programs do confer advanced comprehension skill; but then, who wouldn't understand a second language well after thousands of hours of active exposure? However, the Immersion Approach fails (evidence follows) to produce linguistically competent speech and writing.

Surely an approach to bilingualism resulting in linguistic incompetence is not a valid educational goal and should therefore be neither promoted nor praised.

# 3.3: A Look at the Evidence

That the Immersion Approach results in the internalization of a faulty classroom pidgin has been known for over a decade. While almost all the data available is from French immersion, the result has been the same wherever the Immersion Approach has been tried, regardless of language. Below are listed sample errors of French immersion children under two broad categories, native language (English) interference and second language overgeneralization (both cases of underdifferentiation). The examples are taken from Selinker et al. [1975, coded "(1)" below], who studied children in the second year of early immersion; Spilka [1976, coded "(2)" below], who reported on the French of early immersion children in grades five and six; and my own observations of the speech of children in their second year of either early or late French immersion [coded "(3)" below].

### 3.3.1: Interference Errors

The following is a very small sample of the numerous interference errors that have been observed in the speech (and writing) of children in French immersion programs:

*Il est trois ans* for *Il a trois ans*, from *He is three (years old)*. (1)

*Je vais manger des* for *Je vais en manger*, from *I'm gonna eat some*. (1)

*Il veut les* for *Il les veut*, from *He wants them*. (1)

*Des drôles films* for *Des films drôles*, from *Some funny movies*. (1)

*Avant je vais...* for *Avant d'aller...* or *Avant que j'aille...*, from *Before I go....* (1)

*Un chalet qu'on va aller à* for *Un chalet où on va aller*, from *A cottage that we're gonna go to*. (1)

*Le sac a un trou dans le* for *Il y a un trou dans le sac*, from *The bag has a hole in it*. (1)

*On voit tout le monde mange* for *On voit tout le monde qui mange*, from *We see everybody eat*. (2)

*Jouer un jeu* for *Jouer à un jeu*, from *To play a game*. (2)

*On est allé à une dame* for *On est allé chez une dame*, from *We went to a lady's house*. (2)

*Dormir pour deux jours* for *Dormir pendant deux jours*, from *To sleep for two days*. (2)

*Et puis, elle a vu moi* for *Et puis, elle m'a vu*, from *And then, she saw me*. (2)

*Sur samedi* for *Samedi*, from *On Saturday*. (3)

*Un rouge pomme* for *Une pomme rouge*, from *A red apple*.

### 3.3.2: Overgeneralization Errors

Many errors involve a failure to differentiate irregular from regular forms, a clear case of overgeneralization. Other similar errors are probably due to the learner's belief that a distinction that doesn't exist or isn't important in the native language can't be too important in the second language. These errors are often classified as "simplification" errors, although it's hard to see how a learner can simplify something he has never learned. A few examples of overgeneralization errors follow:

*Le prend un* for *Il (en) prend un* (confusion of pronouns) ("He takes one"). (1)

*Il a couré* for *Il a couru* (regularization of irregular past) ("He ran"). (1)

*Je aller camping* for *Je suis allé faire du camping* (infinitive for

past [or wrong auxiliary, i.e., *J'ai allé camping]?) ("I went camping").
(1)

    *Son voiture for Sa voiture (wrong gender) ("His/her car"). (2)

    *Mon maman for Ma maman (concept of gender obviously not grasped) ("My mom"). (3)

    *J'ai tombé for Je suis tombé (wrong auxiliary) ("I fell down"). (3)

    Harley and Swain [1977, 1978] found that the verb system of pupils in their sixth year of early French immersion was greatly "simplified," that is, that they had failed to master many distinctions. One whole tense, the conditional, was missing, its functions being performed by various circumlocutions.

### 3.3.3: Frequent Errors That Don't Disappear

    The frequency of French immersion pupil errors is high. Spilka [opus cit.] found that over 52 percent of the sentences of early French immersion pupils in grade six (that is, after six or seven years of immersion) were incorrect, as opposed to less than seven percent for native French-speaking children in the same grade. Furthermore, she found that the gap in correctness between these two groups of children increases over time.

    A recent study [Tatto 1983] supports this point. In grade eleven, early French immersion students, exposed to French for thousands of hours since kindergarten or grade one, made grammatical errors of the most basic nature. Although they had superior comprehension, they did not score significantly better, statistically, than Core French students (with only a few hundred hours of formal instruction beginning in grade seven) in free writing or in grammatical exercises.

    Somewhat anecdotal confirmation of the fact that the outcome of French immersion programs is a very faulty and quite terminal classroom pidgin (which has been called "Frenglish") comes from our experience with French immersion graduates at Simon Fraser University. Placed with fourth -semester students of French as a formal subject (in a program which emphasizes audio-oral skills), immersion students with twelve or thirteen years of exposure to French have done poorly, showing little improvement and getting Cs and Ds as final course grades.

    Most recently, in December 1984, one of my graduate students, Micheline Pellerin, completed a study that confirms almost all of the above and adds several new insights. She taped 45-minute interviews with six students in their thirteenth year of French immersion in what has a reputation as an excellent program. She found that, while they had managed to learn (more or less) the conditional tense, 50.7 percent of their sentences were grammatically incorrect —this not counting errors in liaison or pronunciation or false starts, the latter quite numerous. The pronoun "y" was totally absent (except for the idiomatic expression "il y a"). Their vocabulary was adequate for general conversation but quite inadequate for subtle distinctions or specialized purposes. Syntactic structures common to both languages were clearly preferred. Comparing this study with the one by Spilka would seem to indicate that "Frenglish" is internalized in the early grades and that beyond Grade Six there is very little progress, except perhaps lexically —*errors in French structure* don't *disappear with additional years of immersion.*

*Thus, children emerging from many years of French immersion are not* bilingual —they speak English plus a very defective classroom pidgin, Frenglish. Their comprehension of French may be very good, but their production deserves, at most, a rating of 2 (out of 5) on an FSI-type proficiency scale. They are in fact the typical "terminal 2/2 +" cases so well described by Higgs and Clifford [1982], with a large vocabulary and an almost nonexistent control of any second language structures that differ from those of the native language. (Claims that French immersion graduates should be rated as 3 + or 4 on such a scale are no doubt based on giving much greater weight to communicative competence than to linguistic competence.)

*All the available evidence indicates that the Immersion Approach fails to impart linguistic competence.* This has been true not only of French in Canada, but also of Spanish in the United States [Politzer 1980]. I would venture to say that this will be true whenever and wherever the Immersion Approach, as presently known, is tried.

# 3.4: An Approach Based on Myths

The linguistic failure of the Immersion Approach is largely due to the fact that its concept is based on five myths about language learning. Unfortunately, belief in these myths is not limited to the layman. Many people who should know better have exploited these myths rather than exploding them. The five myths are as follows:

**3.4.1:** *To learn a second language, the younger the better* or *Children are better second language learners than adults*

This popular belief is based on faulty observations. A family goes abroad, and after a few months the children speak the language quite well while the parents still have to struggle to say anything; the conclusion: "Children are better second language learners than adults." However, during those months the children interacted linguistically with their host country peers for many hours a day, while their parents probably didn't spend more than one hour a day in such interaction. There is no reason why, given the same amount of linguistic exposure and interaction, adults cannot do as well or better than children at acquiring a second language in the field.

That adults are better learners than children in almost every respect (an exception being motor memory) has been known for nearly sixty years [Thorndike *et al.* 1928]. Adults are cognitively far more powerful, have better learning strategies, are more conscious of learning tasks and goals, have a longer attention span, are capable of a greater variety of associations, can accommodate longer "chunks" in short-term memory, and so forth. The motor memory superiority of children explains why they are better at learning to ride a bicycle or play a musical instrument or at acquiring, unaided, excellent second language pronunciation; but with careful, systematic instruction, adults can also excel in all of these physical activities.

That older children are better second language learners than younger children, at least in the classroom, has been clearly shown in two major studies. The first of these [Burstall *et al.* 1974] showed that British children starting French studies in later grades did better than those starting in early grades. The second study [Carroll 1975] came up with the same finding (among many others) for the teaching of French as a second language in eight countries. It even seems to be the case that late immersion produces somewhat better results than early immersion, something that has puzzled immersion advocates [cf. Genesee 1982:33-4], who apparently believe firmly in the myth of "the younger the better."

### 3.4.2: *Native language acquisition can be recreated in the second language classroom*

Five- or six-year-olds have already internalized a language, so they are essentially *a different kind of learner* from the eighteen-month-old native language acquirer, for they have considerable interference to contend with.

In immersion programs, the child is surrounded *not* by native speakers of the second language but by peers who misuse the language as badly as he or she does. Since peer influence is pervasive in childhood, poor results seem inevitable. As already noted, "immersion" isn't really immersion at all.

### 3.4.3: *A sink-or-swim approach is the best way to learn a second language*

Young children cannot of course be *taught* a language formally, but if surrounded by native speakers they can acquire it unconsciously quite well, as these native speakers serve as "linguistic floaters" who keep them from sinking. In the classroom, however, children lack such support, so they *do* sink linguistically and become "terminal 2/2 + 's."

In the classroom situation, basic pedagogical principles should apply. Such principles as selection, gradation, and progressive integration[1] cannot be abandoned with impunity.

### 3.4.4: *If you just use the second language for communication, linguistic accuracy will take care of itself*

This is of course not a myth but quite true of natural language acquisition by young children in nurseries and streets; but it does not happen that way with older learners, especially in the second language classroom.

Whenever beginning second language students are encouraged to communicate freely without regard to accuracy, many more errors occur than can be effectively self-corrected, so errors soon become fossilized (habitual), with very little hope of their being eradicated later. Under such conditions, linguistic competence has little chance to develop.

The Immersion Approach has been praised because it prevents the development of inhibition about speaking in the second language [Tucker and d'Anglejan 1972]. But a degree of linguistic inhibition is *desirable* if it makes learners think twice before speaking or writing and if it keeps them from constantly venturing into linguistically unknown territory, thereby making numerous errors and internalizing faulty rules.

An emphasis on creative communication rather than accuracy can affect even native speakers. During the late sixties and the seventies many native English-speaking children, encouraged by lax teachers to just be creative and not worry about grammatical errors, developed into young adults incapable of putting a readable paragraph together. Some people seem determined to repeat that story in the second language field, not just in terms of writing but also of speaking.

Producing language program graduates who use a classroom pidgin fluently is not difficult. All it requires is emphasizing communication at the expense of accuracy. But are Frenglish, Spanglish, and the various other classroom pidgins that result from this approach valid educational goals for the United States or even for a country which, like Canada, has a strong need for bilinguals?

Notice that linguistic inaccuracy is not just a concern of purists —as already pointed out in Chapter 2, a good number of studies have shown that linguistic errors are from mildly to strongly offensive to native speakers of a variety of languages. Furthermore the errors French immersion pupils make are not stylistic *faux pas* of the type members of the Académie Française would condemn but errors of the most basic nature which can interfere considerably with communication.

Perhaps the best answer to this myth would be to replace it with the following concise principle: *Communication, yes, but accuracy first.*

**3.4.5:** *Immersion is, given the state of our knowledge, the best we can do to develop bilingualism*

We have already seen that the Immersion Approach does *not* develop bilingualism but the ability to use a classroom pidgin largely composed of second language vocabulary and native language structure. The major reason for the failure of immersion programs to yield productive linguistic competence is that they attempt to recreate natural language acquisition conditions where they do not and *cannot* exist, that is, in the second language classroom. Immersion pupils are expected to learn a second language in the absence of the most fundamental advantage of natural language acquisition (constant interaction with natives), in the presence of considerable linguistic interference, and without any of the numerous advantages enjoyed by older students.

The Immersion Approach could perhaps undergo certain improvements, but their effect would be slight —*the basic model is fundamentally flawed.* Questions such as "Are the children enrolled in the French immersion program more proficient in French than they would be if they took a French-as-a-SL program (20-40 minutes a day of formal French instruction)?" [Swain 1978:240] are misleading. *Of course* twelve or thirteen years of active exposure will result in more receptive competence than a few hundred hours of (generally poor) formal instruction —but is the productive incompetence that results from the former acceptable? We don't have to choose between two bad alternatives; our profession can develop a better option.

# 3.5: Implications

The outcome of the Immersion Approach has important implications for linguistic theory as well as for linguistic theory and research. Eight such implications are discussed below.

### 3.5.1: Linguistic competence

Evidently productive linguistic competence can differ markedly from receptive linguistic competence —Immersion Approach graduates can decode a second language very well but their oral and written production is very far from native-like. If to this receptive/productive distinction we add the audio-oral/graphic modality distinction, we must conclude that the concept of a unitary linguistic competence applies only to the nonexistent ideal native speaker. In the real world languages are learned and used without a unitary linguistic competence but with varying degrees of competence in four intralingual skills and, in the case of second language students, four interlingual skills as well.

### 3.5.2: Receptive and productive skills

I would venture the hypothesis that when we listen (or read) we not only simplify sentences by detransforming them for storage [Lado 1970], but also ignore all input redundancies, if nothing else for the sake of efficiency in processing and storage. The same thing can happen in second language acquisition, with very poor results: Only an active process of disregarding input redundancies seems to account for many of the errors of immersion children.

Since the processing of input seems to be accompanied by subvocal speech, at least in the second language learner, and since this subvocal speech would be nonredundant, this might explain why, when second language students finally start speaking, after a lengthy period of listening, they have a very inaccurate grammar. This is not a matter of their first attempts at production being inaccurate and soon becoming accurate —if they have been producing inaccurate language subvocally, the longer they have done so the more fossilized that defective subvocal speech would have become. This should give second thoughts to those who consider the listening skill central and would train second language students only in listening for weeks or even months before they start speaking.

### 3.5.3: Linguistic and communicative competence

It seems clear that when communicative competence is emphasized early in a second language program, linguistic competence suffers. Furthermore, the condition seems to be terminal —Immersion Approach graduates could perhaps improve their linguistic competence somewhat if they spent many years in a second language-speaking environment, but the pressure would always be there for them to say, "The natives understand me and don't complain, so it doesn't matter if I make a 'few' mistakes."

My argument is that native-like linguistic competence of a limited scope *is* attainable in the second language classroom, but only if linguistic competence is emphasized first and then, gradually, very slowly, communicative competence comes to the fore. This can result, probably in most students, not just in fluency but in *fluency with accuracy*.

### 3.5.4: Linguistic interference

Immersion data abundantly support the view that by the age of five linguistic interference is already an important factor in second language learning. Something not so evident is that, in addition to manifesting itself in the form of intrusions, the native language *precludes* the learning of certain second language structures or distinctions. This *preclusive interference*[2] is often interpreted as second language overgeneralization or, even more simplistically, as a failure to learn for a variety of vague reasons. However, the reason why French immersion pupils persist in such errors as the use of mostly masculine for feminine articles seems to be the internal message, "I can manage quite well without this distinction in English, so it must be unnecessary in French." A hint that this may be the case comes from the fact that speakers whose native languages do have masculine and feminine articles seem to be much more careful with gender in French (they may have, of course, difficulty in remembering the gender of particular nouns, especially if it differs across languages).

### 3.5.5: Natural second language acquisition and formal second language learning

It should be clear from the above that what works in a natural language acquisition environment cannot work in the second language classroom. Different situations and usually different learners are involved. As seen in Chapter 2, Krashen and others have proposed the application of the principles of natural language acquisition to the second language classroom, but this evidently won't do. In a linguistically rich natural environment, a second language may be acquired well (either by young children or by older learners who have first established a formal foundation) by simply using it. However, in the linguistically impoverished environment of the classroom far better results may be obtained by a centrifugal approach in which linguistic rules and elements are learned first and *then*, as each one is learned, they are all used for real or realistic communication limited to the extent of the linguistic competence developed to that point.

### 3.5.6: Linguistic correction

As young children are not responsive to linguistic correction, early immersion programs cannot apply it effectively; this naturally contributes to the early fossilization of faulty rules. Fortunately, older second language learners are not only receptive to correction but *want* to be corrected more than most teachers like to correct them [Cathcart and Olsen 1976]. To suggest, as some do,[3] that linguistic errors need not be corrected is therefore not only highly unadvisable (as it will foster fossilization) but contrary to the wishes of our students.

### 3.5.7: The best age to start learning a second language

Any child, up to the age of twelve or thirteen, who is surrounded by second language speakers can acquire linguistic and communicative competence indistinguishable from those of native speakers. Beyond that age, nearly every second language acquirer retains the characteristic accent of his/her native language. When it comes to formal second language learning, adults seem to do better than children in every respect except, again, pronunciation and intonation. (I think, however, that this outcome is not inevitable but largely due to the generally very poor quality of phonological instruction. As a native speaker of Spanish with thorough training in phonetics, I can attest that several of my adult students have learned to sound like natives; therefore, developing native pronunciation in a second language does not seem impossible for adults.)

It would seem then that, *linguistically* speaking, the ideal time to start learning a second language would be at about twelve years of age, that is, at a point where children still retain much of their motor memory advantage but have already developed considerable cognitive maturity and most of the other learning advantages of adulthood. For *psychological* reasons, however, the ideal point to begin second language study would be at the age of ten or after age sixteen —puberty should be avoided as a starting point because of its excessive self -consciousness and peer pressure (during puberty, for example, few youngsters are willing to make "strange noises"). It seems, however, that with excellent instruction adults of any age can be taught second languages very effectively.

### 3.5.8: Naturalistic, communicative, and/or acquisitionist approaches to second language learning

The Immersion Approach can be considered a naturalistic - communicative-acquisitionist approach, as its emphasis is on exposing students naturally to communicative activities aimed at unconscious language acquisition, not on structure. Naturalists, communicationists, and acquisitionists alike have praised the "success" of immersion programs as evidence supporting their theories.

However, as we have seen, when it comes to imparting basic linguistic competence the Immersion Approach is not a success but a dismal failure. The inescapable conclusion is that *given the best chance it will ever get (twelve or thirteen years of exposure), a communicative approach based on principles of natural language acquisition does not work in the classroom.* Furthermore, there is no reason to believe that other versions of natural, communicative, or acquisition approaches would fare better.

# 3.6: A Better Way to Bilingualism

Neither of the present alternatives, immersion programs or core programs, is desirable. Immersion programs result in good comprehension but very faulty production. Core or regular programs in which a second language is studied formally for a few hours a week may provide a basic structural foundation but rarely lead to the ability to communicate in the language. What would seem a much better way to develop bilingualism in children would progress through the following five stages:

1. **Exploratory courses** [Pei 1973, Bourque and Chehy 1976] from kindergarten through grade four, to establish or strengthen positive attitudes toward other languages and peoples.
2. **Semi-intensive systematic study** (about two hours a day) of a specific second language from grade five through grade eight, taking pupils up to about proficiency level 2 or 2+ a five-point scale) *without allowing linguistic incompetence to develop.*
3. **Partial immersion** (certain subjects taught in the second language) in grades nine through eleven, raising proficiency to about 3 or 3+.
4. **Total immersion** (everything taught in the second language) in grade twelve, so that about level 4 is reached.
5. **Submersion** in a second language milieu for all secondary school graduates for whom this can be arranged.

*Immersion is a situation that should be built up to, gradually, not plunged into at the beginning of the program, for in such deep water a beginner surrounded by other beginners can do nothing but drown as far as linguistic competence is concerned.* If we don't want our students to develop terminal classroom pidgins, they must learn to communicate within the gradually expanding limits of their control of linguistic structure.

# 3.7: Conclusions

Evidence from a good number of sources has been cited to demonstrate that thousands of hours of active exposure to a second language via the Immersion Approach result in a very defective classroom pidgin in terms of both speaking and writing. The theoretical consequences of this are very significant. The failure of the Immersion Approach greatly weakens the case for the Naturalistic, Sociolinguistic (Communicative), and Acquisitionist theories of classroom second language learning. Clearly "being natural" is not the key to second language learning. An emphasis on communication from the beginning of the program seems to do more harm than good. And twelve or thirteen years of the "comprehensible input" so important to the Acquisitionist Theory of Krashen and his associates don't succeed in developing productive linguistic competence.

# 3.8: For Discussion

1. *The failure of the Immersion Approach is the best-kept secret in our field. Why is this so?*
2. *Why are immersion programs popular with educators? Most parents don't speak the languages taught —could this have anything to do with their acceptance of such programs?*
3. *Can a speaker make frequent, serious errors and still be considered linguistically competent? Communicatively competent?*
4. *How serious are the errors frequently made by pupils after thousands of hours of immersion? Try to defend the position (a) that the errors are serious or (b) that they aren't serious. How do these errors resemble or differ from those made by (a) poorly educated native adults and (b) native children?*
5. *What does the outcome of the Immersion Approach tell us about the idea of errors disappearing naturally if just given enough time (something many in our field believe)?*
6. *Should graduates of immersion programs be channeled into further "bilingual" studies? Would a Ph.D. program in bilingual studies be defensible if its graduates came out speaking Spanglish or Frenglish?*
7. *How does a classroom pidgin become terminal? How does any faulty interlanguage become terminal? What are the salient characteristics of terminal interlanguages?*
8. *Is the classroom environment more suitable for conscious or unconscious learning? If one or the other, why? If both, in what propor-*

*tions at what points?*

9. *Do children have any advantage(s) over adults in a formal classroom language learning setting? Do adults have any advantages over children? If so, what are they and how should they affect language teaching theory and practice? Why do older children perform better than young ones in classroom language learning?*

10. *Can natural language acquisition be recreated in the classroom? If yes, how? If not, why not? Explain the basis and the theoretical consequences of your answer.*

11. *Is a new language best approached globally (by a "sink-or-swim" procedure) or step by step? Qualify your response for young children, immigrants, and second language students.*

12. *Why does accuracy suffer when communication among beginners is emphasized? What can be done to develop accuracy without neglecting communication (and viceversa)?*

13. *Can a person be linguistically competent and incompetent at the same time? Can someone be competent in one language skill only (whether intra- or interlingual)? Can there be listening or reading in second language learning without speaking of some sort?*

14. *What is the relationship between linguistic and communicative competence? Explain whether either one can exist without the other.*

15. *Does Immersion Approach data support the view that the native language can be ignored or that it must be attended to in the classroom, even in kindergarten? Has your native language intruded in any other language you have learned? Has it made it more difficult for you to master any feature(s) of a second language?*

16. *Do adults respond differently to correction than children and if so, what are the implications?*

17. *What do immersion programs tell us about naturalistic, communicative, unconscious second language acquisition in the classroom? Would such an approach work better if given more time? Could it be made highly systematic? Can any approach that subordinates structure to communication from the start result in linguistic competence? State the reasons for your answers.*

18. *Would the "better way" proposed at the end of this chapter be more likely than the Immersion Approach to result in fluency with accuracy? Why or why not?*

19. *Has the reading of this chapter affected your views about one or more theories of second language teaching? In what ways?*

20. *In view of what you have read of this book so far, what principles do you think a sound languistic theory should include or leave out?*

**Footnotes**

[1]*Synthesis* 124-5, 209-11.

[2]*Synthesis* 147-8.

[3]Dulay *et al.* 1982:268; Krashen 1982:74-6, 116-9; Krashen and Terrell 1983:177-8.

# An
# Integrated Theory
# of
# Language Teaching

# Introduction to Chapters 4 to 9

Chapters 4 to 9 constitute the main body of the integrated languistic theory presented in this book.

Chapter 4 proposes general definitions/axioms for the theory. Chapters 5 to 8 list and discuss the more specific definitions/axioms, laws, principles, and hypotheses that linguistics can draw, respectively, from linguistics (Chapter 5), psychology (Chapter 6), teaching theory (Chapter 7), and various other sources such as the socio-cultural disciplines, technology, and psychometrics (Chapter 8). Chapter 9 reviews the Two-Cone Model of second language teaching/learning and gives further thoughts about it.

An attempt has been made to define all important new terms as they are introduced; however, some familiarity with the basic concepts and terminology of general linguistics, psychology, and education is assumed.

Certain principles are derived from more than one feeder discipline, e.g., linguistics and psychology or psychology and teaching theory. In that case, the principle may appear more than once, from different points of view, although usually it will be listed with only one discipline, generally the first to appear in the sequence listed above.

The effectiveness of many of the principles proposed in these chapters may be seen clearly only when everything else is equal, which unfortunately is seldom the case. Some of these principles can be effective only when prerequisite or co-requisite principles are also applied.

Several abbreviations are used in these chapters. G stands for "General," D for "Definition," A for "Axiom," L for "Law," P for "Principle," H for "Hypothesis," and C for "Corollary." In terms of the disciplines, the adjectives "Linguistic" (L), "Psychological" (P), "Teaching" (T), and "Various" (V) are abbreviated as indicated in parentheses.

While some of the propositions in this theory are axiomatic or based on logic and may be difficult to test empirically, most are testable. In certain cases where research is particularly desirable and feasible, research suggestions —abbreviated RS— are made.

It should be repeated and emphasized that all the principles in this theory are hypotheses subject to confirmation, rejection or modification depending on the results of empirical research. At the same time, it should be kept in mind that the present author did not arrive at these principles in a haphazard, casual way but on the basis of many years' language teaching experience and research.

# Chapter 4: General Definitions/Axioms

## Introduction and Summary

*In this chapter, definitions (with accompanying discussion) are provided for, among others, the terms "linguistics," "language," "second language," "teaching," "teacher," "student," "language teaching," "the goal of language teaching," "bilingual," "learning," "second language learning," "second language competence," "linguistic competence," "communicative competence," "cultural competence," and "levels of language learning."*

## GD/A 1: Languistics

**Languistics** may be defined as *the science of second (or "foreign" — see below) language teaching and learning.*

There is much need for an autonomous discipline of language teaching if our field is not to be unduly influenced by other disciplines. The history of language teaching has largely been one of a variety of other disciplines becoming dominant and infusing language teaching with their concerns and preferences, which have seldom been appropriate or desirable. Languistics should be like medicine, an applied discipline that makes use of other disciplines, such as biology, chemistry, etc., but does not become subordinated to any of them.

**GD/AC 1.1:** *For languistics to be an autonomous discipline, it must keep other disciplines at arm's length.* Language teaching should not be the application of some other discipline —as implied in terms such as "applied linguistics" or "foreign language education"— but a discipline of its own, with its own name, concerns, and professional standards. Only languists should decide what (if anything) in other disciplines is *applicable* to languistics.

A **science** is *a body of knowledge whose laws and principles are testable by empirical research.* This definition would make it evident that linguistics is not yet a science. It is even debatable whether language teaching is sufficiently distinct from other disciplines to be called a **discipline**, which can be defined as *a branch of knowledge or learning.* This leads to the following conclusion:

**GD/A 1.2:** *For linguistics to become a science, it must establish its own body of knowledge through empirical research.* Of course, empirical research needs to be given direction by one or more theories such as the one proposed in this book.

# GD/A 2: Language

A **language** can be defined, for our purposes, as *a (1) relatively complete, (2) complex, (3) changing, (4) largely arbitrary, (5) rule-governed (6) system of (7) primarily oral (8) symbols (9) acquired or learned and (10) used for communication (11) within the cultural framework of (12) a linguistic community.*

Undoubtedly many linguists would not agree with every detail of the above definition; yet, it will serve our purposes quite well. All twelve points in the definition are important in language teaching, although some are more important than others. Eleven of these points were included and discussed in *Synthesis,* Chapter 2; not much would be gained by repeating that discussion here. The point added to the definition —point (5), that a language is "rule-governed"— was earlier assumed to be included in the concept of "system"; however, perhaps it deserves separate emphasis. Of course, this is unrelated to the penchant of some language teaching methods to stress the memorization and deductive application of rule *statements.* "Rule-governed" simply means that linguistic behavior can be described in terms of certain recurring patterns and operations.

Numerous corollaries and principles of language teaching can be drawn from the above definition of language. They will be presented in Chapter 5.

# GD/A 3: Second Language

The phrase **second language**, as used in this book, refers to *any language other than the native language of the speaker.*

The adjective "foreign," when applied to a language, is a sociopolitical label without any psycholinguistic validity —except, of course, that in many countries it is difficult to generate any interest in the study of anything so labeled. Furthermore, in countries where hundreds, thousands, or even millions of citizens speak, from early childhood, languages other than the official one(s), such languages can hardly be called "foreign," *even* from a sociopolitical point of view.[1]

The distinction between teaching a language widely spoken in the community and teaching one whose native speakers are mostly found abroad is of course very important. But instead of using the traditional terminology ("second" and "foreign" respectively), which is misleading, we shall refer to these two situations as **environmental** and **remote** respectively. A language can be an official language and yet be rather remote, as is the case with French in British Columbia; or it may lack official status and yet be environmental, as happens to Spanish in many parts of the United States. A useful further distinction is between linguistically homogeneous and heterogeneous language classes, either of which can exist in environmental or remote situations.

# GD/A 4: Teaching

**Teaching** can be defined as *a systematic effort to induce learning*. This definition excludes such forms of "teaching" as just *exposing* learners to data, whether it be in the form of quiet (good or bad) moral example, the simple exercise of authority, or largely unsystematic linguistic input. The emphasis in this definition is on active, specific, goal-oriented pedagogical activity of the type that usually takes place in the classroom (or the laboratory, workshop, etc). Implied is at least one person to induce the learning (let's call him or her simply the **teacher**) and at least one person doing the learning (let's be audacious again and call him or her simply the **student**).[2]

The corollaries and principles of language teaching based on the nature of teaching appear in Chapter 7.

# GD/A 5: Language Teaching

**Language teaching** is *a systematic effort by a teacher to induce the learning of a language by one or more students who are native speakers of a different language or languages.*

Note that language teaching is unique. No other teaching involves the learning of a new verbal code that to a considerable extent conflicts (but in some respects agrees) with a known verbal code. Being unique, language teaching should not be directly based on pedagogical principles particular to other subjects in the curriculum. Neither should it be based on activities that do not involve teaching, such as natural first or second language acquisition. Unlike natural language acquisition, which simply is what it is, *language teaching can be what we make it to be*, on the basis of principles we choose because they fit our subject matter and our purposes.

# GD/A 6: The Goal of Language Teaching

**The goal of language teaching** is *imparting second language competence (to be defined below) to students.*

**GD/AC 6.1:** *While a full-fledged language teaching program aims to impart an advanced level of second language competence, there can be limited programs aimed at imparting limited competence.*

Excellent language programs *can* impart native-like control in quality, but not in scope. Even the most ambitious language program will fall quite short of imparting native-like scope of control of the second language, especially of its vocabulary, for this can only be attained after years of submersion in the language. Limited programs with limited goals can help meet urgent needs, but in the long run they may do more harm than good to the students, as such programs may fail to establish a solid linguistic foundation and furthermore tend to encourage the students to communicate far beyond their limited competence. The chances of some-day reaching the goal of advanced, even native-like competence seem to be greatly increased for the student whose teachers insist on full mastery of the fundamentals.

Another way of defining the goal of language teaching is to say that it consists in *the production of bilinguals.* The term "bilingual" has unfortunately been defined too loosely, in ways that include anyone with any knowledge, however limited and faulty, of a second language. The term needs to be redefined both qualitatively and quantitatively. Neither people who speak fluently but incorrectly nor those who speak correctly just a few phrases can be considered bilingual. Perhaps the best definition of **bilingual** would state that *a 100 percent bilingual is a person who can function psychologically (expressing himself directly) and linguistically (lacking structural interference) like a native speaker in each of two languages.* This does not mean equal control of the *vocabulary* of both languages, as very few bilinguals exhibit perfect lexical balance. The extent (percentage) to which a person is bilingual in the various components and skills of the two languages can be determined psychometrically.

# GD/A 7: Learning

**Learning** may be defined as *a relatively permanent change in knowledge or behavior resulting from experience.* This is a general definition of learning which applies both to formal learning resulting from instruction and natural acquisition in which knowledge or behavior patterns are "picked up" unconsciously.

The unconscious learning of behavior applies to both animals and humans; it seems that only humans (at least we would like to think so) are capable of conscious learning and therefore of conscious knowledge — it is doubtful that "linguistically" trained chimps, for example, are conscious learners. Human learning ranges from the simplest, "signal learning" and "stimulus-response learning," to the most complex, "principle learning" and "problem solving," with the more complex forms being ultimately based on simpler forms [Gagné 1977]. The results of learning range from simple associations to elaborate skills, from knowing *about* something to knowing *how* to perform the most complex tasks.

The study of learning in general is one of the concerns of psychologists. Principles of language teaching derived from psychology are presented in Chapter 6.

*As in this book we are interested in learning associated with instruction, the term* learning *will normally be used in that sense, although often preceded by such words as "induced" of "formal," for further clarity.*

# GD/A 8: Second Language Learning

**Second language learning**, as used in this book, refers to *the development of second language competence resulting from instruction.*

Second language learning involves not only developing knowledge *about* a language but primarily developing knowledge *of* a language, that is, the ability to function in it, fluently *and* accurately. This involves a long-term learning task (not something that can be done in a few days or weeks with the help of a $7.95 set of records). It is furthermore a difficult endeavor. Naturally a long-term, complex learning task requires a high degree of commitment on the part of the student.

In languistics, we are much more interested in *induced* language learning than in the natural language acquisition that takes place in nurseries and streets *and about which there is very little we can do.* Furthermore, as we saw in Chapter 3, natural language acquisition *cannot* be successfully recreated in the classroom. It is unfortunate, therefore, that in much of the current literature about language learning (whether general or specific), so many otherwise careful authors fail to indicate whether they mean natural acquisition or formal learning; they often obscure all differences under the phrase "second language acquisition." This difference is very important and should be observed at all times through the use of specific terminology such as *"formal," "induced,"* or *"conscious" (second) language learning* vs. *"informal," "natural,"* or *"unconscious" (second) language acquisition.* The difference is too important to obscure it under general labels.

# GD/A 9: Second Language Competence

**Second language competence** is that *knowledge of a second language that enables a speaker to understand and use the language accurately, fluently, and appropriately to meet all communication needs in the corresponding cultural settings.*

*Second language competence is made up of three types of competence —linguistic, communicative, and cultural. The language (linguistic competence) is used to communicate (communicative competence) within the framework of a culture (cultural competence).* (See Figure 2.1. in Chapter 2.)

As already noted, a fairly advanced degree of second language competence of native-like *quality* is attainable within excellent language programs; but the attainment of second language competence of native-like *scope* requires much unconscious acquisition beyond the best language program. Each language has linguistic rules, communication acts, and cultural patterns that haven't even been described yet and that cannot, therefore, be taught consciously even in the most thorough language program. (Of course, much unconscious acquisition takes place within language programs, regardless of their emphasis on conscious learning.)

# GD/A 10: Linguistic Competence

**Linguistic competence** is defined for our purposes as *both the cognitive and performative knowledge of a language* [Corder 1973].

Linguists, following Chomsky [1957], define linguistic competence as the unconscious knowledge of the language possessed by the ideal native speaker, a purely *cognitive* knowledge which they distinguish from performance. For them linguistic performance is entirely based on competence; this, plus the fact that they include unsystematic mistakes (channel "noise") within performance, naturally turns performance, for them, into something rather "trivial," as some have put it.

Unlike linguists, languists are interested in the largely conscious knowledge of a second language being developed by real non-native speakers, i.e., language students. And again unlike linguists, languists are particularly interested in performance, both mechanical (not based on cognitive knowledge) and systematic (performance based on cognitive knowledge *minus* unsystematic mistakes).

Linguistic competence can be subdivided into four intralingual linguistic skills (listening comprehension, speaking ability, reading comprehension, and writing ability) and two nonverbal intralingual skills (decoding and encoding of such things as gestures). When two languages are in contact, there are also four interlingual skills involved (interpreting and translating, in both directions) and two nonverbal interlingual skills. Each of all these skills may be developed to various degrees. Linguistic competence also relates to each of the subcomponents of language, from sounds/graphemes through morphology, syntax, semantics, and discourse.[3]

In linguistics we would not consider a language learner fully competent until he can *use* the language at all levels (from sound to discourse) accurately and at normal speed. (This of course can only come about at the end of a long process of induced learning followed by natural acquisition.) Using a language at normal speed involves making hundreds of largely unconscious choices of one kind or another per minute. This means that language students need considerable systematic practice in choice-making, slowly and consciously at first, then faster, and finally largely unconsciously.

# GD/A 11: Communicative Competence

**Communicative competence** refers to *the ability to convey socially appropriate verbal messages*. This includes the ability to use "repair" strategies to compensate for breakdowns in communication.

This ability to express oneself in a socially appropriate manner applies to all levels of formality, from an intimate *tête-à-tête* to the most formal presentation before a large audience; of course, very few *native speakers* have the ability to communicate competently in all possible situations. An aspect of communicative competence much more relevant to language teaching is the skillful performance of everyday communication acts such as requesting, agreeing, refusing, and so forth; all communication is made up of such acts, and the competent language student needs to master, over the years, various ways of performing each.

Some would include within communicative competence something called "discourse competence," which refers to cohesion in form and coherence in thought. Cohesion in form is clearly part of the discourse subcomponent of linguistic competence, and coherence in thought would seem a matter of applying, attentively, a normal intelligence to what one is doing with the language. Thus "discourse competence" appears to be an unnecessary concept; moreover, it doesn't seem that such a "skill" needs to be taught.

## GD/A 12: Cultural Competence

**Cultural competence** is *knowledge about a culture and the ability to behave as its members behave*. In terms of language teaching, performative cultural knowledge —knowing how to behave in various situations— is more important than cognitive knowledge and should therefore constitute the emphasis of cultural instruction. Without such "knowhow," the second language speaker risks not being understood or being misunderstood, and as a result being the object of ridicule or causing offense. However, the common knowledge *about* the culture that the average educated native speaker has is also important; without it, the second language speaker will not only fail to understand some messages but will also give the impression of being very poorly educated or of not caring enough about the second culture to bother to learn basic facts about it.

## GD/A 13: Levels of Second Language Learning

Ideally, levels of second language learning should be defined in terms of mastery of specific content; but professional agreement on curricular content is not yet in sight. So it is necessary to define levels in terms of contact hours with the language. This will be done in reference to college or university studies, keeping in mind that due to a variety of factors, the number of contact hours needed to reach the same level of mastery in the schools is about 50-100 percent greater than in college. It should also be kept in mind that the contact hours given below apply to the languages most commonly taught in North America, i.e., Spanish, French, and English (for speakers of Spanish or French). The time required to reach the same level of proficiency in a noncognate, unrelated language can be twice or even three times the number of contact hours given below.

Given the above *caveats*, we can define second language learning levels as follows:

**Beginning level:** The first 250-300 hours of instruction (including study), usually done in the first year of college.

**Intermediate level:** The next 200-250 hours, usually done in the second year of college.

**Advanced level:** The next 150-200 hours, usually done in the third year of college. Apparently many colleges don't offer a third year of *language* study.

**Very advanced level:** The final 150-200 hours of *language* study, unfortunately rarely offered.

This would bring the total hours of the college language program to 750-950, enough to bring most beginners (in the languages mentioned!) up to approximately FSI proficiency level 2 + /3 without their forming bad linguistic habits —assuming the principles of this theory are applied. This would be a good foundation on which to build and go on to acquire native or near-native scope in the use of the second language.

Note that through intensive programs this learning process can be reduced to two or even one year of instruction, thereby enabling students to do many things *in the language*, such as studying its literature, much sooner.

An undesirable current trend is to confuse levels of learning with levels of proficiency, that is, to say that we should aim in language teaching at attaining a series of levels of proficiency as determined by interviews. The problem is that such interviews force learners to communicate beyond their competence and therefore to make many errors. Proficiency levels have therefore built-in inaccuracy. Certainly we should not aim at attaining faulty speech, nor should we condone it at any point. Only positively-stated levels of learning are acceptable.

# 4.14: For Discussion

1. *In what positive and negative ways have other disciplines affected language teaching?*
2. *Compare the definition of "language" given in this chapter with other definitions you have been exposed to. Which of the twelve points in this definition seem most relevant to language teaching?*
3. *What are the advantages and disadvantages of using such phrases as "foreign language" and "second language" in North America?*
4. *Can you think of places other than the classroom where systematic teaching occurs? What do all such situations have in common?*
5. *Would simply exposing learners to language data qualify as "language teaching"? Why or why not?*
6. *Make a list of specific differences between language teaching/*

*learning and other school subjects. Compare your list with those made by other students.*

7. *What goals have been proposed, over the years, for language programs? Discuss the pros and cons of various goals.*

8. *Is it desirable, in the long run, to learn first "tourist Spanish" or "English for stewardesses"? Explain.*

9. *What would be "an 80 percent bilingual"? Is such global quantification possible? Justify your position.*

10. *Can second language learning be effortless? Is it easier for some? What can be done to make it easier for most students?*

11. *Why is it important to differentiate consistently between induced learning and natural acquisition?*

12. *What is your reaction to the relationship between the three components of second language competence proposed in this chapter? Why can't we adopt the linguists' attitude toward performance?*

13. *Is excellent linguistic or communicative competence likely to develop when either is emphasized exclusively from the beginning? When should each be emphasized and why?*

14. *Was cultural instruction attended to or neglected in the language courses you have taken? What kinds of cultural activities were there?*

15. *Suggest principles for the definition of levels of second language learning by content. Is there general agreement among your fellow students about these principles?*

### Footnotes

[1] However, talking about "second" languages and "second" language teaching in the sense given above entails some risk of misunderstanding. Thus, it seems that many potential readers of *Synthesis in Second Language Teaching* failed to see in that the title of a book on language teaching *in general* and assumed instead that it was a book about language teaching in its own native environment, for example, ESL. To minimize such misunderstandings, the present book uses the phrase "second language" as little as possible.

[2] The two *him or her*'s in this sentence are my one linguistic concession to the equality of the sexes. Although I do believe that women are equal to men, I don't believe in awkward English prose, so from now on I'll stick to the generic masculine.

[3] See *Synthesis*, Chapter 10.

# Chapter 5: Principles From Linguistics

## Introduction and Summary

*Despite its voluntary ascent, in recent years, into a stratosphere of greater and greater abstractness and lesser and lesser practical relevance, linguistics —broadly understood— remains an important discipline for us. We teach languages and must therefore be able to describe them clearly and accurately. Linguists can provide us with accurate, explicit descriptions of languages.*

*This does not mean that linguistic grammars are directly applicable to language teaching. They may be a good point of departure for second language authors and teachers, but such grammars are too complex and abstract for pedagogical purposes. It is for us to pick and choose from various linguistic descriptions and adapt and integrate them into useful pedagogical grammars. Rather than use the old term "applied linguistics," even if redefined, we should therefore speak of "applicable linguistics," leaving it entirely to us (not to linguists!) to decide what is "applicable."*

*Language description and comparison is all that linguists as linguists can help us with. Linguists rarely have training in anything other than linguistics. When a linguist speaks about language teaching or learning, therefore, he seldom has any expertise and may in fact say (or write) the most ridiculous and unrealistic things. This has happened in the past and will no doubt continue to happen as long as we endow linguists with an aura of generalized wisdom.*

*This chapter considers first the twelve defining characteristics of language (given in Chapter 4) and some of their pedagogical implications. Then it discusses competence and performance; intra- and interlingual skills; and contrastive analysis, error analysis, and interlanguage.*

# 5.1:The Relative Completeness of Language

All languages are relatively complete vis-à-vis the communication needs of their speakers. If new needs arise, in technical vocabulary for example, the gaps are soon filled, mostly through borrowing or word coinage. No language can therefore be said to be "better" as a whole than any other language, although some languages adapt to changing needs faster than others.

**LP 1.1:** *Language students should be encouraged to feel that their native language is not better than the second language.* This recommendation is related to the following hypothesis:

**LH 1.1.1:** *Linguistic ethnocentrism (sense of linguistic superiority) has a negative effect on second language learning.* **RS:** There are no significant studies of this that I know of. Perhaps the best way to test this hypothesis would be by correlating a preprogram questionnaire on linguistic ethnocentrism with overall and *specific-skill* outcomes at the end of the language program. Note that I think it is the *linguistic* aspect of ethnocentrism that needs to be isolated.

No one has a complete knowledge of his native language, especially of its vocabulary. (For example, it has been said that no one knows more than about ten percent of the vocabulary of English.) The important thing is to know what is needed to meet one's communication needs. These communication needs vary from one individual to another, but there seems to be a common communicative and linguistic core.

**LP 1.2:** Given that far less than the whole language can be taught or learned, *what will be taught should be carefully selected, with special emphasis on the core of communication needs of language students.* (This principle of selection is discussed in greater detail in Chapter 7.)

It seems that young children often find themselves frustrated by linguistic limitations, which may explain some of their tantrums (a *very* tentative hypothesis). When adults suffer from linguistic limitations they will either use circumlocution or, if bilingual, switch languages; when they can't do either, they, too, can feel quite frustrated and upset. The language student who cannot express himself and does not know how to talk around his gaps in linguistic knowledge will (1) overgeneralize and thus misuse what little he knows of the language, (2) revert to his native language, (3) try to communicate nonverbally, usually without success, or (4) adopt a stance of stony silence.

**LP 1.3:** *Do not ask students to participate in communicative activities without providing them first with the necessary linguistic tools.* Most of these tools should be provided in advance, some as the communicative activity takes place.

**LH 1.3.1:** *Greater accuracy and less frustration will result when language students are provided with the tools they need for communicative activities.*

**LP 1.4:** *As soon as possible, teach the "art" of circumlocution.* This is especially useful in instances of faulty recall. However, circumlocution requires considerable linguistic skill, so perhaps it can only have a very limited role with beginners.

# 5.2: The Complexity of Language

Unlike animal "languages," whose messages are unitary, human language involves a theoretically infinite number of sentences which involve recombinations of many rules and a very large number of elements. Two principles follow from the great complexity of language.

**LP 2.1:** *As there is so much to be learned, learning a second language is a long-term endeavor.* A young child acquiring his native language needs thousands of hours of interaction to attain audio-oral mastery. Conscious second language learning by adults may be more efficient; still, it would be unreasonable to expect basic control of even the easiest languages in less than about 900 hours of instruction and study, and much longer for the harder languages.

**LP 2.2:** *The most efficient and effective way of teaching something complex is step by step.* This principle —gradation— has been challenged by many in recent years. Gradation is discussed in some detail in Chapter 7. Suffice it here to say that with the limited number of hours our language programs have, efficiency is essential. In natural language acquisition situations there are few time constraints, so the complexity of language can be dealt with globally, unconsciously, and more or less at leisure. That is not the case in formal language teaching and learning.

# 5.3: The Changeability of Language

Phonological, morphological, and syntactic changes are generally rare in established modern languages, but their vocabularies change frequently. Many words and phrases, and occasionally forms, are quite transitory —this is especially true of slang.

**LP 3.1:** Given that the main purpose of language learning is to be able to communicate in the language and that people communicate in the present-day form of the language, *the current form of the language should* *be taught.* One does not learn to communicate in, for example, modern English by studying Shakespeare or the King James version of the Bible.

**LC 3.1.1:** *Only words and forms having some permanence should be taught.*

**LC 3.1.2:** *Language teaching materials should be updated linguistically every eight to ten years.* This would enable authors and language teachers to incorporate semipermanent slang and colloquialisms in the language program.

**LP 3.2:** *Optionally, older forms of the language could be taught to very advanced students, for cultural, historical, and literary purposes.*

# 5.4: The Arbitrariness of Language

Languages have certain universal characteristics, but they also differ from each other in many arbitrary ways. The fact that the currently dominant school of linguistics emphasizes universals and shows less interest in differences should not distract us from the importance of the latter in linguistics. Even if we could explain all differences historically, from a present-day, synchronic point of view we would have to say that the differences are largely arbitrary. There is no logical reason for a language to have or not to have an extensive morphology, for adjectives to precede or follow nouns, for the verb to occur in the middle or at the end of the sentence, and so on.

**LP 4.1:** *In language teaching, appeals to logic or to history to explain differences between languages have very limited usefulness.* The very question "Why?" which so many of our students like to ask either has no answer or has an answer that contributes little to language learning. "How does it work?" would be a frequently answerable and much more useful question (this is what most students seem to have in mind when they ask "Why?").

As languists, whatever is universal is of little or no interest to us, for linguistic universals are, by definition, already known to our students before the first day of class. Moreover, everything the *two* languages — native and second— have in common is also already known to our students; they only have to be shown what they *can* use of the native language in the second language. So we need to concentrate our attention on the differences between the two languages.

**LP 4.2:** *Language learning is largely a matter of learning to use whatever in the second language differs from one's own.* Note however that much practice is needed in using the language in an integrated fashion, i.e., what is new plus what is the same, for communication.

# 5.5: A Language Is Rule-Governed

A language is governed by rules that a successful natural acquirer or formal learner internalizes and can use without conscious awareness. In the case of the conscious language learner, this is much the same as saying that he internalizes a system of linguistic habits (if we understand by such **linguistic habits** *any structured linguistic behavior which practice has made unconscious*). Thus the *substance* of linguistic "rules" and "habits" is essentially the same. The difference is in point of view: "rules" emphasize cognition, "habits" behavior.

**LP 5:** *A language should be taught in such a way that the rules governing it may be internalized (be made unconscious) and may control linguistic behavior.* This does not mean that language teaching has to be entirely or even largely deductive. Whether the point of departure in internalizing a rule is conscious (a "rule statement") or unconscious does not seem as important as ensuring that it ends as an accurate, unconscious way of controlling linguistic behavior.

# 5.6: A Language Is a System

In fact it is a system of systems, for it is made up of a hierarchy of subsystems or components. These are, from the lowest, most specific, and most concrete to the highest, most abstract, and most general: phonology, morphology (including vocabulary), syntax, semantics, and discourse. These components are interrelated in many ways, the whole forming an integrated but very complex system.

The complete structure of a language is described (not prescribed) in a "grammar." A **grammar** is not a book; nor prescriptive rules to be memorized; nor a discussion of just morphology and syntax (this is now best referred to as "morphosyntax," to prevent confusion); nor something to stay away from in language teaching — it is simply *a description of the (entire) structure of a language.*

There are several types of grammars, the main ones being traditional, popular, scientific, and pedagogical. A scientific grammar has to be precise and explicit, and as long, complex, and abstract as necessary to fully describe all of the unconscious knowledge an ideal native speaker has of his language. By meeting the requirements of suitability for scientific purposes, such grammars become quite unsuitable for pedagogical purposes. In Chapter 7 pedagogical grammars will be discussed, as will their relationship to other types of grammars.

**LL 6.1:** *The structure of a language is the framework or "skeleton" that supports the entire "body."*

**LP 6.1.1:** *Language teaching must concentrate on the mastery of structure first.* This is not to say that vocabulary and the communicative activities lexical knowledge allows are unimportant for beginners. They are. It is just a matter of emphasis. This can be put as a hypothesis:

**LH 6.1.1.1:** *While considerable communicative competence at the end of the program can be attained by emphasizing communication early or late, better linguistic competence (more accurate use of structure) will be attained by students whose programs emphasize structural accuracy at the beginning and intermediate levels.* **RS:** Comparisons of the outcomes of whole programs exhibiting these two different emphases are called for. The structural inaccuracy of Immersion Approach graduates should be an indication of what to expect.

**LL 6.2:** *All modern languages have sound systems with phonemes (contrastive sound units) and allophones (variants of phonemes).* The number of phonemes in the languages of the world vary greatly, from about twelve to nearly one hundred, but they all have phonemes and allophones. It is possible, however, for a phonemic contrast to be neutralized in certain contexts, as happens with North American English /t/ and /d/ in, for example, *latter* and *ladder*. Such problems are hardly adequate grounds for abandoning the phonemic principle, which is particularly useful in language teaching, whatever its status may be in theoretical linguistics.

**LP 6.2.1:** Because everything that is said in a language makes use — rightly or wrongly— of its sound system, *the phonemes and allophones of a second language must be mastered very early in the program.*

Many, including some people whose opinions I respect, argue that control over the sounds of the language should be allowed to come about very gradually, over a period of months or even years. My informal observations over many years lead me to disagree: It seems that best results in pronunciation are obtained when bad habits are not allowed to form and good habits are established from the start. Curiously, some of the same scholars who advocate gradual improvement in pronunciation would not allow students to initially form bad habits in the use of morphology, syntax, or vocabulary. To state my position as a testable hypothesis:

**LH 6.2.1.1:** *Fewer pronunciation errors will occur at the end of the program when pronunciation is taught systematically at the beginning of the program, and corrected throughout as needed, than when good pronunciation is expected to be "picked up" gradually.* **RS:** One could treat three or four "difficult" sounds both ways. (How pronunciation should be taught at the beginning of the program is discussed in Chapter 7.)

**LP 6.3:** *Syntax isn't necessarily the most important component of language structure.* In some languages, such as Latin, syntax is fairly free and doesn't convey as much meaning as morphology, which is quite elaborate and rigid. In other languages, such as English, much more meaning is carried by syntax, and morphology is relatively less important. In Chinese, syntax is extremely important, as there is no morphology to speak of.

**LC 6.3.1:** It follows from the above that *in language teaching, the relative emphasis given to morphology or syntax should depend on their importance in the second language, as well as on how the two languages relate in this regard.*

**LP 6.4:** *Ultimately, a language system is a system of identities, contrasts (including differences), and distributions.* Two utterances or **writtances** (*instances of written language, from a single letter to the longest encyclopedia*) are either the same or different, and each has a characteristic distribution in the language.

**LC 6.4.1:** Accordingly, *language teaching should concentrate on creating awareness of intralingual (and interlingual) identities, contrasts, and distributions.* If students are not led to see the correct identities, contrasts, and distributions, they will reach their own conclusions about these basic relationships, conclusions that will often be wrong.

# 5.7: A Language Is Primarily Oral

The many reasons for concluding that modern languages are primarily oral were reviewed in *Synthesis* [pp. 34-8]. Perhaps the most significant points are that spoken language is much more common and fundamental, and that it is precisely the audio-oral aspect of the second language which the great majority of language learners would like to master.

**LP 7:** *The main stream of the language program should emphasize listening and speaking, without neglecting to teach, at the right time, reading and writing.* Of course, this does not apply to classical languages or to courses with the limited goal of developing reading skill.

**LC 7.1:** *For best results in developing listening and speaking ability, audio-oral emphasis must be maintained throughout the program.* This could be tested empirically, but it doesn't seem necessary to do so, for it seems highly logical that one will develop best the skills one practices most. And yet, the "audiolingual" programs of the sixties and seventies and many other "oral" programs, while starting instruction with an emphasis on listening and speaking, have soon shifted to an emphasis on the written language, with corresponding results.

**LC 7.2:** Given that the language program should be primarily audio-oral, *language learning should be based primarily on audio-oral activi-*

*ties and media (such as recordings) and only secondarily on graphic activities and media (such as textbooks and computers).* It should be obvious that one cannot best develop skills in one modality through activities in a different (and often conflicting) modality.

## 5.8: A Language Is Made Up of Symbols

Symbols are meaningful and arbitrary; both characteristics must be present for efficient communication to be possible. These symbols are the lexical and grammatical morphemes of the language. Note that, by themselves, sounds and letters are not meaningful. In the sense above they are not symbols but subsymbolic elements, the stuff symbols are made of. Language symbols are social conventions, and as such their semantic boundaries will often differ from those of "equivalent" symbols used in other languages.

**LP 8.1:** *We should be wary of assuming vocabulary equivalences across languages.* An apparent equivalence can only be a "working hypothesis," and the door of the mind should always be left open to the likelihood that there will be some difference after all.

**LP 8.2:** On the other hand, *very many words do have interlingual equivalences in their basic denotations.* We should therefore not fall for the "myth of the missing equivalent" [Butzkamm 1973], in which many seem to believe.

## 5.9: Languages Are Acquired or Learned

To review, *acquiring* a language is "picking it up" informally and unconsciously in a natural environment, while *learning* a language is internalizing it formally and (at least initially) consciously in the classroom. Native language acquisition follows the first process and is almost invariably successful. When it comes to second language learning, both processes may or may not result in the ability to use the language fluently and accurately.

There are many conditions under which a language may be acquired or learned. The six that we will distinguish are: (1) native language acquisition; (2) bilingual development from infancy, certainly the "least painful" way of becoming bilingual; (3) second language acquisition in childhood, when a monolingual child is surrounded by speakers of another language; (4) second language learning in childhood, when the second language is a subject in the curriculum; (5) adult second language acquisition, such as what adult immigrants go through; and (6) second language learning in the classroom by linguistic adults. (**Linguistic adults** can be defined as *persons who have reached linguistic maturity as well as a considerable degree of cognitive maturity*; the onset of linguistic adulthood is about age ten, which is of course years before most people reach emotional or legal adulthood). Situation (6) above is the main concern of languistics and therefore of this book. We have already considered a further situation, immersion programs, which try to reproduce situation (1) later in childhood and in the classroom.

Acquirers and learners (and therefore acquisition and learning) differ markedly in many respects. They differ in the linguistic environment available to them; their motivation and initial knowledge; the amount of exposure to the language; the role of linguistic interference, if any; the presence or absence of language ego, anxiety, and inhibitions; the degree of flexibility of the brain; the relative power of motor and general memory; the existence of spelling-boundness; the possession of a system of concepts; the degree of linguistic awareness and interest in linguistic accuracy; overall learner characteristics; and probably several other variables.

**LP 9.1:** *Natural language acquisition and formal second language learning are very different processes that take place in very different situations and often involve very different learners.* To be successful, natural language acquisition requires much linguistic interaction with native speakers, whose influence must be far stronger than that of linguistically incompetent fellow acquirers. This is an *essential* condition for successful natural language acquisition.

**LC 9.1.1:** *Successful natural language acquisition cannot take place in the second language classroom.* The failure of the Immersion Approach to produce linguistic competence (as shown in Chapter 3) is strong evidence of this. This leads to the following hypothesis:

**LH 9.1.1.1:** *Significantly better linguistic competence will be obtained in the second language classroom by starting with semi-intensive formal learning in late childhood (at about age ten or eleven) or early adulthood (age 16 or older) and shifting, a few years later, to natural acquisition than by relying on natural acquisition from the start.* **RS:** This hypothesis can only be tested by comparing the outcomes of entire language programs, although the fossilization of faulty rules is observable quite early in acquisition-oriented programs.

**LP 9.2:** *Classroom second language learning differs markedly from classroom native language learning.* This is so obvious that it shouldn't need to be said; but, alas, it has to, for some people are claiming that second language teaching isn't very different from native language teaching! The native language classroom involves teaching literacy and better means of expression to children *who already know the language.* Beginners come to the second language classroom *without* any knowledge of the language, and it takes them many years of study to attain the scope and flexibility of a six-year-old's native control of the same language.

**LC 9.2.1:** *While certain native language teaching techniques may be usable, especially after the beginning level, second language teaching cannot be based on native language teaching.* The usable techniques are *some* of the techniques used in teaching literacy, reading comprehension, and writing ability to native speakers.

# 5.10: The Main Purpose of Language Is Communication

Very few uses of language are noncommunicative; two examples are very deliberate thought and singing in the shower. Even literature and media programs are uses of the language to communicate, though the recipient of the communication acts is indeterminate. Not surprisingly, the desire to communicate orally is the main reason for study given by a majority of second language beginners who have been surveyed at various times. Yet, most students don't want to learn to communicate in any old way —they want to learn how to do it *accurately.*

**LP 10.1:** *The main purpose of language teaching should be to impart the ability to communicate fluently and accurately in a second language.*

**LC 10.1.1:** Students find communication highly motivating, so, if for no other reason, *there should be some communicative activity from the beginning of the program, even if very brief and simple at first.* As the program progresses, communicative activities can become longer and more challenging.

**LC 10.1.2:** *We should insist on accurate use of what is learned as it is learned, for accuracy enhances both the intelligibility and the acceptability of communication.* Implied here is the avoidance of communicative activities beyond the students' linguistic competence and the correction of errors.

**LH 10.1.3:** *Under typical classroom conditions, an early emphasis on free communication will result in linguistic incompetence.* Rare is the student who doesn't disregard accuracy when he is constantly encouraged to communicate beyond his competence. **RS:** The difference in outcome between a program that emphasizes free communication from the start and one with an early emphasis on accuracy should become apparent in as few as one hundred hours of differentiated instruction. The outcome I would expect is that the students in the former type of program would be able to say many things, yes, but incorrectly and those in the latter type of program would be largely accurate within a limited (but slowly growing) communicative repertoire. Of course, the difference in treatment between the two groups should be limited to this one variable. Comparing, for example, the Communicative Approach to some form of the Grammar-Translation Method is comparing apples and oranges.

**LL 10.2**: *Languages are communication systems that contain much (useful) redundancy.* This is true of all subcomponents of a language. To give just one example from English morphology, the *-s* in *He works at home* is quite redundant, as the subject is already expressed by *He*. However, this and other redundancies greatly facilitate communication, for they repeat important parts of messages. Unfortunately, language students tend to ignore what is redundant to the bare-bones message they want to communicate. In so doing, not only do they produce socially unacceptable utterances but make the comprehension of their messages more difficult even for listeners endowed with much goodwill and patience.

**LC 10.2.1**: In language teaching, *we must insist on the students learning and using the redundant elements and rules of the language.* Under classroom conditions, omissions cannot be allowed, for there is no guarantee that the gaps will be filled in later.

**LH 10.2.2**: *Early leniency with the omission of linguistic redundancies will result in the nonuse or underuse of redundant features at the end of the program.* What tends to eventually appear during the normal development of native language acquisition may never appear under classroom or even second language acquisition conditions. **RS:** The long-term two-group comparison this calls for should involve students of the same native language background learning the same second language.

# 5.11: A Language Is Used Within a Cultural Framework

As noted in Chapter 4, cultural competence involves knowledge about the second culture and knowledge of how to behave in it, that is, both cognitive and performative cultural knowledge. Linguistically, this involves primarily the cultural connotations of words and phrases and the nonverbal behavior that accompanies language in various situations.

**LP 11.1**: *As words and phrases are taught, their cultural connotations should also be gradually taught.* The emphasis here is on "gradually." It can take a long time to learn all the important cultural connotations of certain words and phrases; the learning process should not be rushed.

**LP 11.2:** *Behavior appropriate to the second culture should also be taught.* Probably the best way to do this is to model such behavior and have the students act it out. Situations and simulations seem especially suitable.

**LP 11.3:** *Knowledge* about *the culture should also be imparted.* It would seem best to do this on an *ad hoc* basis until the advanced level, and then study the second culture systematically in the second language.

**LP 11.4:** *A systematic comparison of the two cultures offers the greatest insights into both, so it should also be offered.* For such a comparison to be really profitable, the students need to know the second language and the separate cultures quite well. It seems therefore that this is a type of study best left for the advanced or very advanced level. Of course, the *ad hoc* noting of specific differences and similarities is possible —and desirable— throughout the program.[1]

# 5.12: Languages Are Used in Linguistic Communities

Linguistic communities range from a few people within a country where another language is spoken to the populations of several countries plus speakers scattered around the world, as in the case of English. Within the boundaries of a linguistic community there is usually a considerable number of linguistic subcommunities or dialects which are distributed geographically, occupationally, and socially.

**LP 12.1:** *We should teach, for active use, a standard dialect spoken by educated native speakers.* This may have to be a "hybrid" dialect with features from several dialects, as no one really speaks, for example, Standard American English, Latin American Spanish, or Standard French. It would not be in the students' best interests to learn a dialect with minority or substandard status.

**LC 12.1.1:** *Teachers who are not speakers of the standard dialect used in the program should receive training in its use and be encouraged to use it.* Abandoning, for classroom language teaching purposes, the peculiarities of one's regional dialect seems very difficult but really isn't if one is clearly aware of the differences involved. Exposing beginning students to markedly different dialects seems only to confuse them. This is a matter of the teacher making a little concession for the benefit of the students.

**LP 12.2:** *As an advanced activity, we should teach comprehension of all major dialects.* It isn't enough to be able to understand and use a standard dialect spoken by educated people. Language program graduates will usually come in contact with native speakers of a variety of dialects. A good language program will train advanced students auditorily for this experience.

**LC 12.2.1:** *Collections of recordings with conversations, speeches, etc. in a variety of dialects of major languages should be made widely available.*

# 5.13: Competence and Performance

**LL 13.1:** *All verbal communicative performance is based on some sort of linguistic competence.*

**LL 13.2:** *There is nonverbal communicative performance (and competence) that is largely independent of linguistic competence.* Beginning language students who succeed in communicating many ideas generally do so on the basis of nonverbal communicative competence and at the expense of linguistic performance and competence. Nonverbal communicative competence may thus hinder the full development of linguistic competence.

**LP 13.3:** *Language programs should emphasize linguistic competence and the nonverbal behavior that accompanies linguistic performance.* What should be discouraged in language classrooms is the substitution of the nonverbal for the verbal. Such substitutions show that communication has been allowed to exceed the limits of linguistic competence. They also seem to retard or even prevent the development of the corresponding linguistic competence.

**LP 13.4:** *There is also noncommunicative (or precompetent) performance, such as mechanical performance, that is not based on linguistic competence.* Mechanical performance involves the imitation, repetition, and/or manipulation of utterances. This is found in young native language acquirers in the form of the imitation and repetition of "routines" and the manipulation of many of these as "patterns" for substitution and combination. Competent performance seems to emerge from such precompetent performance, as mechanical activity is cognitively easier than free, creative activity.

**LC 13.4.1:** *The teaching of any element or rule of a language should lead the learner to competence in its use by taking precompetent, mechanical performance as the point of departure.* Note that initial performance has to be mechanical but *not mindless.* Mindless performance is boring and not conducive to learning.

**LH 13.4.1.1:** *Better (faster and more accurate) competence-based linguistic performance will be the outcome of language programs that don't skimp on precompetent but intelligent mechanical performance.*

**LP 13.5:** *A learner's attempts to communicate verbally beyond his competence will lead to faulty performance which can easily "fossilize" into linguistic incompetence.* Faced with having to communicate a message beyond his limited linguistic competence, a language learner will rely on (1) native language transfer, (2) overgeneralization of what he knows of the second language, or, usually, (3) both. The result is very inaccurate speech (or writing) which, if continued for some time, becomes the norm.

**LC 13.5.1:** *Language students should be discouraged from communicating beyond their competence.* One doesn't learn to swim long and well by just jumping in deep water and thrashing about without any preparation, although one could, that way, manage to learn to stay afloat for a while with an unsightly dog paddle.

# 5.14: Intralingual Skills

There are four verbal intralingual skills and two nonverbal intralingual skills. As Figure 5.1 shows, these six skills can be classified and interrelated on the basis of *modality* (audio-oral, graphic, or nonverbal) and *activity* (receptive/decoding or productive/encoding).

**LP 14.1:** *The central skill of language is speaking.* I realize this runs counter to the view of many who see other skills as central. But consider the following: gestures normally accompany speech, rather than the other way around; we say what we write to ourselves before or as we write it; we transform what we read into subvocal sounds, especially if it is new and difficult (as much in a second language is); and it seems we echo, match and reorganize subvocally, that is, via silent speech, all spoken language we hear and understand. When we hear something we don't understand within an intelligible context, we repeat it subvocally in an attempt to store it until we can check it. When speech is totally unintelligible, as when listening to a strange language, we can retain very little because even mechanical subvocal speech (not to speak of cognitive processing) cannot take place. A trained phonetician would be able to retain more and longer strange utterances, and visualize and transcribe them, precisely because he *can* produce the necessary subvocal echoing. (One of the earliest tasks of language teaching is to train beginning students to do this.)

**LC 14.1.1:** *Language teaching must emphasize the speaking skill from the start while not neglecting listening and introducing, in due time, reading and writing.* One important reason for having students speak from the start, even if only mechanically at first, is that students can respond nonverbally quite correctly to complex auditory stimuli while developing faulty subvocal speech at the same time. For example, after many hours of responding nonverbally to increasingly complex commands and other auditory stimuli, when Total Physical Response students start to speak their speech is full of the most basic errors. No doubt their accuracy improves in time; but I believe better results can be obtained when all important errors (especially early errors, which set the pattern for future performance) are corrected —and subvocal errors are not accessible for correction.

| | | MODALITY | | |
|---|---|---|---|---|
| | | AUDIO—ORAL | GRAPHIC | NONVERBAL |
| ACTIVITY | RECEPTIVE/DECODING | Listening Comprehension | Reading Comprehension | Gestural Interpretation |
| | PRODUCTIVE/ENCODING | Speaking Ability | Writing Ability | Gestural Expression |

Figure 5.1

**LP 14.2:** *While nonverbal skills are dependent on verbal skills and graphic skills are ultimately based on audio-oral skills, all skills have certain independent characteristics.*

**LC 14.2.1:** *Gestures should be taught in connection with the verbal behavior they accompany.* There wouldn't seem to be much point in learning a second language gesture or other form of nonverbal communicative behavior without learning the language (and the situation) with which such nonverbal behavior is appropriate.

**LP 14.3:** *Since writing is an attempt, however imperfect, to represent speech, the introduction of the graphic skills should follow the develop-*

*ment of an audio-oral foundation.* Written language has the same referents as speech, but often writing fails to represent or misrepresents important details of speech. Logographic systems such as Chinese characters, for example, represent only the semantics and syntax of speech, not its sounds. Many alphabetic systems represent speech partially and inconsistently; this largely accounts, for instance, for the considerable difficulty native speakers of English have in becoming literate.

All standard writing systems have been designed with the needs of fluent native speakers —*not* beginning second language learners— in mind. Interpreting a different alphabet, for example, usually involves facing many contradictory stimuli —often difficulties with internal inconsistency and *always*, or so it seems, problems of interference from native language sound-spelling correlation habits. The inevitable result of such early exposure to contradictory stimuli is that the visually dependent older child and adult language learner disbelieves his ears and follows the visual stimuli [Hammerly 1970], with disastrous effects on their pronunciation and intonation.

**LC 14.3.1:** *Because most linguistic adults are visually dependent, they should be provided with visual aids to pronunciation and intonation at the beginning of the language program.* Specialized alphabets such as phonetic alphabets allow phoneticians and other scholars to communicate, but such universal systems fail to meet the needs of speakers of a particular native language trying to learn a particular second language; such alphabets fail furthermore to provide a bridge between pronunciation and spelling, forcing the separate treatment of each. The unavoidable conclusion is that, *if* excellence in pronunciation and intonation is considered important (which I think it should be), then the introduction of standard alphabetical writing in a second language should be delayed until an audio-oral foundation has been established in the language with the help of carefully designed *pedagogical* aids to pronunciation, intonation, and then the transition from these to spelling.

**LP 14.4:** *One skill does not result automatically from another; each skill should be taught.* While the development of a more basic skill facilitates the subsequent development of a less basic one, each skill has particular characteristics that must be attended to and each skill must be taught and practiced. Thus, while learning the basics of speaking will facilitate the development of listening comprehension, skill in understanding fluent native speech needs to be taught and practiced as such. Learning to read is greatly facilitated by developing an audio-oral foundation first, but many aspects of reading still have to be taught, and of course there must be extensive practice in reading. The same principle applies to writing, which is facilitated by, but does not result automatically from, listening, speaking, and reading skill.

# 5.15: Interlingual Skills

When two languages come in contact, there can be four verbal skills (oral interpretation and written translation in either direction) and two nonverbal skills that accompany interpretation (nonverbal interpretation in either direction).

**LP 15:** *When two languages come in contact, vocal or subvocal interpretation or translation are inevitable.* It is impossible *not* to relate the unknown to the known —that's the way our minds are made up. It is impossible therefore not to try to find a native language equivalent for new words and phrases —at some point some sort of equation *is* made. Even the most determined advocates of a Direct Method find themselves translating in their minds, as Harold Palmer noted long ago.

**LC 15.1:** *Rather than spend time and energy in a vain effort to impede translation, language teachers should* direct *this unavoidable process by overtly making the differences and similarities between the two languages quite clear to the students.* Much language teaching has lost efficiency and effectiveness through elaborate and time-consuming procedures for avoiding using the native language of the students, when all the while the latter are letting the native language run rampant in their minds and are assuming incorrect covert equivalences that often do not emerge "in public" until it is too late to correct them.

# 5.16: Contrastive Analysis

**Contrastive analysis** (CA) is *the systematic comparison of the rules and elements of two languages aimed at describing their identities/ similarities and contrasts/differences in form, distribution, function, and meaning.* Together with transfer theory and the principle of reliance on the familiar (both to be discussed in the next chapter), CA can tell us in what ways the native language will facilitate or interfere with the learning of particular aspects of the second language. CA can also explain many of the errors that result when a language student tries to communicate beyond his competence.

CA is predicated on the existence of universal (or at least bilingual) bases for comparing two languages. The universal basis for phonological comparisons is phonetics. For meaning, semantics provides the universal basis of comparison; more narrowly, good bilingual dictionaries have offered us semantic CA analysis for centuries. When it comes to morpho-syntax, James [1980:178] demonstrated that neither surface structure nor deep structure plus transformations is an adequate basis of comparison, and that it is best to rely on translation equivalence —something bilinguals seem to do with ease.

**LP 16:** *Language teaching should rely on contrastive analysis for a description of the identities/similarities and contrasts/differences between the second language and the native language(s) of the students.* This may be the most unfashionable proposal in this book, for, at least in North America, the interest in CA has gone down greatly since the late sixties. And yet, nothing *can* replace CA as a way of comparing two languages and as the basis for certain pedagogical insights and decisions dependent on such a comparison.

**LC 16.1:** *Contrastive analysis is useful in the preparation of first-generation language teaching materials and in their presentation and manipulation in the classroom, in the correction of errors, in language testing, and in research on language learning, especially in the area of transfer.* CA predicts areas of interlingual difficulty and facilitation. Once a careful record of actual student errors with given materials has been obtained, reliance on experience is possible and prediction becomes less useful.

Note that the predictive power of CA seems to be greatest with phonology, which involves motor habits. It is weaker with morphosyntax and perhaps weakest with semantics, which is arguably the most cognitively oriented subcomponent of language. And yet, until recently CA had not been applied to the development of pedagogical transcriptions.[2]

# 5.17: Error Analysis

**Error analysis** (EA) is *the analysis of the deviations of second language learners from native-speaker norms.* The purpose of such an analysis is to determine the nature and causes of errors so as to better understand the language learning process. It also has certain practical applications.

EA enables second language specialists to revise teaching materials and procedures in order to improve their effectiveness. By understanding the causes of errors, language teachers can better help their students. EA has also been the basis of many studies of the order of natural language acquisition. As has already been explained, the natural order (whatever it may turn out to be) has little relevance to the order in which rules should be learned in the language classroom, where students should not be required to meet global communication needs.

**LP 17:** *Error analysis should be used in language teaching on an* *ongoing basis.* The careful observation of student errors by the classroom teacher enables him not only to understand the difficulties of his students but also to evaluate the effectiveness of his teaching, to provide the most suitable correction, and to offer remedial work as needed.

For the researcher, EA is a tool that makes possible confirmation or rejection, and thus refinement, of the predictions of transfer theory and linguistic theories. Unfortunately, some research work of this nature has been deficient (for example, some researchers have approached errors with a certain theoretical bias, minimizing the influence of the native language, ignoring the different effect of interference at different levels of language learning, and so forth).

# 5.18: Interlanguage

An **interlanguage** (IL) [Selinker 1972] is *a linguistic system based on the output of second language learners.* It is, in other words, a linguistic system intermediate between two languages. Although the term "interlanguage" has become established in the professional literature, it is something of a misnomer, since "language" implies stability and regular use in a linguistic community, but ILs are very unstable (except maybe for the last one or "terminal" IL) and are frequently used outside linguistic communities. A better term for the nonterminal systems used in second language classrooms would be *transitional systems* [Hammerly 1982], a term that does not imply linguistic inaccuracy; perhaps the stable terminal system, short of the second language, that the second language learner or acquirer does not go beyond should be referred to as an IL.

**LP 18:** *Language teaching should try to prevent the formation of faulty interlanguages.* This may sound idealistic, for errors are unavoidable when our students are encouraged, as they must be, to produce novel sentences using what they know. But the last thing language students need is to develop more-or-less *stable* faulty systems, for such systems tend to become permanent the moment they are seen to satisfy perceived communication needs. In language teaching, the early formation of faulty ILs can be prevented by encouraging students to communicate only within their limited but growing linguistic competence and actively discouraging them from going beyond it and thus internalizing faulty rules.

# 5.19: For Discussion

1. *If a student asked you which is the best language for him to learn, what would your reply be? Why?*

2. *Have you had the experience of being expected to communicate beyond your competence in a second language? What did you do? What was the outcome (short-term and long-term)?*

3. *Think of complex tasks you have undertaken in the past, such as learning to type, to play a musical instrument from sheet music, or to operate complex equipment. How do they compare with learning a language in terms of time commitment? In terms of the degree of difficulty involved?*

4. *How have you mastered complex learning tasks in the past — globally or step by step? Are some such tasks more suitable for one or the other approach?*

5. *What do you think of the idea that an ancestor language should be learned first and then one or several of its offspring? For example, would it be a good idea to require that English speakers learn Latin before they attempt to learn Spanish and/or French?*

6. *Is the following statement a realistic one: "Each second (or 'foreign') language should be taught as a unique, independent linguistic system." Why or why not?*

7. *Explain the different meanings of "rule" in traditional grammar, popular grammar, the Grammar-Translation Method, transformational-generative grammar, and languistics. What do you understand by a "rule statement"?*

8. *What position do various scholars and language teaching methods take regarding (a) the importance of a structural foundation? (b) the need to master the sounds at the beginning of the program? and (c) the teaching of intralingual and interlingual identities/similarities, contrasts/differences, and distributions?*

9. *List what you see as the pros and cons of an audio-oral emphasis for the language program. How do textbooks, recordings, computers, and classroom activities fit with an audio-oral emphasis?*

10. *Do most words have equivalences (though not necessarily one-word equivalences) across languages? Would this apply to the basic meanings of the word? To its cultural connotations? To its occurrence in idioms and proverbs?*

11. *What is your reaction to the assertion that "Successful natural language acquisition cannot take place in the second language classroom"? Argue the case for and against it.*

12. *What types of brief and simple communicative activities could possibly be carried out in the first hour of the language program?*

13. *What would you do to ensure that inaccurate communication does not become the norm in the classroom?*

14. *What is the likely effect, in the long run, of ignoring, in the second*

*language classroom, such "developmental" errors as* \*He want a apple, *on the grounds that these are "late-acquired rules"?*

15. *Rank the following activities for their suitability at the early beginning, intermediate, advanced, or very advanced levels: (a) a study of the role of marriage customs in the two cultures; (b) notes and asides about the common cultural connotations of words; (c) role-playing in a typical shopping situation; (d) a realia exchange; (e) culture-specific humor; (f) culture-oriented literature; and (g) reading in the native language about a foreign custom.*

16. *Which dialect of the language you plan to teach would be best to teach to your students? Defend your choice on such grounds as number of speakers, internal simplicity, prestige, usefulness, etc.*

17. *Is precompetent (imitative or manipulative) performance necessary or useful? If so, why? If not, why not? How can such practice be made acceptable (even if not welcome) to second language students?*

18. *Discuss the advantages and disadvantages of starting the study of a second language with a long period of (a) listening only, (b) reading only, or (c) listening and reading only.*

19. *Describe what happens when a beginning student of the language you plan to teach reads it in its standard written form from the start. What specific errors result? What can be done about this?*

20. *When you were a beginning second language learner, did you find it possible not to translate new words and phrases in your mind? What role did mental translation play for you at more advanced levels?*

21. *What do you see as the ideal roles of CA and EA and as the ideal relationship between them?*

22. *Are you a speaker of a terminal IL? If so, how did that come about? Do you think it is possible to prevent the development of stable, faulty ILs within the language program? How?*

### Footnotes

[1]Chapter 20 of *Synthesis* discusses cultural competence and 30 types of cultural activities for the language program.

[2]*Synthesis* devotes a whole chapter, Chapter 9, to CA, error analysis, and interlanguage.

# Chapter 6: Principles From Psychology

## Introduction and Summary

*Psychology, the science of the mind, has very much to contribute to linguistics, since cognition, emotion, and volition —three major concerns of psychology— are all involved in most language learning activities. But again, it should be remembered that, as with linguistics, the choice of "applicable" psychological theories and concepts is up to us. Enough psychological pet theories have been unwisely foisted on language teachers for us to be cautious of any strong claims or unusual procedures based on vague "psychological studies" or "findings." "Good" psychology, like "good" linguistics and "good" almost-anything, is balanced and objective, not extreme and subjective.*

*This chapter does not go into all the implications of psychology for language teaching but concentrates on what seem to be the most significant ones. It discusses such topics as the organization and gradation of learning tasks, attention, transfer, sound perception, subvocal speech, practice, errors, integration, the subsumption of lower-level skills, memory and forgetting, and learner factors. Since most of these and other topics considered in this chapter could be the subject of separate books, the reader should not expect, in a few pages, more than a brief discussion of each.*

## 6.1: The Human Learner

**PL 1.1: Cognition:** *Human beings are cognitive creatures; they can't help being cognitively active.* Except for short periods of deep sleep and for incidents of unconsciousness, human beings are always cognitively active, one way or another. Of course, some forms of cognition are higher than others and therefore more challenging and rewarding. (The degree of cognitive maturity required for formal learning is not fully reached until the age of ten or eleven; see PP 9.4 below.)

**PC 1.1.1:** *To fully involve a learner in the learning process, his higher cognitive abilities must be called into action.* (John B. Carroll pointed this out long ago.) While a certain amount of mechanical conditioning is necessary, especially early in a language program, it is far from sufficient. A higher cognitive organization is very useful because it serves as a sort of "hat rack" on which the various facts involved can be "hung."

**PH 1.1.1.1:** *Second language teaching that makes considerable use of higher forms of cognition (a) will be more interesting to the learners and (b) will be more effective, resulting in better retention.* **RS:** This is the kind of common-sense statement that wouldn't seem to need formal validation, but, if so wished, it could be tested formally; one semester should be enough, although, frankly, I would consider it unconscionable to submit the control class to mechanical teaching for so long.

**PL 1.2: Emotion:** *Human beings are emotive creatures; they can't help having feelings.* There are persons who don't seem to feel anything; when this is truly the case (which it seldom is), it can be considered pathological.

**PC 1.2.1:** *Language programs should attend to what has come to be known as "the affective domain," by providing an emotionally favorable atmosphere.* This is not to say that language teaching must be highly emotional; but it does mean that an effort must be made never to offend or hurt and to accentuate positive emotions. This recommendation seems obvious, and yet some language classrooms are filled with fear and hostility, and in many the teachers maintain an emotional neutrality that fails to enlist the emotions of the students in the learning process. (See also PP 9.3 below.)

**PL 1.3: Volition:** *Human beings are volitional creatures.* Whether they want or do not want to do anything, including learn, is crucial to its outcome.

**PC 1.3.1:** *The desire of the language student to learn the language must be secured.* If it isn't there at the beginning of the program, every effort should be made to develop it as soon as possible. (See also PC 9.1.2 below.)

**PC 1.3.2:** *As language teaching to unwilling students tends to be ineffective, there seems to be little point in doing it.* It can be argued, of course, that all students should be exposed to another language and that if, through extrinsic motivation (such as grades), they do study, they will learn. This is probably true, but far from ideal; and being far from ideal, it isn't likely to produce very good or long-lasting results. No doubt some learning results simply from responding to stimuli, even if unwillingly, but successful language learning involves far more than mechanical responses; some of the activities essential to it require willing long-term participation.

# 6.2: Types of Learning

**PP 2.1: Learning Hierarchy:** *According to Gagné's [1977] theory of learning, which is a continuity theory, there are eight types of learning and the more complex forms are based on the simpler ones.* From the simplest to the most complex, the eight types of learning Gagné distinguishes are: (1) *signal learning*, more commonly known as "classical conditioning"; (2) *stimulus-response learning*; (3) motor *chaining*; (4) *verbal association* or verbal chaining; (5) *multiple discrimination*; (6) *concept learning*, in which generalization plays a very important role; (7) *principle learning*; and (8) *problem solving*. Examples of each of these are provided in Chapter 3 of *Synthesis*. Here only key aspects of certain forms of learning will be discussed.

**PL 2.1: Conditioning:** *Much behavior in a willing learner can be conditioned, both with or without the mediation of higher cognitive activity.* In natural acquisition situations, stimuli and reinforcements are largely indirect and often not easy to observe; but formal teaching can make careful use of schedules of stimuli and reinforcements to facilitate and speed up the learning process.

**PC 2.1.0.1:** *All the mechanical aspects of language learning can and should be conditioned, so that they can be used automatically.* Note that this applies to far less than the whole language and not at all to the *use* of a known language. As we learn a language we need to internalize, through conditioning, the lower-level skills; however, the more we learn the less time needs to be spent on conditioning, as this should have become built in.

**PC 2.1.0.2:** As learning that avoids the higher cognitive skills is generally inefficient and ineffective, and uninteresting and unchallenging to the learners, *language programs should rely on intelligent, cognitively-mediated conditioning.*

**Intelligent or cognitively-mediated conditioning** [*Synthesis* 48-54] means that *(a) at all times the learner knows what is going on, knows the basis for the limited choices facing him, and is encouraged to choose consciously among the apparently possible responses to each discriminative stimulus; and (b) initially slow, conscious response choices are speeded up through increasingly faster and more meaningful practice until the responses can be generated largely unconsciously, at normal*

84

*conversational speed, with attention on the meaning of the utterance.*
The formula for intelligent conditioning appears in Figure 6.1.

Figure 6.1

According to this formula, physical, emotional, and volitional conditions must be met before there can be cognitive mediation. Cognitive mediation, for which an understanding of the basis for the choice is a prerequisite, intervenes between the stimulus and the chosen response, which is then reinforced through some form or reward, praise, or simply noncorrection. Note that intelligent conditioning relies on *discriminative* stimuli and responses —there must be a (limited) choice, a certain degree of built-in unpredictability to provide the intellectual challenge we want. Practice in which a predictable stimulus has a predictable response can only bore intelligent students.

**PH 2.1.0.2.1:** *Language programs that rely on intelligent conditioning to internalize the mechanics of the language (a) will be more efficient and result in better understanding and more accurate communicative skill than those that rely primarily on purely mechanical conditioning and (b) will result in greater linguistic competence than those that do not use conditioning procedures at all.* Intelligent conditioning should be better than mindless conditioning because there seems to be little transfer from the fixed routine of pattern practice to the improvisation of conversation; , it should also be better than no conditioning at all because lower-level skills have to be automatic or habitual, and conditioning is the most efficient and effective way to internalize rules to the point that they become habits.

**RS:** Purely mechanical (mindless) pattern practice has been compared with intelligent contextualized practice [Oller and Obrecht 1968], with the not-surprising result that the latter was significantly better; but as far as I know no one has experimented formally with intelligent conditioning.

**PP 2.1.1: Visual Stimuli:** *Visual stimuli are mnemonically powerful.* Written language is a particularly powerful stimulus for literate linguistic adults. Pictures are especially useful as reminders of sequences and contexts.

**PC 2.1.1.1:** *Language programs should make considerable use of visual stimuli for mnemonic purposes.* That is, visual stimuli will help students remember better something they understand. This does not mean visuals are reliable as initial *conveyors* of meaning [Hammerly 1974-b, 1984].

**PP 2.1.2: Competing Stimuli:** *When two different stimuli compete or conflict, learners tend to respond in a familiar way to the more familiar stimulus.*

**PC 2.1.2.1:** *Beginning language students should not be asked to decode competing or conflicting stimuli.* Competing stimuli should be avoided because they will slow down the learning of new responses as the students continue to rely on the more familiar stimuli. For example, to the extent that students are helped to understand a dialogue or story through the use of pictures they are relying on the pictures rather than on the linguistic input. (Similarly, it has been found that the frequent use of specific visuals in literacy readers retards the development of literacy.) Conflicting stimuli are confusing and more or less force the students to respond in familiar ways. For instance, by the time a child is twelve years old or so he has become to a great extent graphemically dependent; for him and for older learners, trying to decode the strange sounds of the new language from the familiar letters of the native language is fraught with contradictions and conflicts that are naturally "resolved" in favor of the native sounds long associated with those letters.

**PP 2.1.3: Individual Production:** *Learners learn best through individual production.* A response that is part of a group response is not as conducive to learning as an individually constructed response. Far more cognitive effort is involved in the latter, since in group responses many learners simply "follow the leaders," who may be those students who are capable or popular or who have the loudest voices. Learning requires individual effort and feedback.

**PC 2.1.3.1:** *Language teaching should rely primarily on individual responses and production, relegating choral responses to an occasional, echoic function.* I shudder to think of the millions of language students in the sixties and early seventies who each went through hundreds of hours of largely choral response practice, a type of practice which does not encourage individual learning effort, does not allow individually geared feedback, and ultimately does not result in either linguistic or communicative competence.

**PP 2.1.4: Overt Production:** *To be accessible for discriminative feedback, the learner's production —whether self-generated or in response to stimuli— must be overt.* It is not possible for the teacher to reward or correct covert, mental production; a result of covert production is that future production cannot be guided or affected.

**PH 2.1.4.1:** *Covert production, generative or echoic in nature, accompanies, respectively, deliberate thinking and receptive activities — such as listening and reading— containing unknown elements; such production is in the form of* subvocal or "silent" speech. When we come across anything strange in reading or listening (a foreign word or a name, for example), we "say" it to ourselves subvocally. When we think about something very carefully, we carry on an internal monologue. **RS:** Subvocal speech has been definitively demonstrated to exist in the reading of strange, unfamiliar words and in differentiating the initial sounds of written words on lists. The other two suggested domains of subvocal speech — listening and deliberate thinking— remain to be further explored.

**PC 2.1.4.2:** *Language teachers should emphasize overt production so as to be able to guide their students in the formation of correct linguistic habits (or "the internalization of correct linguistic rules").* Subvocal speech can be quite incorrect. If allowed to continue uncorrected for weeks or even months, the inevitable result is the formation of incorrect subvocal habits. When such students finally start producing overtly and the teacher finally becomes aware of their problems, it is generally too late —work must be *remedial* at that point; remedial work is of course neither efficient nor very effective.

**PP 2.1.5: Feedback:** *Feedback (reinforcement) is essential to learning.* Some learning is possible without feedback, through the contiguity of stimuli; but where behavior is involved, the learner must know whether his behavior is satisfactory or not if he is to know how to behave in the future.

**PC 2.1.5.1:** *Language teachers should provide their students with consistent feedback on a continuous basis.* Failure to keep feedback consistent can lead to student confusion; failure to provide it continuously can lead to mislearning. What is considered reinforcing will vary with each learner and with the level of the program. Thus, while initially it may be necessary to provide praise, or at least a smile or a nod, for most correct responses, soon these forms of reinforcement can be reserved for the latest rule being learned or for unexpectedly good production, and the average correct response is reinforced through noncorrection (of course, this works only if incorrect responses *are* corrected).

**PP 2.1.6: Temporal Proximity:** *For an association to be formed between a stimulus and a response, reinforcement must not be delayed.*

This has been shown to be the case in numerous experiments. It isn't so much the passage of time itself that reduces the effectiveness of the reinforcer, but the intervening cognitive activities, which tend to be incorrectly associated with the delayed reinforcement when this finally comes.

**PC 2.1.6.1:** *The language program should avoid activities that do not lend themselves to prompt feedback.* Probably the worst culprit in this regard is the typical composition, which comes back to the student, full of red marks, days after he wrote it. By then the student has forgotten the rationale behind his errors —it is this rationale, rather than the resulting surface errors, which needs to be corrected— and so this delayed correction is largely ineffective. (Perhaps early writing should be group writing in the classroom, with an overhead projector and with immediate feedback.

**PP 2.1.7: Shaping:** *Through conditioning procedures, a new response can be shaped step by step from a known response.* The old response is modified one step at a time until it becomes the new response. This is particularly useful in teaching certain new sounds and in the correcton of pronunciation errors when a student does not respond to more direct correction techniques.

**PP 2.1.8: Vicarious Reinforcement:** *Learners can be reinforced (and thus, learn) by observing the explicit feedback given to other individual learners' production.* Most learners are not dumb. They see another learner being rewarded or corrected for a certain behavior and of course they will try to behave or not behave accordingly themselves.

**PC 2.1.8.1:** *Language students should be encouraged to observe very carefully which production by the other students is deemed acceptable or unacceptable, and act accordingly.* Perhaps to promote this kind of careful observation the students could often be invited to correct the errors of their classmates (this would be desirable only where the right attitude towards error correction and peer assistance has been created).

**PP 2.1.9: Deconditioning:** *Undesirable human behavior can be modified or eliminated via the conditioning of alternate responses or deconditioning.* What this involves is learning to behave in a new way *in the presence of old stimuli.* This of course is involved in language learning whenever the two languages differ.

**PC 2.1.9.1:** *To a large extent, learning a second language involves learning new responses to familiar stimuli; consequently, if the old responses to these stimuli are to be blocked, the learner must be made aware of their inappropriateness as the new responses are being learned.* In other words, it isn't enough to teach a new response as if it had nothing to do with previous responses. Until a fairly advanced level in the program the old responses will come first to mind, even if never produced overtly.

The interference of the old responses will not be eliminated by ignoring them. Such interference, where it exists, needs to be tackled directly and openly. The learner has to be made aware of the two responses, of the extent to which they differ, and thus of the extent to which the old response is inappropriate and must be replaced by the new. None of this can be accomplished if the old response is ignored in the simple hope that it will just go away; it just *won't* go away, unless the language learner forgets his native language, which of course cannot happen (nor should happen) during the language program.

**PP 2.3: Rule Learning:** *Rule learning is a complex form of conceptual learning involving analogy and analysis.* Analogy is a more fundamental form of learning than analysis, for all learning involves analogy while analysis is used in higher forms of learning only.

**PC 2.3.1** *To teach language rules, we should rely on analysis based on analogy.* Although very simple aspects of language learning, such as sound discrimination, can be handled analogically, that is, at least without *conscious* analysis, most things that need to be learned, and especially rules, can only be handled efficiently by making use of higher cognitive skills, that is, by making some use of analysis.

Analogy (comparing particulars) is the foundation of inductive learning (going from the particular to the general). Analysis is associated with deduction (going from the general to the particular). There is no experimental evidence conclusively showing the superiority of either induction or deduction. In fact, the best way to handle most language rules may be a third alternative, **guided discovery**, which consists in *helping the students "discover" and state the rule from a series of appropriate examples.* Which approach is more suitable to a particular rule seems to depend more on the nature of the rule rather than on individual learning strategies.[1]

**PC 2.3.2:** *Whenever it can be done efficiently, students should be encouraged to "discover" the rule.* Discovering a rule is not only more challenging than simply being presented with a rule statement but may also facilitate recall. Except for certain rules which are very difficult to discover, even with help, and therefore require a deductive explanation, rules can be discovered efficiently, in a matter of minutes. Simple rules may require no more guidance than the careful selection of examples. Many difficult rules can be subdivided into subrules, each of which can be discovered in a short time. Let me emphasize that this process is much more interesting for the students than being given predigested statements; it lets them play the challenging role of "minilinguists."

Guided discovery may be contrasted with (a) a purely deductive approach, in which there is no challenge, no chance to test hypotheses, and (b) a purely inductive approach, in which guessing in the face of numerous apparent ambiguities can stretch out for hours or days. The latter is not only frustrating but also an inefficient, totally unnecessary roundabout way of dealing with rule learning (or lexical learning, for that matter).

**PP 2.4: Problem Solving:** *The highest form of cognitive activity, problem solving, is also the most interesting and challenging.* Complex problem solving is at the top of the learning hierarchy. There is, however, a wide range of difficulty in problem solving, with very simple problems at the bottom.

**PC 2.4.1:** *To make language learning interesting and challenging, plan it as a series of "miniproblems" for the students to solve.* Note that (a) for something to be a problem, there has to be a possibility of reaching a wrong "solution," and (b) for something to be a *mini*problem, the chances of error must be limited.

# 6.3: Three Basic Learning Processes

After reviewing types of learning in general and certain types in particular, we come to three basic processes that are ultimately present in all learning.

**PP 3: Basic Processes:** *All basic, lower-level learning is cognitive reorganization that results from the (1) comparison, (2) equation or differentiation, and (3) association of cognitive data.* By "cognitive data" I refer to all kinds of stimuli, responses to stimuli, and thoughts, and to the environmental responses (feedback, if any) to them.

**PP 3.1: Comparison:** *The learner's mind will naturally compare cognitive data.* The learner wants to know, *must* know what is the same and what is different, and that requires comparison. But comparison of largely unrelated data is confusing and inefficient. And the active avoidance of overt comparisons makes for inefficient and ineffective learning.

**PC 3.1.1:** *Language teaching efficiency and effectiveness can be enhanced by arranging for the systematic, overt comparison of related data.* This speaks against the idea of simply surrounding language students with more or less haphazard language data. It also points to the necessity of overt comparison, including interlingual comparison —such overt comparison is neglected or even actively avoided in many language programs.

**PP 3.2: Equation or Differentiation:** *The learner will decide in his mind whether data is the same or different and the extent of the difference if any.* A big problem is that previous learning affects this basic process, so the learner often needs help in equating or differentiating correctly. The point is that, whether helped or not, whether correctly or not, the learner *will* equate or differentiate.

**PC 3.2.1:** *Language students should be helped to equate or differentiate correctly.* The brief clarification of equivalences and differences, and various types of drills, exercises, and other activities can help students do this.

**PP 3.3: Association:** *The learner will naturally associate cognitive data; the more associations, the better is retention and the easier is recall.* Associations can of course be wrong if they are based on wrong equations or differentiations; but perhaps in our field the greatest source of incorrect associations is the noncorrection of wrong responses. Adults, being more experienced learners, can make more associations than children and can organize them better into a cognitive structure.

**PC 3.3.1:** *To facilitate retention and recall, language programs should provide, for each new item, numerous contexts that help establish numerous associations.* Many language teaching materials fail to observe this principle, as they frequently present new items in only one or two contexts.

# 6.4: Steps in Classroom Learning

**PP 4: Teaching/Learning Steps:** *Classroom learning (as well as much learning outside the classroom) usually follows five steps: (1)* identification, *i.e., what the item is, how it sounds, what it looks like, etc.; (2)* reproduction, *either overt or covert; (3)* understanding, *that is, awareness of how the item works (what its functions are) and how it relates to other items; (4)* manipulation, *by that meaning practice with the item, at first (often briefly) mechanically, then meaningfully; and (5)* application, *putting the item to realistic or real use.*

*It should be clear that in learning one needs first to identify an item as same as or different from previously encountered items and, if it is different, to determine the extent of the difference. Next comes being able to reproduce the item, either mentally or in the form of overt production such as speaking or writing. Further progress in learning is made by understanding the item, both in terms of its makeup and of its relationship to other items; generalization is an important process at this stage. If skill is aimed at, there should then be manipulation of the item, mechanically and in limited contexts at first, then gradually more meaningfully and in freer contexts. Finally, the item should be put to use, first in realistic situations such as simulations, then in real life. It would seem that, while these steps in classroom learning —identification to application— apply* particularly well to the learning of second language items, they also apply to many other forms of learning, in or out of the classroom.

# 6.5: Seventeen Principles of Classroom Learning

**PL 5.1: Organization:** *Organized material is easier to learn than disorganized material.* The human mind prefers organization and will impose it on disorganized data. Failure to lead learners to establish the right kind of organization of the data is not only inefficient (it may take them a long time to see the correct organization) but may be ineffective (they may establish the wrong kind of organization).

**PC 5.1.1:** *Systematic instruction that presents organized data is more efficient and effective than unsystematic exposure to data.* Rather than unsystematically exposing learners to a second language as if they were in nurseries or streets, we should therefore carefully follow the principles of selection, gradation, integration, etc. which have characterized sound teaching for centuries.

**PL 5.2: Gradation:** *A complex learning task is best accomplished step by step.* The people who, in their impatience, want to learn globally seldom seem to attain the high level of skill reachable by those who carefully master each subskill.

**PC 5.2.1:** *Language teaching should consist of a series of learning steps ordered in a principled manner.* Ordering principles include "from simple to complex," "from regular to irregular," "from frequent to infrequent," and so on. Such principles have been known for centuries, having been explicitly stated by Comenius in the 17th century and by many others. It is symptomatic of our confused age that many educators have been ignoring gradation or minimizing its importance.

**PC 5.2.2:** *A step must not be taken before its prerequisite steps.* Appendix A, "Prematurities in Language Teaching," points out that much of the failure of language teaching to produce linguistically compe-tent graduates is due to our doing many things prematurely. Among other "prematurities," we introduce our students to reading before they have an audio-oral foundation, we encourage them to communicate freely before they should, we have them read literature long before they are ready, and we expect them to behave like coordinate bilinguals (something that may be attained after *many* years) from the start of the program.

**PL 5.3: Attention:** *Learners can fully attend to only one thing at a time.* One can give partial attention to two or more things, but only one thing can get all of our attention. If something is to be learned thoroughly, there are obvious advantages in concentrating on it to the temporary exclusion of other matters.

**PC 5.3.1:** *Often language students need to attend to one thing at a time.* An example is the beginner who needs to concentrate, for each item, first on form and then on meaning, for otherwise control over form suffers.

**PH 5.3.1.1:** *Increased attention to meaning means decreased attention to form, and vice versa, at least at the beginning of a learning task.* **RS:** This hypothesis and the one below lend themselves to short-term experimentation.

**PH 5.3.1.2:** *In order to have full attention to meaning with full control of form at the end of a learning task, emphasis should be on form first, then on meaningful uses that presuppose control of form.*

**PC 5.3.2:** *Student attention should be directed to the crucial.* At any particular point in a learning program there is something specific (sometimes several things) which is crucial to the learning process. Student attention should be concentrated especially on that.

**PP 5.4: Emphasis:** *In a skill-learning program, students can become highly proficient only in those activities that the program emphasizes.* While learning one skill may incidentally help develop a related skill, it is the skills that are practiced that are learned best.

**PC 5.4.1:** *Language practice should concentrate on the skills that it has been decided should be learned.* This seems very obvious; yet there are language programs where, for example, students are supposed to learn to communicate orally after spending most of their class and study time reading and writing! This principle is frequently violated.

**PP 5.5: Sound Perception:** *Sound perception is a cognitive activity which is aided, like all such activities, by the systematic development of awareness of identities/similarities, differences/contrasts, distributions, and functions.* Such awareness can soon become fine-tuned by the systematic presentation of perceptual data.

**PC 5.5.1:** *Language students should have, very early, discrimination, differentiation, and distribution training in the perception of second and native language sounds.* Traditionally in applied linguistics, "discrimination" refers to phonemic contrasts in the second language, "differentiation" involves distinguishing second language sounds from their closest native language counterparts, and "distribution" refers to the phonic contexts in which allophones or phonemes occur. All three perceptual activities are necessary; all three require the application of basic linguistic, psychological, and pedagogical principles.

**PP 5.6: Sound Production:** *The production of new sounds requires careful habit-formation training.* While early attempts at the production of a new sound may involve conscious control of the speech apparatus, clearly sound production soon needs to become automatic, i.e., habitual. Since good habits rarely result when initial incorrect behavior is condoned, careful early training and correction must characterize the learning of second language pronunciation in the classroom.

**PC 5.6.1:** *Language students should be given careful, step-by-step training in sound production very early in the program.* Everything that is said, correctly or incorrectly, reinforces similar early production. Moreover, there should be early training in pronunciation because of the mutual feedback between receptive and productive activities and the necessity of overt responses in the classroom.

**PP 5.7: Reception and Production:** *Discriminative reception and correct production reinforce each other through mutual feeback.* Thus, reading a word or construction should make it easier to write it; conversely, writing it should make it easier to understand it next time it is seen in print. Another example: Each act of successful sound perception facilitates the following production of that sound, and (what is seldom recognized) it seems that each act of correct sound production facilitates the next act of perception of that sound. Through systematically guided mutual feedback between perception and production, it becomes possible to zero in on the correct perception/production of all sounds in a second language within the first ten to fifteen hours of instruction.

**PC 5.7.1:** *Language programs should not separate receptive from productive activities (other than for brief periods of time).* In language teaching, a common violation of this principle is to begin language study with a long period of listening and/or reading before there is any speaking. While this no doubt results in greater initial proficiency in the receptive skill(s) taught, it fails to take advantage of the reinforcing effect of productive activities. (Furthermore, it does nothing to prevent the formation of incorrect subvocal habits and it fails to capitalize on language students' greatest motivation, which is to *speak* the language.)

**PL 5.8: Practice:** *While it may be possible to develop theoretical knowledge in the abstract, no skill can be developed without practice.* Without practice, theoretical knowledge does not readily translate into active skill. Practice ranges from repetition (with attention on form only) through manipulation (with increasing attention to meaning) to creative application (with attention on meaning only, control of form having been previously built in). Loosely, a "skill" is any ability. But for our purposes, we will define a **skill** specifically as *the ability to use correctly and with ease an integrated set of linguistic habits.* A skill involves conscious attention to certain higher-level cognitive processes, mostly semantic in nature, with everything at lower levels falling into place automatically.

One definition of **habit** is: *Specific, unconscious (automatic) behavior that has been internalized through practice.*

In terms of classroom conditioning, the progression from the first S-R-R experience to a skill involves practice which results first in (1) a trace, then (2) an association, then (3) discrimination and generalization, followed by (4) (preferably intelligent) conditioning which, if sufficiently strengthened becomes (5) a habit which, combined with other such habits, constitutes (6) a skill.

**PC 5.8.1:** *Practice is essential to language learning.* Without sufficient practice of the right kind, language students will try to apply performative knowledge they don't have; the long-term result of this will be linguistic incompetence.

**PC 5.8.2:** *In language teaching, practice should start with repetition and manipulation, but it is essential that this be followed by application in communicative activities.* While little habit formation will occur without mechanical practice, mechanical practice is useless if it does not lead to communicative skill. A problem which seems to be common in language programs is lack of habit integration and application. As communication is a higher cognitive activity, it will not result automatically from the process of conditioning, especially if this process is handled mindlessly.

**PL 5.9: Inevitability of Errors:** *Errors are inevitable in any complex learning task.* Learning can be made nearly error-free by (a) breaking down the learning task into very small steps and (b) not applying lower-level knowledge thus developed to higher-level tasks. But such purely mechanical learning is boring to the students and fails to fulfill any worthwhile goals.

**PC 5.9.1:** *Language students should be led to realize and accept the inevitability of errors without adopting the attitude that they are unimportant.* Unless the students accept the production of some errors as unavoidable, they may be nervous and frustrated throughout the program; unless they consider errors important, they will either ignore or resent error correction and thus become linguistically incompetent. Errors occur particularly the first few times a newly learned rule is tried out in conversation. The proper student attitude toward errors can be established during the orientation at the beginning of the program. At that time, an effective technique is for the teacher to relate, with some humor if possible, his own experience with errors in early language learning.

**PC 5.9.2:** *Within reason, errors should be minimized.* It would *not* be reasonable to minimize them by dividing learning into very small (and boring) steps or by keeping it largely mechanical. There never need be *many* errors at any given point. If there are, it means one of two things: (a) learning steps have been too large, so that what should have been learned well has not been learned well or (b) the students are being allowed or encouraged to communicate beyond their competence, i.e., they are applying lower-level skills they don't control.

**PL 5.10: Error Correction:** *Errors must be corrected; if they go uncorrected often enough or long enough, they become resistant to correction as the faulty rules underlying them become habitual ("fossilized").*

**PC 5.10.1:** *Language students' errors should be corrected consistently and as persistently as necessary to ensure the formation of correct linguistic habits.* Failure to correct errors, for whatever reason (for some it is a matter of philosophy) is contrary to the interests of our students. Furthermore, almost all language students very much *want* to be corrected. This does not mean that all errors in all learning activities must be corrected. In some activities, all errors should be corrected; in others, certain errors can be left uncorrected.

**PC 5.10.2:** *In language teaching, the best policy regarding the correction of errors seems to be to ignore* **mistakes** (unsystematic errors such as slips of the tongue), correct all **deviations** (systematic errors with what has already been taught), and insist that students express themselves within the boundaries of what they know, so that they won't commit **faults** (errors with what hasn't yet been taught).

**PC 5.10.3:** *Error correction should deal cognitively with the incorrect presupposition(s) that caused the error, not just provide mechanical repetition.* To involve the learner cognitively in the correction of the error, a good technique is to try to elicit self-correction from him by providing him with clues that lead him to "rediscover" the presupposition(s) necessary for correct performance.[2]

**RS:** Several research questions need to be answered in regard to error correction, among them the following: (1) What exactly happens when second language errors are not corrected? (2) How frequently or for how long a period of instruction must various types of second language errors go uncorrected to become habitual? (3) What is the maximum number of second language errors of various types that can be corrected in a given period of time while retaining corrective effectiveness? (4) How can the high effectiveness of error correction while attention is on form be maintained when attention shifts to meaning?

**PP 5.11: Control Before Use:** *What is to be used with accuracy should come under a high degree of control before it is used freely.* This principle could also be stated as "Knowledge before application." Of course, each skillful use of an item strengthens control over it and each improvement in control facilitates use —this is another type of mutual feedback loop. Lacking control over an item, learners will rely, for their use of it, on transfer, which is often inappropriate. Emphasizing control before use seems to be particularly important in early instruction, as at that level allowing free use before control is very likely to result in a defective foundation.

**PC 5.11.1:** *Language teachers should insist that their students master each item in a limited but growing number of contexts before they try to use it in free recombination.* As noted, this is imperative at the beginning level, when the most basic linguistic habits are formed.

**PP 5.12: Higher- and Lower-Level Skills:** *In learning a complex, multilayered skill, it seems best results are obtained by mastering the lower-level skills before the higher-level skills that contain them.* Lower-level skills never seem to be quite fully mastered when the learner rushes to practice higher-level skills.

**PC 5.12.1:** *Language programs should first concentrate on the lower-level mechanical skills, then on the higher-level communication skills that include them.* Since attention must be, gradually more and more, on the higher-level skill of meaningful communication, everything else needed for it should have been so thoroughly mastered in advance that it can automatically fall into place. If it hasn't been, production will be from moderately to highly inaccurate.

**PC 5.12.2:** *The successful generation of accurate and fluent sentences, whether consciously or unconsciously, requires that lower-level mechanical skills be mastered to the point of automatic, unconscious control.* It is impossible to generate fluent sentences while consciously attending to lower-level rules.

**PP 5.13: Integration:** *Complex knowledge or skills that are to be used as a whole should be integrated at all levels.* As subskills come under control, they should be progressively integrated with everything learned previously.

**PC 5.13.1:** *Progressive integration of what is learned is essential if we want language students to function competently in the language.* Competence in a second language is not developed by simply attaining linear mastery of one item after another. It is instead a matter of mastering gradually growing transitional systems, which ideally should grow one rule at a time. It is like a cone growing out of its apex. It is like the process of crystallization, which starts at one point and then gradually builds up outwards while maintaining all parts structurally interrelated.

**PP 5.14: The Importance of Memorization:** *Memorization seems to be important to many forms of learning.* A substantial amount of memorization goes on in native language acquisition, where there is considerable evidence that children memorize early utterances as "routines," before understanding their structure, then manipulate them to some extent as "patterns," and finally use them as the basis for freely recombinatory speech.

**PC 5.14.1:** *Some early memorization of language samples should be used in language teaching as a point of entry into the language and to facilitate further work.* A memorized sample can be manipulated in various ways and thus serve to bridge the gap between initial exposure to forms and their correct and meaningful use. But since most language students dislike memorization tasks rather intensely, the memorization of language samples should be kept to a minimum and should be facilitated by all reasonable aids.

**PP 5.15: Memorization and Recall Effort:** *Memorization requires recall effort.* The passive repetition of utterances, no matter how frequent, doesn't usually lead to their memorization. For instance, church goers can testify that, although they have sung certain hymns and repeated certain prayers maybe hundreds or even thousands of times, they cannot produce them unaided unless they have made a systematic effort to recall them.

**PP 5.16: Recall and Recurrence:** *For something to be available for immediate recall, it must have recurred with recall effort and with some frequency in the learner's experience.* It is true, of course, that some things appear to the learner for the first time in such a dramatic manner that he will always remember them even in the absence of a pattern of recurrence; but such things are the exception, not the rule. (In fact, they cannot be made the rule, for if we tried to teach *everything* dramatically the impact of each individual item would be lost.)

**PC 5.16.1:** *Language programs must reintroduce items for recall effort at intervals that will maintain initial memory strength and result in entry in long-term memory.* Materials that, for example, introduce a word or rule in Lesson 3 and do not reintroduce it until Lesson 17 are not acceptable — yet many materials show this shortcoming.

**PH 5.16.1.1:** Several hypotheses with various wordings could be formulated about the best pattern of reintroduction for various second language items. One thing that is clear from recall studies in other fields is that the intervals need not be of the same length but can gradually increase in duration. An important variable would be the receptivity/productivity of each encounter with the item. **RS:** The curious thing is that very little research has been undertaken to study this important area of language teaching.

**PP 5.17: Forgetting:** *Forgetting seems to be due to the interference of intervening activities and to proceed in the inverse order of learning.* According to this principle, forgetting would not result from the mere passage of time but would depend on the nature of the intervening activity.

Unrelated activity would not result in forgetting, partially similar activity would (see 6.6 "Transfer" below). It also seems to be the case that what is learned last —and presumably practiced least— is forgotten first, and vice versa.

**PC 5.17.1:** *There should not be long interruptions in the language program.* Such interruptions result in forgetting through the interfering effect of using the native language to communicate the same meanings as in the second language program; we can expect this forgetting effect to be the more marked the closer the two languages are. In light of this, it might be better for a learner not even to start the study of a second language until he can be assured of program continuity.

**PH 5.17.1.1:** *The longer an interruption in a language program, with intervening activity in another language, the more of the second language will be forgotten.* **RS:** The above hypothesis would seem to be an obvious truth. What researchers should concentrate on is studying the specific effects of interruptions of various types and duration.

**PC 5.17.2:** *Considering that they will be forgotten last, items for early presentation should be selected so as to ensure that they are truly fundamental and useful.* Such items should include, in language teaching, the sound system, high-frequency vocabulary, and the most basic rules of morphology and syntax.

**PH 5.17.3:** *Second language items will be forgotten in inverse order to the degree to which they have been learned; this usually means late-presented items are forgotten first and early-presented items last.* **RS:** Note that an early item may not have been thoroughly learned and a late item may have. This is therefore a complex research question, as in addition to the chronological introduction of the item it would be necessary to take into account its dramatic impact, its frequency of occurrence in classroom communication, its pattern of recall activation on the part of the students, and so on.

# 6.6: Transfer

(Transfer is such an important psychological principle for languistics that it deserves a chapter section by itself.)

**PL 6: Transfer, Generalization, and Underdifferentiation:** *In an unfamiliar situation, a learner will generalize previous knowledge, whether appropriately (positive transfer or correct generalization) or inappropriately (negative transfer — "interference"— or overgeneralization); unable to differentiate properly for whatever reason, he will underdifferentiate and thus be in error.* Another way of putting this is to say that *given similarity between them, a learner will relate the unfamiliar to, and base it on, the familiar.* There seems to be inevitability about this process; it appears to be a basic way in which our minds function.

**PC 6.1:** *Rather than ignore the inevitable process of transfer, language teachers should take it into account by overtly fostering positive transfer and counteracting negative transfer.* This means using what the learner knows, that is, his native language. Why should language teaching be the only subject in the curriculum in which previous student knowledge is ignored? You might wish to ponder what the usual effects of ignoring reality are, in any sphere of life.

**PP 6.2: Learning Unfamiliar Responses:** *For an unfamiliar response to be learned in the presence of interference from a familiar response, the inappropriateness of the familiar response must be made clear and the new response must be adequately practiced.*

**PC 6.2.1:** *Sound language teaching offers considerable practice based on the findings of contrastive and/or error analysis (CA or EA).* In the absence of many years' teaching experience that allow at least informal EA, a language teacher would be well advised to rely on CA for an idea of what will be difficult or easy for his students. CA makes it clear where positive transfer can be encouraged and where negative transfer can be expected.

**PC 6.2.2:** *Contrastive analysis must be practiced overtly.* It isn't enough for the textbook author or the language teacher to be aware of interlingual identities and differences. The students must be made aware of them too if they are to avoid interference errors and transfer "sames" with any efficiency. Note that just as it is important for them to know what they should *not* transfer, they should also be made aware of what they *may* transfer, for otherwise they may hesitate to use anything that resembles the native language.

**PC 6.2.3:** *There is nothing wrong in transferring items from the native language to the second language when they are the same in both languages.* Not only isn't it wrong but it is *desirable* to foster such transfer, as it will greatly increase the efficiency of the learning process. Some (in some cases most) sounds, the basic meanings (denotations) of most words, and many of the syntactic rules of, for instance, any two Western European languages *are the same.*

**PC 6.2.4:** *As they do not know enough of the second language to base all their production on it, beginning second language students will tend to rely primarily on what they know, i.e., their native language; as they progress in the program, they will tend to rely more and more on what they have learned of the second language.* This requires further experimental testing. If it is true (as two or three studies so far seem to indicate), then we can expect beginners to make many interference errors at first and then more and more second language overgeneralization errors as they progress in the program. Incidentally, native language interference errors are also overgeneralization errors, except on an interlingual basis; second language overgeneralization errors are also a form of interference —of one second language form on another. Both are basically one and the same process: underdifferentiation.

**PP 6.3:** **Types of Interference:** *While interference is traditionally thought of in terms of intrusions, previous knowledge can also have the effect of* precluding *the development of new knowledge.* This **preclusive interference** is sometimes a more serious impediment to learning than intrusive interference. That preclusive interference is a reality can be seen in the greater difficulty of the Chinese, as compared to Spanish speakers, in mastering English articles, or in the greater difficulty of English speakers, again as compared to Spanish speakers, in mastering the difference in usage between the two past tenses in French. What seems to lie behind these difficulties is the learner's belief that he doesn't need to learn a form or distinction without which he has long performed a function in his native language. The new form or distinction appears to seem redundant to him, something he can ignore.

**PC 6.3.1:** *Language teaching should concentrate on the points of intrusive and preclusive interference.* Here is where the greatest difficulties in learning a second language lie.

**PP 6.4: Degree of Interference:** *The most persistent intrusive interference is caused by subtle differences; identity facilitates; and totally unrelated items of knowledge show neither facilitation nor interference.* Figure 6.2 shows a tentative representation of the intrusive interference curve.

**PC 6.4.1:** *In second language learning, subtle phonetic, graphemic, syntactic, and semantic differences cause more persistent interference than more obvious differences; morphological differences seldom cause interference.* Tentative hierarchies of difficulty in these areas were given and discussed in Chapter 9 of *Synthesis*, so only a few points will be made here.

While phonemic interference is a more serious phonological problem from the point of view of communication, it is phonetic/allophonic problems that are most persistent and largely characterize the accent of near-bilinguals. The problem is exacerbated, in early language learning, by exposure to alphabetic second language writing (for those whose native language is also written alphabetically). Standard writing interferes with the development of accurate pronunciation in many specific and often subtle ways. What makes its negative influence most insidious is that it also *supports* comprehension and recall in *broad* ways, so that many teachers and students do not want to be without it. Native language sound-spelling correlations facilitate or interfere with the learning of second language sounds and sound-spelling correlations according to the same principles of transfer that affect the learning of syntactic rules, meanings, etc., except that sound and sound-spelling correlation problems seem to exist at a more unconscious, more habitual level.

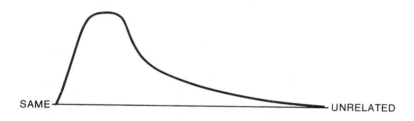

SAME                                                                    UNRELATED

Figure 6.2

Only very closely related languages, like Spanish and Portuguese, or German and Danish, seem to present significant morphological transfer effects. In other cases, the usual absence of such effects may be due to the fact that morphologies tend to be closed systems that are language-specific. In any event, syntactic rules generally cause far more interference than differences in morphology (this can be taken as an indirect comment on the very limited applicability, for us, of the morphological order-of-acquisition studies of the late sixties and the seventies). This doesn't mean that the morphological learning task will necessarily be easy; there may not be any interference, but in terms of absolute difficulty the task of learning the morphology of Russian, Finnish, or even French can be quite great for a speaker of English. Even the simple morphology of English can present a major problem for learners whose native languages, like Chinese, have no grammatical morphology.

Unlike phonological learning, in which intrusive interference is paramount, the most persistent syntactical problems in learning a second language seem to be caused by preclusive interference, that is, situations in which the second language has a syntactic category or distinction absent in the native language.

With respect to vocabulary, each basic meaning (denotation) of a word almost always has a one- or two-word equivalence across languages; if not, a paraphrase can always be provided. It would seem, therefore, that there shouldn't be serious semantic problems in learning the vocabulary of a second language. The reason there usually are such problems seems to be that either the semantic boundaries of words (not only what they mean, but what they *don't* mean) or their cultural connotations have not been made clear to the students. Of course, when a second language is taught as a monolingual guessing game, such lack of semantic clarity is inevitable.

# 6.7: Learning Difficulty

**PP 7: Absolute and Relative Difficulty:** *The degree of difficulty of a learning task depends on absolute factors such as complexity and abstractness, and on relative factors such as previous learning and learner characteristics.* How readily observable an item is and how frequently it occurs are also difficulty factors.

**PC 7.1:** *The absolute learning difficulty of various languages, if it is different, doesn't seem to affect native language acquisition, as young children seem to master any native language at about the same age. The fact that markedly different learning times are needed to master various second languages later in life would seem to confirm the great importance of transfer.*

**PC 7.2:** *The same level of proficiency will be reached faster in a second language closely related to the native language than in an unrelated language.* This seems something of a paradox, for a related language is likely to cause far more interference than an unrelated one. The explanation lies largely in the magnitude of the lexical learning task, which is far smaller with related languages.

**PH 7.2.1:** We can hypothesize, quite tentatively, that *The time it will take the average second language learner to reach FSI proficiency level 3 will increase as (1) the number of cognate words decreases, (2) syntactic rules differ, (3) morphological complexity increases, (4) the writing systems differ, and (5) pronunciation and intonation differ, in that order of importance.* **RS:** Something that needs to be looked into is the question of which poses a more serious barrier to second language learning, absolute or interlingual difficulty, and in what specific ways.

# 6.8: The Results of Learning

**PP 8.1: Knowledge or Skill:** *The final outcome of learning is knowledge, which is cognitive, or skill, which is behavioral (although ultimately based on cognition).* One could also emphasize the cognitive foundation of skill and refer to it as "performative knowledge," in which case the outcome of learning would be two types of knowledge, cognitive and performative.

**PC 8.1.1:** *The final outcome of second language learning is skill in the use of the language, that is, performative knowledge of the language.* Cognitive knowledge about the language will speed up the learning process but is not essential to the final outcome.

**PP 8.2: Intuition:** *Intuition seems to be a pattern of response or production based on a very rapid unconscious review of a large store of knowledge and experience.* It would seem that without much previous relevant knowledge there can be no intuitive behavior.

**PC 8.2.1:** *Until they reach a fairly advanced level, second language learners lack the necessary knowledge and experience —conscious or unconscious— to be able to produce rapid and accurate intuitive responses.* If forced, prematurely, to respond rapidly and nonmechanically, language learners will therefore rely on their *native language* intuition plus what little they know of the second language —the result being inaccurate second language production.

**PP 8.3: Creativity:** *Creativity involves conceptual novelty based on making new associations among known items; it depends therefore on previous knowledge. Creativity based on faulty knowledge will likely lead to error.* "Creativity" is a meaningful term at the conceptual level only, as defined above. It makes very little sense to refer to any novel sentence as an act of "linguistic creativity" —there is nothing creative about prosaically recombining, without any conceptual novelty, thoroughly known sentence parts. What linguists call "creativity" should therefore more accurately be called "recombinatory power."

**PC 8.3.1:** *Language students should be encouraged to be conceptually creative with, or to recombine, only items they know thoroughly, following recombination rules they know thoroughly.*

**PH 8.3.1.1:** *Emphasis on conceptual creativity or linguistic recombination without the prerequisite thorough knowledge of the items and rules involved will result in language students making many more errors than can effectively be corrected, with the result that such errors will soon become habitual.* **RS:** As far as I know no careful study has dealt with this predictable and herein predicted effect of premature "creativity." It may be possible to study this question in just one semester of classes.

# 6.9: The Learner

(As a whole chapter —Chapter 6— of *Synthesis* was devoted to learner variables, only a few points will be raised here.)

**PP 9.1: The Learner's Requirements:** *Given sufficient (1) aptitude and (2) motivation, learning will take place if the learner is given (3) data, (4) guidance, and (5) adequate time to learn.*

**PP 9.1.1:** *Aptitude, including language aptitude, is normally distributed.* For second languages, this has been confirmed by the distribution of scores on standardized language aptitude tests. But although specific language aptitude can vary considerably among individual learners, it seems that all learners with normal IQ *can* learn a second language.

**PP 9.1.2:** Apparently not much learning can take place against the learner's will; this underscores the importance of motivation. *The earliest goal of the language program, most important during the first few hours of instruction, should be to secure the students' desire to learn the language; throughout the program, a high level of motivation must be maintained.*

**PC 9.1.2.1:** *Language teachers should foster the student attitudes and types of student motivation most suitable to the learning situation.* For two obvious examples: An attitude of independence should be fostered in self-instructional programs, one of cooperation for many activities in regular classroom programs. Integrative motivation (wanting to be part of the other linguistic group) would enhance learning in an environmental ("second language") situation, as it would lead to increased use of the language for communication. Instrumental motivation (learning for a practical purpose) would be most conducive to learning in many remote ("foreign language") situations. Intrinsic motivation (learning for the satisfaction of learning) would be helpful in any situation but particularly so when language study is voluntary. Extrinsic motivation (that is, grades and the like) can be used in language programs to enhance learning effort and may be the most effective type of motivation for many students taking required language courses.

**PP 9.1.3:** *Learning is facilitated when data is presented to the learner in an organized, principled manner.* Simply surrounding learners with haphazard data will retard whatever learning there is or may even result in no learning at all.

**PP 9.1.4:** *All learners either need guidance for a learning task or perform it on the basis of knowledge or skill previously developed under guidance.* The question is how much guidance to provide at each point in the learning process. Insufficient guidance will retard learning; too much guidance will interfere with individual initiative and will therefore be resented.

**PC 9.1.4.1** *At the beginning level, language programs should provide considerable guidance, but as the learner progresses in the program and he develops a knowledge base he should be guided less and less and encouraged to be more and more self-reliant.*

**PC 9.1.5:** *As different learners require different amounts of time to learn the same things, each should be given —within reason— the time he needs.* It seems incredible that, with this sound idea of self-pacing having been around for such a long time, we continue to penalize language students who are working hard and learning the language just because they do not meet our standards by rather arbitrary deadlines.

**PP 9.2: The Learner's Personality:** *Personality characteristics affect learning and performance; personality extremes are generally disruptive to learning.*

**PC 9.2.1:** *In the terminology of Eric Berne's Transactional Analysis, the type of personality relationship most conducive to language learning in the classroom is Adult-to-Adult.* The teacher as Parent will tend to be very strict and demanding, although at times he must act that way. The student as Child will tend to be irrepressible and irresponsible. Of course, part of the task of language teaching is to build a linguistic Parent, a *second language superego*, in the student's unconscious. But, by and large, language classroom activities benefit most from an Adult-Adult relationship, which most students appreciate.

**PC 9.2.2:** *Extroverts are not necessarily better language learners.* There is no question that extroverts become more fluent as language students. Informal observations, however, lead me to believe that extroverts are less accurate, as in their desire to communicate they seem to be less reflective and don't seem to worry too much about *how* they communicate. Inhibition, far from being an entirely negative quality, is *desirable* in the language classroom to the extent that it will make a learner think twice before speaking or writing and also to the extent that it keeps the learner from frequently venturing into linguistically unknown territory, thereby making more errors that can effectively be corrected and thus internalizing faulty rules. In any event, with respect to extroversion/introversion what the teacher must do is compensate for the extremes, i.e., limit talk by the excessively extroverted and encourage the excessively introverted to speak, and of course insist that all should be reflective, for the sake of accuracy.

**PH 9.2.2.1:** *From the point of view of extroversion/introversion, the best language students (the most accurate and, eventually, also fluent) are moderately introverted.* **RS:** Such a hypothesis would have to be tested via correlation between a personality scale and end-of-program scores based on a test that emphasizes speech accuracy, not just fluency (extroverts win hands down on the latter).

**PC 9.2.3:** *Learners benefit from a healthy degree of self-esteem and from reasonable perfectionism.* Self-esteem should be fostered, as it facilitates learning. There is, however, such a thing as "loving oneself too much," with results such as excessive independence and unwillingness to accept correction. Perfectionism correlates with reflectiveness and maybe also with introversion. The opposite of perfectionism, sloppiness, should never be allowed in the language classroom. Perfectionism is desirable and should be encouraged up to a point; extreme perfectionism should be discouraged, as it has a paralyzing effect.

**PP 9.3: The Learner's Emotions:** *The emotions of the learner should be observed and attended to, as they can seriously affect learning.* Learning a language in particular is an emotionally charged experience involving such emotions and attitudes as (1) infantilization and dependence, (2) anxiety, and (3) empathy (or lack thereof) toward the teacher and/or native speakers of the language.

**PC 9.3.1:** *Everything within reason should be done to prevent language students from feeling infantile helplessness or any other negative emotions.* In some ways, learning another language involves a return to the helplessness of early childhood and to dependence, this time not on the mother but on the teacher and the teaching materials. This is a very uncomfortable feeling for many older learners. It can and should be minimized by providing dependable modeling and Adult-Adult guidance and counsel. Otherwise, students left to their feeling of infantilization can develop considerable anxiety.

**PC 9.3.2:** *Efforts must be made to reduce student anxiety to manageable proportions.* A moderate amount of anxiety may be desirable, as it seems to sharpen performance. But a high level of anxiety interferes with learning. A major cause of excessive anxiety in the language classroom is ambiguity. This is a completely avoidable source of anxiety, as there is no reason why everything should not be made perfectly clear, if not immediately certainly within a few minutes. Unfortunately in certain language programs —monolingual programs in particular— ambiguities pile up on top of ambiguities and continue to plague students for hours or even weeks. Another important cause of excessive anxiety are unpleasant surprises such as unannounced tests or tests with unexpected contents —again, this is perfectly avoidable.

**PP 9.4: Child and Adult Learners:** *Children are superior in motor memory but otherwise inferior to adults as learners.* Perhaps children "pick up" unconscious knowledge more readily than adults, but they also seem to forget it faster, probably because they have less of a cognitive apparatus to anchor it to (that is, children seem capable of making fewer, weaker associations than adults). The superiority of adults as learners has been known for a long time [Thorndike *et al.* 1928].

**PC 9.4.1:** *Except for pronunciation, where children have a flexibility/ motor memory advantage, young adults are better language learners than children.* Psychologically, then, the best age to start learning a second language in the classroom would be at the onset of linguistic adulthood, that is, at the age of ten or eleven. Before that age, children are largely unreceptive to formal language instruction; two or three years later they lose their motor memory advantage and can no longer "pick up" native-like pronunciation. However, with proper phonological instruction many older learners *can* develop excellent, native-like pronunciation of a second language.

# 6.10: For Discussion

1. *How far can one go in learning a second language in the classroom without conscious attention to what one is doing? How efficient and effective does such an unconscious approach seem to be? How interesting and challenging?*

2. *What specifically can be done to create an emotionally favorable atmosphere in the second language classroom?*

3. *Do you agree that unless a student wants to learn a second language it is rather pointless to try to teach it to him? What can be done to motivate unwilling students?*

4. *Do mechanical drills have to be performed under the illusion that the mind does not exist? Is conditioning a form of mindless behavioristic manipulation when the students are willing participants who choose their responses intelligently?*

5. *How can visual stimuli (for example, visual representations of sounds) be made to support, rather than compete with, auditory stimuli?*

6. *Why does group instruction have failure built in? Do students learn as groups or as individuals? What can be done to emphasize the individual learner within lockstep programs?*

7. *Why is it necessary to phase out reinforcement for each item and rule taught?*

8. *Give two or three examples of phonetic shaping.*

9. *Have you learned from the errors of your classmates? What if they were not corrected?*

10. *Is analysis of second language structures desirable? Is it enough? How can linguistic habits be formed efficiently? What should be the relationship between* knowing about *and* knowing how*?*

11. *To what an extent can we rely on the students to "discover" rules and*

*solve "miniproblems"?*

12. *Do language students compare second and native language items and rules in their minds? What advantages or disadvantages are there in doing this overtly —at least with certain bothersome items— in the classroom?*

13. *Why do many (if not most) language materials present each new item in only one or a few contexts? Why are textbook authors in such a rush to "cover the language"?*

14. *From the presentation of the first example to the correct use of a second language item or rule in communication, what steps would you follow in teaching it? How long would you be at each step? Defend your choice of steps and their duration in light of the possible consequences.*

15. *Have language programs to which you have been exposed done certain things prematurely? What and with what results?*

16. *How can the conflict in having to pay attention to both form and meaning best be solved? Why?*

17. *Discuss the pros and cons of emphasizing the formation of correct pronunciation habits during the first 10-15 hours of instruction.*

18. *Have you experienced "silent speech"? On what occasions? What does this suggest about the role of silent speech in second language learning? Does this have any pedagogical consequences?*

19. *What are the different attitudes second language scholars, teachers and students have toward errors? Describe what you consider the attitude most conducive to the development of second language competence.*

20. *Which language skills are "higher-" and "lower-level" skills? To what an extent must both levels of skills be developed simultaneously in the language program?*

21. *What activities could be used to ensure progressive integration?*

22. *Do students resent having to memorize short language samples when they are made aware of the rationale for, and likely advantages in, doing it?*

23. *In what ways does transfer —positive and negative— affect the learning of the various components of a second language? Would awareness of transfer effects by the students help or hinder their language learning?*

24. *What role has transfer played at various points in your second language learning? If you are now a near-bilingual, are most of the occasional errors you still make due to native language interference or second language overgeneralization?*

25. *Compare observations with the other students in your class regard-*

*ing the relative difficulty in learning various languages. Do appar-
ently valid generalizations emerge from these observations?*

26. *How much guidance do language students need? As a language
learner, have you had the "right" amount of guidance?*

27. *What are the practical implications of giving each student the time
he needs to master each step in a language program? Why is the
educational establishment largely unwilling to accept self-paced
learning and what can be done about this?*

28. *In your own language learning experience, has a moderate degree
of anxiety improved or hurt performance?*

### Footnotes

[1]See *Synthesis* 409-17 on this topic.

[2]The correction of errors in general and of various specific types of errors
is discussed in several places in *Synthesis*.

# Chapter 7: Principles From Teaching Theory

## Introduction and Summary

There have been excellent teachers since earliest times, thousands of years before the establishment of faculties of education. Even today, some of the most outstanding teachers are people who never set foot in an education classroom. It cannot be said, therefore, that the study of education is a prerequisite for good teaching. At the same time, it must be recognized that educators are the people who have studied teaching in greatest depth and that certain educators have elaborated teaching theories that are comprehensive and probably quite valid. The discipline of education has therefore much to contribute to linguistics.

The philosophy of education that may dominate a particular period cannot help but affect our endeavors in major ways. We ignore the history of education at our own risk. Curriculum theory provides us with very useful principles to guide our activities. Educational technology —as we shall see in Chapter 8— can make a very significant contribution to language programs. The problem with assigning to education the same degree of importance as a feeder discipline that has been assigned in this book to linguistics or psychology is that, of all the possible feeder disciplines, education is the one most subject to capricious trends and fads. Should we really give much input into language teaching to the ones who gave us the wonders of new math, open classrooms, pass/fail, and now the Immersion Approach? I don't think so.

The proprietary rights that educators claim over language teaching (to wit, calling our field "Foreign Language Education") are quite undeserved. Ours is a unique subject that requires a unique, multidisciplinary treatment, not subservience to any one discipline. We should therefore resist and do everything possible to stop the use of phrases such as "foreign language education" —first because language teaching ("linguistics") should not be an appendage of any other discipline, least of all education; second because few languages are really foreign (not spoken by citizens) to North America.

*For all these reasons, the title of this chapter refers to "teaching theory," not education. Teaching theory is something all teachers can contribute to and apply, whether there have been education courses in their backgrounds or not.*

*This chapter deals first with the importance of teaching in terms of the difference teaching makes. It then presents 15 principles of teaching. A linguistic (or pedagogical) grammar is defined and some of its particulars given. Next there is a discussion of how to teach a rule. The chapter concludes with sections on teacher qualifications and behavior, teaching materials, and the need for instructional continuity.*

# 7.1: Teaching Makes a Difference

A recent careful, scientific study —better left unnamed— *demonstrated* the self-evident fact that teaching makes a difference. It seems ridiculous that such an obvious fact should have to be the object of experimental research, and yet, maybe it was necessary, for in the sixties and early seventies certain misguided visionaries and *enfants terribles* were saying that probably teaching made no difference at all, that all that mattered was the cognitive activity of the learner. We can state it as a law:

**TL 1:** *Teaching makes a difference.* This means not only that learners can learn faster and better with the help of instruction, but also that good teaching will produce better results than poor teaching (another truism). That this law is true is evident from the fact that human beings are affected by all their relationships with other human beings, so it is the extreme of unreasonableness to think that teaching may make no difference. That the quality of teaching may have a positive or negative effect is also self-evident, a truth that can be attested to by any human being who has been exposed to both superior and poor teaching.

**TP 1.1:** *Teaching approaches, methods, procedures, and techniques make a difference.* An **approach** may be defined as *a general pedagogical orientation based on one or a few assumptions related to an explicit or implicit theory.* For example, one can speak of an "oral" approach, which assumes that language is primarily an audio-oral phenomenon; a "linguistic" approach, which assumes that linguistic principles should guide the teaching process; or a "natural" approach, which assumes that languages are to be "picked up" naturally rather than taught formally (and which should not be confused with Terrell's "Natural Approach," which is only a *method*).

A **method** is *any of the sets of teaching procedures that follows an approach, each method's procedures being based on numerous specific assumptions that are in harmony with the assumption(s) of the approach.* It follows that within each approach there can be several methods, and that each method can vary in its procedures as long as these agree with the approach.

Several studies have shown that methods make a considerable difference in the results that can be attained with them. For example, at the end of one year of audiolingual instruction, Scherer's students of German were markedly superior in listening and speaking to students taught traditionally [Scherer and Wertheimer 1964]; reduction of these differences at the end of the second year of instruction is clearly due to the fact that during the second year *all* students in the program were taught the same way. My year teaching "experimental" audiolingual Spanish at Ohio State University (1964-65) confirmed Scherer's findings: after three quarters, the audiolingual students were vastly superior to the traditionally taught students in listening and speaking; furthermore, the audiolingual students did a little better on the dictation of unknown words, even though they had *never* had dictation practice and the traditional students had practiced dictation in almost every class throughout the school year.

A **procedure** is *a method-wide way of doing something.* For instance, the use of bilingual word lists, the memorization and deductive application of rule statements, and written translation exercises are procedures of the Grammar-Translation Method. The presentation of samples of the spoken language (usually dialogues) and their manipulation in the form of oral drills and exercises are procedures in the Structural Method, which follows both the oral and linguistic approaches. The prohibition on the use of the native language is a procedure in the Direct Method, another method which follows an oral approach but not necessarily a linguistic approach.

A **technique** is *a specific way of implementing a procedure.* While techniques can be to some extent a matter of the individual teacher's choice, no technique should be used that contradicts the principles of the method and the approach within which it is being implemented. For example, the oral procedure of teaching the voiced/voiceless contrast as it applies to certain consonant sounds can be implemented via at least three techniques —touching the laryngeal area, stopping an ear, or placing the palm of a hand on top of the head— any of which is acceptable and the choice of which can be left to the preference of the teacher (I suppose a lady teacher with an elaborate hairdo would want to avoid the third technique mentioned); however, for the teacher to try to explain the voiced/voiceless contrast in terms of letters of the alphabet would be against the principles of the oral approach, as much as it might be desirable, at some point, to introduce some sort of visual symbols as mnemonic aids.

**TP 1.2:** *Some approaches and methods are more suitable than others to the goals of the program, the knowledge and personality of the teacher, and the goals, personality, and learning strategies of the learner.* For instance, if the only goal of the program is imparting reading ability, an oral approach is unsuitable; conversely, a method that emphasizes reading and translation is clearly unsuitable if the goal of the program is overall second language competence. A teacher who cannot speak the second language or is extremely introverted can hardly be expected to function competently within an oral approach. Students with narrow goals, extreme personality characteristics, or rigid learning strategies may find it very difficult to learn under certain methods.

**TH 1.2.1:** *Students with high second language aptitude and high motivation may do well with (or in spite of) any approach or method; but logically they can only do best with one —the one most suited to their goals, abilities, personalities, learning strategies, etc.*

**TH 1.2.2:** *Students with low second language aptitude may do best with a method that breaks the learning process into small tasks and makes the conditions for success in each very explicit.*

**TP 1.3:** *Teaching should be not only effective but also efficient.* If an inordinate amount of time and effort is being spent to achieve effective learning of something, this should be a hint that perhaps efficiency is being sacrificed and that there might be a more efficient way of attaining the same results.

It seems incredible how little efficiency is valued by some members of our profession. On "principle" they will spend 20 minutes or longer to convey *monolingually* the meaning of a word or phrase, when the bilingual conveyance of its meaning would take only seconds. On "principle" they will spend several hours trying to teach a difficult rule more or less mechanically and *inductively*, when cognitively oriented procedures would be much faster and just as effective. Such methodologists and teachers choose to ignore the fact that we have our students for just a few hundred hours, and that therefore efficiency is essential.

**TP 1.3.1:** Some teaching procedures are much more efficient and/or effective than others. *Up to a point, efficiency should be sacrificed for the sake of effectiveness; but when there is no proof that a procedure really is more effective, then efficiency should be the decisive factor.* This implies an obligation on our part to determine which procedures are both effective and efficient and to use them in our teaching.

**TP 1.4:** *For teaching to make a major positive difference, a standard of* *excellence must be maintained.* This applies both to what the teacher demands of himself and to what he demands of the students. If the aim is not high, the attainment won't be high either. Students will rarely reach higher than the teacher's standards require, and many will reach lower. Without the challenge of excellence, very few students will learn as much as they are capable of.

**TP 1.5:** *Simply exposing students to data is not teaching.* Teaching follows definite principles such as those discussed in 7.2 below. In second language teaching, only "input" that is manipulated meaningfully seems to become "intake." Just providing "comprehensible input" is not enough to develop accurate productive competence —"manageable output" is required, and this means careful selection, gradation, presentation, correction, integration, and so forth.

**TC 1.5.1:** *Providing a "natural" linguistic environment is not teaching a language.* There is nothing "natural" about the linguistic environment of the language classroom —nor can it be made natural unless almost everyone in it is a native speaker of the second language (in which case it obviously ceases to be a *second* language classroom!). Furthermore, even in environmental language learning situations (such as ESL), where the language is spoken natively outside the classroom walls, it seems undesirable (leading to the formation of faulty habits) to expose beginners to that very rich linguistic environment before they have developed a basic knowledge of the language within the classroom program.

In other words, second language learning should not be based on the classroom linguistic environment or, until basic competence is developed, on using the language in the community outside the classroom. Instead, *second language learning —at least through the early intermediate level— should be based on* instruction.

# 7.2: Fifteen Principles of Classroom Teaching

The 15 principles discussed in this section were derived from a variety of sources, including curriculum theory; however, most emerged from the comparison of successful and less successful language teaching practice as observed and tried by me and as reported in the professional literature.

**TP 2.1: General objectives:** *To be successful, teaching must have clear general objectives.* General objectives are overall statements of what needs to be learned and to what level of mastery. They are based on an often implicit philosophy that ideally takes into account both the needs of society and the general needs of the learners.

**TP 2.1.1:** *Except for programs with limited aims, the general objective of language programs is to impart overall second language competence.* By that is meant not just knowledge *about* the language but also the ability to perform competently —fluently and accurately— *in* the language —in other words, a high level of proficiency.

Note that global control and use of the language as a whole is the *terminal* aim of the program. Partial, imperfect proficiency should never be aimed at. Intermediate degrees of faulty proficiency short of high proficiency should never be the basis for a language curriculum, as that would imply the acceptance of faulty production, which should be consistently discouraged. By aiming at faulty proficiency we ensure incompetence in the end.

**TP 2.2: Specific Objectives:** *Successful teaching is based on specific objectives at every step.* Unless the teacher knows why he is doing what he is doing at every step of the program, teaching effectiveness will suffer.

**TP 2.2.1:** *For a student to be able to perform at his best, he needs to know what the general and specific objectives of instruction are.* Statements to the students of specific objectives and how to reach them have been referred to as "performance objectives." Although certain objectives can be left implicit in lockstep programs without much harm, explicit objectives are a must in individualized or self-instructional programs.

**TP 2.3: Means of Instruction:** *How something is taught should depend primarily on its nature.* It is true, of course, that there are other factors in choosing the means of instruction, such as the age and interests of the learners, the abilities of the teacher, the availability of materials and facilities, and so forth; but teaching can be successful even when these factors are far from ideal. On the other hand, it seems that teaching cannot be successful when it goes against the nature of what is being taught.

A few examples from language teaching should make this clear:

Since a language is primarily an audio-oral phenomenon, it is against its nature to teach it on the basis of reading and writing.

Since writing is a representation of speech, it is again against the nature of language to teach sound -spelling correlations before a basic knowledge of the spoken language has been developed.

Since meaning is largely based on context, the teaching of vocabulary out of context (such as in one -to-one bilingual word lists) also goes against the nature of language.

Since languages are meant to be used for communication, a language program that does not allow some communication from the start — however simple and limited at first— goes against both the nature and purpose of language (as well as against student motivation).

Many such examples of language teaching against the nature of language could be given.

**TP 2.4: Selection:** *Given the time constraints of the classroom, it is very important to decide what to teach and what not to teach.* Again, there are other factors, such as the aptitude of the students and the knowledge of the teacher; but time constraints are the main reason for selecting what will be taught.

Selection involves several criteria, such as frequency of occurrence, availability, learnability, etc.[1] It should be clear that while teaching a language involves teaching all its sounds and all the letters of its alphabet (or syllabic symbols), not all the grammatical morphemes, maybe only about 50-60 percent of the syntactic rules, and just a very small percentage of its total vocabulary can be taught within the usual language program. Such limitations call for selection. Selection is unavoidable, for whether we are conscious of it or not what we teach is a selection from the universe of the teachable —better of course that selection be *principled* rather than haphazard.

**TP 2.5: Gradation:** *Teaching should proceed step by step, the simple before the complex, the frequent before the infrequent, the concrete before the abstract, the independent before the concomitant, etc.* For example, one would first teach children the numbers from one to five, relating them to the five fingers of a hand; one would then expand this to ten, later to 20 (all fingers and toes), then to other units of ten to 100; only much later could concepts such as one thousand, and still later, one million, be taught.

**TP 2.5.1:** *Gradation in language teaching refers to the ordering of (a) competences and the performance that leads to them and results from them; (b) components within competences; and (c) elements and rules within components.*

**TP 2.5.1.1:** *Language teaching should concentrate on linguistic competence first, then on communicative competence (at the advanced level, once the basic structure of the language is under control), and finally on cultural competence.* Note that this is a matter of emphasis — *some* communicative activities and at least *ad hoc* cultural information should be part of language instruction from the start.

**TP 2.5.1.2:** *Within linguistic competence, the gradation principle dictates that emphasis should be first on phonology (phonetics and phonemics), then successively on morphology, syntax, the lexicon, and discourse.* Clearly the sound system has the smallest number of elements and rules, and most sounds occur more frequently than any particular morpheme, syntactic rule, or word. While the discourse component may not contain very many rules (certainly fewer than syntax), a fairly advanced knowledge of a language is needed to understand lengthy connected speech or writing. Still, keep in mind that this is a matter of emphasis.

Note that the above order proceeds from concrete to abstract. It also follows the order of discovery as opposed to the order of sentence generation, which presupposes precisely the competence that we are trying to teach.

**TP 2.5.1.3:** *Gradation also applies within linguistic components.* For example, in terms of pronunciation, English [š], a fairly easy sound to produce, should be taught before [r], a difficult sound for most learners of English. Another example, this time both in terms of difficulty and frequency, is the teaching of the English progressive before the past tense.

Note that when it comes to language gradation, "the concrete before the abstract" does not refer to ideas or vocabulary —most beginning language learners old enough to be *taught* a language are perfectly capable of (and interested in) handling abstract concepts in structurally simple language, provided limited use is made of the native language to initially put the equivalences across. There is no reason for beginners to talk endlessly and inanely about chairs, books, and chalk.

Note also that what must be accompanied by something else (i.e., what is "concomitant") has to be learned after what must accompany it. For instance, the present tense of *have* has to be learned before the present perfect —while the application of this subprinciple is obvious in this example, at times it is not so obvious.

**TP 2.5.2:** *Violating the principle of gradation leads to incompetence.* The higher blocks on a pyramid need to lie on top of firmly placed lower blocks or it will hardly be a well-formed and stable pyramid. Skipping important steps in the learning process, or even proceeding to higher steps before the lower ones have been fully mastered seems to result, almost always, in faulty learning.

**TP 2.5.2.1:** *In language teaching, premature second language behavior leads to linguistic incompetence.* This is the reason why, for example, students should be discouraged from engaging in linguistic adventurism, that is, in free conversation that calls for rules they don't know sufficiently well or don't know at all.[2] Perhaps this principle can be formalized as a hypothesis:

**TH 2.5.2.1.1:** *Engaging in any second language activity without developing sufficient mastery of the activities that should precede it will result in faulty control over (or at least significant difficulties with) that aspect of the language.* It seems that good language teachers have always been aware of this.

**TP 2.6: Guidance:** *Guidance should be provided whenever needed throughout the program of instruction.* Students must be informed what to learn and how to learn it, as few seem able to realize this without help.

**TP 2.6.1:** *Language students should be eased into the second language so as to avoid "language shock" and minimize "language stress."*

There is no reason for allowing disorientation and confusion to develop. The best way to avoid them seems to be giving an orientation at the beginning of the program. Students need it, as second language learning is very different from the study of other subjects in the curriculum. An orientation allows us to obtain information about the students' background and interests and to make quite clear what is expected of them. Inappropriate goals —on the part of the student *or* of the program— can be modified at the time of the orientation. Of course, the orientation should be in the native language of the students, or it won't be understood.

One of the goals of an orientation is to train students to become good second language learners. Some student language learning strategies are appropriate, others not. Students need to know too what the program emphasizes. If the students are to make a decided effort to learn something, they must perceive it as important. What a program *really* emphasizes —as seen in its evaluation procedures— is by and large what the students will make an effort to learn.

**TP 2.6.2**: *Throughout the language learning process, guidance should make the purpose, nature, and expected outcome of each activity perfectly clear.* Guidance can manifest itself in the choice of examples that highlight the crucial point to be learned, in the presentation of the examples, in the description of what is to be learned, in the manipulation of elements and rules through carefully chosen drills and exercises, in correction, in the choice and conduct of communicative activities, and so forth. Should ambiguities and confusion develop at any point in instruction, they should be clarified, if necessary by using the native language.

**TP 2.6.3**: *Guidance should be provided only to the extent that it is needed.* To a considerable extent, and especially as their knowledge of the second language increases, students should be encouraged to be self-reliant, i.e., to make maximum use of what they already know. This means, in particular, involvement in guided discovery procedures (although such procedures would be inefficient with the more complex rules).

**TP 2.7: Presentation:** *Presentation consists in exposing the students to examples of what is to be learned for simple manipulation in the form of repetition and/or memorization.* In the case of language programs, these samples would consist of sentences (often in pairs for intra- or interlingual contrast), short dialogues, narrations, anecdotes, sayings, verse, and so on. An important requirement is that language samples be in some sort of natural context; real or even realistic language occurs in a context and derives much of its meaning from it.

**TP 2.7.1**: *Imitation is a very important first step toward communication.* Even young children acquiring their native language find it necessary to engage in a great deal of imitation —much more so should second language students, who have such a limited time to learn the language. It should be noted that below slow-normal speed, speech is considerably distorted, so imitation should be at normal speed from the start, only adding pauses *between* sentence parts if needed. (Speeding up, later, speech which was initially slowed down to the point of distortion results in *fast distorted speech*.) Long utterances can be broken up for imitation into phrases, maintaining normal speed within each phrase.

**TP 2.7.2**: *The memorization of very basic material provides a foundation for further progress.* It would seem that memorization of a number of carefully written short dialogues will help establish a solid foundation on which to build second language competence. This applies especially to the early beginning level (first semester of college or equivalent) and occasionally later. Asking students to memorize long dialogues or other long material is not only inefficient but counterproductive —most students resent, with justification, having to spend so much time on what is essentially a mechanical activity.

**TP 2.8: Understanding:** *We should make use of the students' intelligence and knowledge by helping them understand what is being taught.* Learning consists primarily in the making of discriminations and generalizations, which is a cognitive activity.

**TP 2.8.1:** *Language teaching should make full use of what the students know.* This is generally done in all other subjects in the curriculum. Why should any language teacher treat his students as if they didn't know anything?

**TP 2.8.2:** *An appeal to the intelligence and knowledge of the student doesn't mean an emphasis on analytical, deductive language teaching.* Analytical explanations and deduction have their place —they can greatly increase efficiency in teaching certain very complex rules— but most language instruction can best proceed by guided discovery and, occasionally, induction. Guided discovery accommodates both inductive and deductive learning styles. Less intelligent students seem to benefit more from analogy than analysis —they would benefit, for instance, from remedial work with such an emphasis.

**TP 2.9: Practice:** *Internalization requires practice.* This practice should be graded from mechanical practice with full attention to form (i.e., repetition and mechanical manipulation) to free use with attention on something else (for example, free conversation with attention on meaning, not form).

**TL 2.9.1:** *Practice doesn't necessarily make perfect, but it makes permanent.* Premature practice (practice beyond the learner's competence) or practice without error correction *makes imperfection permanent.*

**TP 2.9.2:** *Since a language is a system of internalized rules (i.e., of habits), much time and effort must be spent on activities that facilitate rule internalization.* These activities include, in particular, choice-making drills and exercises that present learners with a series of miniproblems to be solved. Very little seems to be learned by mindless, rapid-fire substitution, and what can be learned that way seems to be learned much faster through initially conscious choice -making drills. Of course, solving miniproblems involves being given adequate time to solve them, so pauses to think of the answer are typical of the first few choice-making drills on any rule. These pauses soon get shorter and then almost disappear, with the advantage that with this approach the students have internalized *the cognitive criteria* for the choices.

**TP 2.9.3:** *There will be errors during practice.* If gradation is carried to such an extreme that (a) no choice-making or problem-solving exists (and therefore no challenge), and that (b) what is learned is never used freely, it is possible to have very few errors; but clearly neither approach to the minimization or errors is acceptable.

**TP 2.9.3.1:** *Desirable minimization of errors involves (a) simplifying and grading instruction so that no more errors are made than can be effectively corrected while (b) retaining the possibility of error so as to keep the learning task challenging.* This involves a trade-off, a balancing act so that only an acceptable range of error incidence is maintained. Thus, the occurrence of *many* errors on any activity is a clear indication that instruction has not been properly graded and that it is necessary to go back to earlier steps and establish mastery at that lower level first.

**TP 2.9.3.2:** *Error correction needs to deal with the cause(s) of each error.* Of course, before he can deal with the cause of his error the student needs to be aware of what he has done wrong. Thus, in correcting a pronunciation error the first step would be for the teacher to ensure its perception by isolating the error, down to its minimal context (the word or syllable), and then differentiating it from what should have been said by putting both utterances side by side. Should the problem involve articulation rather than perception, articulatory pointers would be in order. Lexical and structural errors would necessitate more cognitively oriented correction —inter- or intralingual depending on the suspected cause— that deals with the faulty criteria underlying the errors, not with their surface manifestations. Surface error correction is a temporary measure, like aspirin for a tumor; criterion correction can be permanent, like surgery.

**TP 2.9.3.3:** *Students must be trained to monitor their own practice.* Most of the time —even in the language laboratory— students are not under direct supervision, so they must develop the ability to monitor their own speech. I believe that with appropriate training language students can develop into good self-monitors. What we must do is build accurate discrimination and choice-making criteria —the "voice" of the teacher— first into their conscious and with practice into their unconscious —in other words, provide them with a "languistic superego."

**TP 2.10: Integration:** *Anything that is taught and learned must be integrated with what has previously been taught and learned.* That is, to the extent that this is possible, new items should be used in conjunction with previously learned items. This is a call for progressive integration in teaching rather than the much-too-common linear approach in which a series of things are taught without relating them to each other. Progressive integration is particularly important in a subject which, like language teaching, involves imparting ability to function with a complex interrelated system of knowledge. Other subjects, such as literacy and mathematics, are in the same position.

**TP 2.11: Variety:** *Without variety in teaching activities, attention wanders off, boredom sets in, and little or no learning can take place.* This principle means that the classroom should offer a variety of activities, maybe none for longer than about ten minutes. An extension of this principle is to have courses taught by a variety of instructors and aides, as in team teaching, thus ensuring student exposure to the varied and unique contributions of each.

**TP 2.12: Evaluation:** *The results of teaching should be evaluated continuously.* Careful evaluation makes it possible to estimate the relative success of the teacher, the materials, and the program in teaching anything and of individual students, a given class, and various classes (in the same school or across schools) in learning anything.

Evaluation within the teaching process is essential if student or class deficiencies and errors are not to become permanent. Much of the time such diagnostic evaluation can be informal and can consist simply of ongoing, cumulative evaluation of classroom responses. But formal diagnosis via quizzes and tests is also necessary, if nothing else because it is expected, it seems to motivate students to greater study effort, and the results of it are taken more seriously than informal feedback.

Formal evaluation doesn't necessarily mean the teacher must administer and score all tests. Responsible students can administer and score many of their own quizzes and tests, leaving it to the teacher to do this only with a few tests that would account for most of the course grade.

Note that students form much of their idea of what is important to learn in a course by what the teacher gives greatest weight to in his evaluation; thus evaluation has a direct effect on the direction and degree of student effort.

**TP 2.13: Reintroduction:** *To ensure learning, each item should be reintroduced for active use many times, frequently at first and then at* *increasingly longer intervals.* This principle would seem to apply to any subject of study. In second language teaching, it appears, for example, that a word needs to be reintroduced *meaningfully* about 10-20 times before it is learned —fewer times when used in speaking, more when exposure is only receptive.

A research question which has not at all been adequately explored in this regard is what would constitute the most effective pattern of reintroduction for sounds, morphemes, words, syntactic rules, idioms, etc.

**TP 2.14: Meaningful Use:** *Full internalization of an item requires considerable meaningful use.* Only through meaningful use is it possible to establish the strong associations that allow ready recall. Mechanical use by itself is not enough for an item to "sink in," for cognitive reorganization to take place.

**TP 2.14.1:** *In language teaching, meaningful use should emphasize controlled, realistic communication rather than free, real communication.* Communication that is allowed to roam freely beyond the boundaries of what the students know will result in an unmanageable (and damaging) number of errors. In the long run, the result of classroom linguistic "creativity" with what is not known seems to be terminal incompetence.

**TP 2.14.2:** *Meaningful language use requires small group activities.* It isn't possible to converse in large classes, so *supervised* small group activities are necessary. This supervision can be provided by aides or even by advanced students who can absolve some of their course requirements by directing the small group conversation activities of beginning or intermediate classes. As to the activities themselves, they would be largely situations and role-playing, as well as games and, at a more advanced level, discussions, drama, etc.[3]

**TP 2.15: Mastery:** *Only teaching for mastery is worthwhile —mastery of each item as it is taught.* If programs cover material more superficially or more rapidly than required by the students to master it, the inevitable result is faulty learning.

**TP 2.15.1:** *The most important factor in the attainment of mastery is having adequate time to learn.* Given sufficient motivation and normal intelligence, it seems that even students of below-average aptitude can learn quite well if given adequate time to do so.

**TC 2.15.1.1:** *As different students require different amounts of time to master the same item, ideally the pace of learning should be individualized.* Pace individualization means that the best students need not be held back and that the slow students need not fall so far behind the pace of the class that they must either drop the course or fail it.

When pace individualization is not possible, the only way mastery can be attained by most students is if the best students are continually kept in "holding patterns" (through so-called "enrichment" activities) while the slow students are forced to constantly try to catch up through remedial work —hardly an ideal situation.

**TP 2.15.2:** *In addition to pace, goals to be mastered and means to attain mastery can be individualized.* For example, at the advanced level the various interests of the students can be attended to by means of partially self-instructional minicourses on a variety of topics.[4]

# 7.3: Pedagogical Grammars

**TD 3.1: Types of Grammars:** *We can distinguish four types of grammars: traditional, popular, scientific, and pedagogical (including linguistic).* A **traditional grammar** is *a prescriptive grammar based on the written language and (at least for the Western languages) on the structure of Latin.* A **popular grammar** would be *a compendium of popular beliefs about the structure of a language*; it is a set of beliefs largely influenced by traditional grammar and not lacking in folk myths. A **scientific grammar** is *a descriptive grammar developed by linguists*; in North America we recognize two main varieties of scientific grammars, i.e., structural and transformational, each of which has something to offer to language teachers.

A **pedagogical grammar** is *a grammar designed for teaching purposes.* One type of pedagogical grammar is a **linguistic grammar**, which is *a grammar designed to take a learner where he is (taking into account his knowledge of the native language and his traditional and popular notions about language) and lead him step by step to the internalization of the structure of a second language, describing the rules as they are learned (in as concrete a way as possible) but making sure that the outcome is not just cognitive knowledge but fluent and accurate performative knowledge.*

**TP 3.1.1: Transfer:** *A linguistic grammar fosters positive transfer and counteracts negative transfer (interference), both* overtly. By ignoring the native language, the problems it causes are perpetuated.

**TC 3.1.1.1:** *To be most effective and efficient, language teaching must be bilingual.* This doesn't mean, of course, constant translation, much less word-to-word "translation," which isn't translation at all. It does mean that the native language should be used in certain ways that increase the effectiveness and efficiency of instruction. Examples of this are an orientation at the beginning of the program, any explanations to beginners, and the conveyance of meanings that cannot be readily guessed from context. At the same time, the native language most emphatically should *not* be used as the basis for generating second language sentences —model sentences in the second language are a much better basis for sentence generation. When the aim is to teach the *second* language, not to produce professional translators, use of the native language in the program should gradually be phased out.

A good linguistic grammar will *ease* beginners into the second language. As they will tend to base their production on the native language, overt interlingual equation and differentiation must be used to make clear to them what they may and what they must not transfer from the native language to the second language. Only overt contrast will make really clear to them the inappropriateness of much transfer. Not tackling such negative transfer directly and overtly virtually guarantees that it will continue to occur.

**TP 3.1.2: Ordering of and within components:** *In a linguistic grammar, components and elements within components are ordered according to the principle of gradation.* Gradation —from concrete to abstract, from frequent to infrequent, etc.— and the nature of habit formation dictate that the earliest emphasis of the language program should be on pronunciation, followed by morphology, syntax, vocabulary, and discourse. This is a matter of emphasis, of course —most activities most of the time would include all components.

**TP 3.1.2.1: Teaching pronunciation:** *Teaching the perception and production of sounds and basic intonation patterns involves four steps: (1)* sound discrimination, *i.e., learning to differentiate sounds, especially from those with which they would tend to be confused; (2)* understanding *of what is involved in production, a step that usually requires a brief descriptive explanation; (3)* articulation, *that is, producing the sound or intonation pattern; and (4)* integration, *i.e., using it in combination with what has been previously taught.*[5]

Something that is often forgotten in dealing with pronunciation for beginners is that such instruction must refer strictly to sounds rather than be based on the standard writing system. Standard writing systems are either totally unrelated to pronunciation (such as Chinese characters) or are internally inconsistent (such as English, French, and, yes, Spanish), with few exceptions; most are also externally misinterpretable. For these demonstrable reasons, standard writing should be withheld from the usual beginners (maybe not from sophisticated linguists) as long as necessary to develop a basic audio-oral foundation in the language. However, most beginners seem unable to work strictly audio-orally for more than a few hours; without something on paper they find themselves rather confused and unable to memorize or review material efficiently. This points to the need of transitional graphic representations, that is, pedagogical transcriptions.

**TP 3.1.2.1.1:** *As standard writing systems were designed for native speakers, not for second language learners, the latter need a pedagogical transcription as a transitional learning aid.* With nonalphabetic writing systems, a pedagogical transcription is needed as a reminder of the way words sound; with alphabetic writing systems, a pedagogical transcription can be not only a reminder of the correct pronunciation but can overtly counteract phonological interference and provide a step-by-step bridge between pronunciation and spelling. Note that the availability of tape recorders doesn't make transcriptions unnecessary (as Stern [1983:93-4] suggests); recordings are rather unsuitable for both memorization and review purposes. Note also that the International Phonetic Alphabet and various other transcriptions, such as phonemic ones, are quite inadequate from a languistic point of view, as they ignore transfer effects and do not provide a bridge to spelling.[6]

**TP 3.1.2.1.2:** *Dictation does not seem to improve either sound discrimination or listening comprehension.* There are better, more direct ways to do either. This should not detract from the value of word dictation as a way to practice spelling patterns or of textual dictation as a quick means of evaluating overall language proficiency.

**TP 3.1.2.2: Teaching morphology:** *Teaching grammatical morphemes should involve, first of all, choice-making manipulation in which different morphemes (or allomorphs) are matched to different linguistic environments —i.e., correlation and replacement drills and exercises.* Languistically speaking, to try to derive morphemes from syntactic transformations is to put the cart before the horse.[7]

**TP 3.1.2.3: Teaching syntax:** *Teaching syntactic rules should be primarily a matter of manipulating sentences (involving rules that differ from native language rules) through the addition, deletion or transposition of words and phrases —i.e., via transformation exercises— or through translation.* Of course, as in the case of morphemes, full internalization of syntactic rules requires that more mechanical practice be followed by considerable application of the rule in communication.[8]

**TP 3.1.2.4: Teaching vocabulary:** *The teaching of vocabulary should follow closely the principles of selection, gradation, and integration and should present each item in the context of sentences and the larger context of discourse, i.e., in real or realistic language samples.*

**TH 3.1.2.4.1:** *One-to-one word lists and vocabulary cards encourage word-by-word "translation" which usually results in very unauthentic language.* This hypothesis shouldn't be hard to test.

**TH 3.1.2.4.2:** *Early emphasis on cognates will aggravate phonological problems, lead to false cognatization, and probably strengthen the tendency to "translate" word by word.* Maybe cognates and their formation should not be emphasized until the late intermediate level.

**TP 3.1.2.4.3:** *For reference, beginning students should use specially prepared bilingual glossaries; intermediate students should use good, large bilingual dictionaries; only advanced students can use monolingual dictionaries with any efficiency.* Pocketsize dictionaries, whether bilingual or monolingual, are a bane for anyone other than people who already know the second language quite well, for their lack of contextual information leads learners to make innumerable lexical errors. Monolingual dictionaries are a major source of frustration for beginning and intermediate students, for they force them to waste their time chasing after one word to understand another word to figure out another word, and so on. Only large dictionaries (first bilingual, later monolingual) that do provide contextualized examples of each word meaning (and not just many more entries) are worth having in the classroom; each language classroom *should* have such dictionaries, while forbidding the use of pocketsize dictionaries.[9]

**TP 3.1.3: Teaching the language skills:** *If the overall goal of the program is (accurate and fluent) communication, an audio-oral emphasis must be maintained throughout.* Programs that start with an audio-oral emphasis but soon switch to an emphasis on reading and writing are unlikely to develop the maximum student potential for communicative competence. Of course, an audio-oral emphasis does not exclude the teaching of reading or the use of literary selections, at the right time, to promote reading skill or stimulate conversation.

**TP 3.1.3.1:** *The receptive skills of listening and reading do not develop automatically but must be taught as such.*

**TP 3.1.3.1.1:** *In a full-fledged program, neither listening nor reading (nor both) should be taught first apart from speaking.* During what may seem purely receptive practice at the beginning of a program the students are subvocally quite active; as this subvocal speech is often inaccurate and goes on uncorrected for weeks or even months, by the time the students start speaking they have gone a long way toward internalizing faulty rules and so need remedial (and largely ineffective) instruction.

**TP 3.1.3.1.2:** While visual aids seem to be motivating, can stimulate output, and can provide general semantic orientation that facilitates comprehension, *it must be recognized that to the extent that comprehension of a passage is based on visual aids it is* not *based on the linguistic message.* Excessive reliance on visual aids —even in comprehension tests!— makes it unnecessary for the students to make a real effort to understand the language involved.

**TP 3.1.3.1.3:** *Comprehension breaks down when ambiguities pile up on top of ambiguities.* This means that, at key points in the course of comprehension activities, the teacher (or the materials) should provide checks on comprehension before proceeding any further.

**TP 3.1.3.1.4:** *Comprehension improves when there is considerable input that is slightly more difficult than what the learners readily understand.* This has been shown to be the case in natural language acquisition; but the classroom situation requires careful selection of what will be added rather than something like Krashen's vague *"i + 1"* input.

**TP 3.1.3.1.5:** *Comprehension improves significantly faster when the learners respond physically to the input.* James Asher [1977] has demonstrated this in numerous experiments with different languages and with groups of various ages. It may be —it is at least an interesting hypothesis— that responding physically to the linguistic input helps even when a student is studying alone.

**TP 3.1.3.1.6:** *All comprehension materials should be carefully graded through the advanced level.* If readings have more than 1:30 or at most 1:20 new words to known words, then the process becomes one of laborious decoding rather than reading. (Of course, this refers to extensive readings; short texts that are going to be studied intensively to a high level of mastery may contain far more unfamiliar vocabulary.) To ensure comprehension, new words should be glossed, with brief explanations as needed.

**TP 3.1.3.1.7:** *As all literature has been written for fluently literate native speakers, very little literature is linguistically simple enough to be used without adaptation in the second language program.* An appreciation of literature, a very valid and desirable academic goal, is counterproductive within the *language* program, as it will almost invariably result in the language students having to read texts that are far beyond their competence. So within the language program the reading of literature should be limited to the few linguistically simple texts available or should use adapted texts. If a good language program is allowed to follow its ideal course, the students will be ready to read most literature in the second language, in its original form, at the end of the program. If it is felt that literary appreciation must be developed within a short time, only two logical solutions that do no harm to the language program are available: (a) to speed up the language program by making it intensive or at least semi-intensive or (b) to rely on good translations. Literature cannot really be appreciated, anyway, when it has to be decoded with a dictionary in one hand and a grammar in the other.

**TP 3.1.3.2: Teaching writing:** *It is essential that, in teaching writing, careful gradation be followed.* Clearly since writing is largely based on (at least potential) speech, a solid foundation in the spoken language should be established before attempting to write (or, for that matter, to read) in a second language. A typical mistake is to start writing "compositions" too early. It can even be questioned whether free writing of any kind belongs in the language program or should be delayed until after having spent at least a few months in a country where the second language is spoken. Certainly the greatly delayed feedback offered by free writing assignments seems to be ineffective, as it does not deal in a timely way with the faulty decision criteria that led to the errors; as a result, compositions keep on coming with the same errors over and over again. It may be far more effective to have group compositions with the help of an overhead projector and with immediate discussion of any errors that occur. (Herein lies the potential for an interesting experiment.) Matters of style also tend to be dealt with very prematurely in our language programs; they would seem to belong at the advanced or the very advanced level.

**TP 3.1.4: Teaching a rule:** *The teaching of a rule should involve (1) presentation, (2) understanding, (3) practice, and (4) communication.*

**TP 3.1.4.1:** *The presentation should consist of examples from real or realistic language samples.* The students would repeat the examples with understanding of their meaning, if necessary provided bilingually — without understanding what the examples mean, how could the students relate the new structure to its usage? The examples must clearly highlight the structure being taught, by contrasting it with another second language structure, with the closest native language structure, or both.

**TP 3.1.4.2:** *Since intelligent practice seems to be much more effective than mindless practice, the students should be led to understand the rule before trying to apply it.* This understanding need not be imparted deductively except for a few very complex rules; much more challenging —and perhaps resulting in better recall— is the process of gaining understanding through guided discovery, with help from the teacher as needed.

**TP 3.1.4.3:** *Practice should be fairly mechanical at first, which will make it easier for the students, and then gradually more and more meaningful.* Language teachers should not hesitate to use *some* mechanical practice —what should be avoided is having *nothing but* mechanical practice. Practice can be made more meaningful in a variety of ways. This is the crucial and often neglected stage in learning a rule —having practice in which there is attention to both meaning *and* form.

**TP 3.1.4.4:** *Communication is essential to the full internalization of a rule.* At the beginning of the program, communication has to be quite limited and at best realistic; later real (though controlled) communication can be used more and more. At no time should communication beyond the learners competence be encouraged; such communication can only lead to linguistic incompetence, as much as it may help develop functional communicative "competence."

**TH 3.1.4.5:** The above leads to the testable hypothesis that *if any of the above steps in teaching a rule is eliminated or unduly shortened, the rule will be imperfectly learned.* This means that the teacher should never go on to the next step in teaching the rule until the previous step is mastered.

**TH 3.1.4.6:** Furthermore, it is hypothesized that *if steps are skipped or shortened for many rules, the final result will be linguistic incompetence.* For example, rather than providing beginners with opportunities to use the language freely, they should be actively discouraged from doing so until they control the necessary linguistic tools. Unless accuracy comes before communication, communication will remain inaccurate. Classroom language teaching should be centrifugal —first learn something, then use it for communication.

# 7.4: The Teacher

**TP 4.1: General Qualifications:** *All teachers need to (1) know their subjects; (2) understand the psychology of learning; (3) know how to teach, how to test, and how to use the technology associated with their subjects; (4) understand human nature; and (5) have the right personality and attitudes —sensitivity, a sense of humor, enthusiasm, neither rigid perfectionism nor permissiveness, etc.*

**TP 4.2: Qualifications of Language Teachers:** *Specifically, language teachers should (1) be highly proficient in the second language (this is a* sine qua non*); (2) if possible, be proficient in the native language of their students, something that can greatly enhance the teacher's effectiveness; (3) have a transmittable linguistic knowledge of the structures of the two languages (much linguistic knowledge is not transmittable to language students); (4) have a good knowledge of linguistic psychology, methodology, testing, and technology; (5) know the facts about, and understand the behavior in, the two cultures; and (6) if possible, be skillful in consecutive interpretation and written translation.* [10]

In the language program there is much occasion for humor, especially if a healthy attitude is maintained toward errors, some of which are quite humorous; it is important of course that students should not feel laughed at. Sensitivity to personality differences permits the teacher to promote desirable characteristics and attitudes and compensate for personality deficiencies in his students. The good teacher will always take into account his students' emotions.

Permissiveness has no legitimate place in language teaching. Without a considerable amount of discipline and hard work, a second language cannot be learned (or at least cannot be learned well). Steady, regular study should be encouraged, as language is not a subject amenable to "cramming" before tests. Since class time is limited, whatever the students can do outside of class they should do. Homework (though not necessarily involving reading and writing) should be assigned and given important weight in course grades.

The good language teacher is not reluctant to have extensions of his skills and presence as part of his program. I am referring here to technological aids such as recordings, visual aids, and (at the right time) computers and also to human assistants such as native paraprofessionals, advanced students as aides, etc. Properly incorporated into the program, technological aids and adequately trained aides multiply the presence of the teacher and should be welcomed by any good (and confident!) teacher.

# 7.5: The Teaching Materials

**TP 5:** *The teaching materials should match the specific goals of the program and should be used, not allowed to control the teaching/learning process.* Unfortunately many language teaching materials go counter to the stated aims of language programs and are followed slavishly, thus allowing the materials to control all teaching.

**TC 5.1:** *When the aim of the program is audio-oral competence, the teaching materials must provide primarily audio-oral rather than reading and writing practice.* The typical textbook or, for that matter, the latest computer programs (unless synchronized with recordings) cannot therefore be the best tools for developing the listening and speaking skills. Such materials tend to defeat the whole purpose of an *audio -oral* program. It would be far better to rely at first on recordings and scripts, then add workbooks, and only much later add readers and maybe computer-assisted instruction —nowhere in the program sequence is there any need for the ubiquitous traditional textbook (sorry, publishers).

# 7.6: Instructional Continuity

**TP 6:** *Unlike purely cognitively oriented subjects, language teaching requires instructional continuity.* All performative knowledge seems to be hurt by lack of temporal and methodological continuity; this seems to be especially true of a very complex set of skills like a language.

The effects of temporal and methodological discontinuity on second language learning have not been adequately studied. It seems clear that it isn't worth starting the study of a language if such study is to be interrupted for several years before having achieved basic competence. It also seems clear that methodological discontinuity is in the best of cases upsetting and in the worst frustrating and discouraging to the point where study is abandoned. These observations should lead to taking seriously all matters of articulation within and across programs.

**TH 6.1:** It can be hypothesized that *temporal and methodological continuity (or the lack thereof) in language teaching will especially affect results while basic competence is being developed but will have a lesser effect after basic competence has been attained.* It seems that once one "knows" a language, relatively long periods of time of nonuse can elapse without substantial forgetting. On the other hand, an interruption of more than two or three months seems to have very negative effects (in terms of forgetting) at the beginning or intermediate levels of language learning. (If nothing else, a person who has achieved basic competence can largely maintain it by occasional reading, something the precompetent student cannot do.)

**TP 6.2:** *To ensure continuity until the students attain basic competence, language programs should, if possible, be semi-intensive or intensive.* This would also have the advantage that students would be ready for very advanced work, such as reading literature or systematically studying the second culture, in half or even one forth of the customary time.

# 7.7: For Discussion

1. *Do you share the author's misgivings about educators playing a dominant role in language teaching? Why or why not?*
2. *In your experience as a language learner, have teachers and teaching made an important difference? In what ways, if any?*
3. *Which method would be most suitable for someone who just wants to learn to read? For an academic who will be attending an international conference in a foreign country? For a student who would like to be able to communicate fluently and accurately in the second language? See what other possibilities you can come up with.*
4. *Section 1.3 above gives two examples of efficiency being sacrificed for the sake of doubtful principles. Can you think of other examples? Why do some leaders propose and many language teachers readily follow such "principles"?*
5. *Have the language programs you have known been characterized by a standard of excellence? What specific consequences did the pursuit or nonpursuit of excellence have on the outcomes of those programs? How can we induce students to adopt the goal of excellence?*

6. *If no goals of instruction are set, can language teaching succeed? (Hint: Succeed at what?) Do goals need to be explicit? If so, for whose benefit?*

7. *Can you think of additional examples —other than the four given in Section 2.3 above— of language teaching procedures that are contrary to the nature or purpose of language?*

8. *In your opinion, what types of phonological rules, morphemes, syntactic rules or vocabulary items need not be taught in a full-fledged language program? Why?*

9. *Propose a gradation for the main features of the language you plan to teach or of a component thereof. Defend the order of your choice. (This could be expanded into a major term project.)*

10. *How would you go about providing language students with sufficient guidance without becoming overbearing or motherly?*

11. *What is your reaction to the "law" stating that "Practice makes permanent"?*

12. *Why would teacher provision of a corrected form be "superficial" and teacher-prompted self-correction (of the criteria underlying the same error) by the student be "deep"? Which type of correction was used in the language programs you attended?*

13. *How can a new rule or element be integrated with those previously learned? List specific ways of effecting integration.*

14. *Can the observant teacher, without formal evaluation or record-keeping of some sort, know exactly which student (in a class of 20 or so) knows what?*

15. *In what ways do tests help students learn? In what ways can they hinder the learning process?*

16. *Try to learn two or three new words in a second language. Keep a record of the number of times you need to (a) encounter them and/or (b) use them before you can readily understand them or use them correctly without hesitation. Report your results to the class and compare them with the results obtained by other students. Keep in mind that your special attention to these words will facilitate their learning. (This, again, is a long-term activity suitable for a class term project.)*

17. *How can language students be guided to use what they have learned meaningfully without being encouraged to communicate freely beyond their competence?*

18. *If pace individualization to ensure mastery is a sound idea, why isn't it widely applied? Can the practical difficulties of pace individualization be overcome? (You may wish to refer to* Synthesis, *Chapter 23.)*

19. *Discuss the specific ways in which a languistic grammar would have to differ from (a) traditional grammars, (b) popular grammars, and (c) the two main types of scientific grammars.*

20. *Why are the International Phonetic Alphabet and the various phonemic transcriptions unsuitable as languistic tools? Consider the way they represent the "problem" sounds —are these representations that make their articulations clear, foster positive transfer, counteract negative transfer, and lead step by step to spelling?*

21. *Tell the class of your experience as a beginning language student with various kinds of dictionaries —bilingual, monolingual, pocketsize, unabridged, and so on. State whether or not you agree with the author's views about dictionaries, and why.*

22. *Why is mechanical practice important? Is it strictly necessary? Could the same degree of control over rules and elements be attained by engaging in meaningful practice only? (Hint: Consider the amount of specifically linguistic feedback a language class would offer in the latter case.)*

23. *Why is the communicative use of a new rule or element essential to its full mastery?*

24. *Tell the class which qualifications in your language teachers you have appreciated the most, and why.*

25. *What's wrong with textbooks (or computer programs) as the be-all and end-all of comprehensive audio-oral language programs? What constraints and limitations do they impose?*

26. *Discuss the effects any temporal or methodological discontinuity may have had on your second language learning.*

### Footnotes

[1]For a full discussion of these see Mackey [1965]; for a brief discussion re vocabulary see *Synthesis* 459-61.

[2]For a discussion of "prematurities" in language teaching see Appendix A.

[3]See *Synthesis* 294-303 for many suggestions.

[4]For a concise discussion of second language individualization, see *Synthesis* 617 -31.

[5]See *Synthesis* Chapter 15 on the teaching of pronunciation.

[6]Tentative pedagogical transcriptions, based on new principles, for Spanish, French, German, and English were proposed in *The Articulatory Pictorial Transcriptions* [Hammerly 1974].

[7]See *Synthesis* 406-8 and *passim* on the teaching of morphology.

[8]See *Synthesis* Chapter 17 on the teaching of syntax.

[9]See *Synthesis* Chapter 18 on the teaching of vocabulary.

[10]These qualifications are discussed in *Synthesis*, Chapter 8.

# Chapter 8: Principles From Various Sources

## Introduction and Summary

*Sociolinguistics, which is concerned with the use of language rather than its structure, has contributed several important principles to language teaching. These principles provided the basis for the Communicative Approach in its several versions, including the teaching of "SLSPs" —second languages for specific purposes. As we shall see early in this chapter, a sociolinguistic point of view was overdue and is welcome in language teaching; but it isn't the solution to all our problems, as it has certain inherent limitations.*

*Language evaluation and testing have benefited from substantial psychometric research in the seventies. We are now in a position to enunciate tentative principles on the role and nature of testing in language teaching. Much has been learned, for example, about how to measure language proficiency; our profession must be cautioned, however, against basing curricular decisions on the descriptions of proficiency levels.*

*Technology can play a very important role in language teaching, freeing the teacher from everything mechanical in language teaching and thereby enabling him to concentrate on what only a creative human being can do. Only teachers whose incompetence limits them to mechanical teaching activities need fear being "replaced by machines." How the machine can extend the "presence" of the teacher is one of the concerns of this chapter.*

*Where circumstances require it, language teaching may have to be largely self-instructional. Principles for self-instruction are discussed.*

*A second language learner cannot be deemed fully trained until after he knows the essential facts about the second culture, appreciates its accomplishments, understands the behavior of its members, and can behave accordingly. This chapter ends by considering principles about the teaching of culture —principles based both on the nature of culture and on pedagogical desiderata.*

# 8.1: Principles From Sociolinguistics

Sociolinguistics (SL) is primarily concerned with rules of communication rather than linguistic rules. It sees sentences as having not only structural meaning but also communicative meaning. Children acquiring their native language learn simultaneously the form of words and sentences and their communicative meaning, i.e., how they are used in communication. Language students, on the other hand, may be trained in linguistic competence and performance —the production of correct sentences— without being sufficiently trained in communicative competence and performance —the production of situationally appropriate sentences.

**VSLP 1.1:** *As language students will not necessarily develop communicative competence on their own, skill in the appropriate use of the second language must be imparted.* It is possible to produce numerous linguistically correct sentences that are nevertheless contextually or situationally wrong.

Language students are even less likely to develop linguistic competence on their own, so it is clearly a matter of imparting *both* linguistic and communicative competence, as well as, as we shall see, cultural competence. None of these three types of competence should be emphasized exclusively, although it seems desirable to stress each at a different point in the program.

**VSLP 1.2:** *Language students should be made aware, among other things, of (a) various communication acts and their relationship to linguistic acts, (b) what makes sentences cohesive and coherent, (c) register and style differences, and (d) paralinguistic behavior.*

**VSLP 1.2.1:** *Language students need to be shown how the same sentence may be used in a variety of communication acts and how the same communication act may be carried out with a variety of sentences.* Communication acts include greeting, stating, questioning, agreeing, disagreeing, requesting, persuading, commanding, commenting, arguing, criticizing, complaining, apologizing, accusing, insulting, changing the subject, and so forth.

That the same sentence can perform a variety of communication acts is seen in a sentence like "It's hot in here," which may be a statement of fact, or a request that a window be opened, or a complaint against whoever set the thermostat, or a question about whether the air conditioner is working properly, etc. Even the same morpheme may have different functions; for instance, English -*ing* may refer to present action, action in the immediate future, future action, and repeated actions, and can furthermore nominalize a verb.

A communication act can be performed with many different sentences. For example, a chart by Wilkins [1976:60-1] shows that there are at least 57 ways of asking permission to use a telephone. The communicatively competent second language learner would know most ways of carrying out communication acts as well as which ways are most appropriate to various situations.

**VSLP 1.2.2:** *Language students need to be shown how to produce cohesive and coherent sentences.* A sentence is cohesive if it is appropriate to its linguistic context. In other words, cohesion involves formal relationships between sentences which are linguistically signalled, i.e., through syntactic or semantic rules, in an overt manner [Widdowson 1978:27]. For example, the answer "Yes, he went to the party" is not a cohesive response to the question "Did he go to the party?" —cohesion in this case demands the response "Yes, he did," as linguistic rules dictate the elimination of redundancies.

Coherence, on the other hand, involves an often covert relationship between sentences that can be inferred from the situation. Coherence applies not to sentences as linguistic acts but as communication acts, and to the relationship between communication acts. An exchange can be coherent without being cohesive. For example, the comment "I'm in the bathroom" in reply to "The phone is ringing" shows communicative coherence even though it lacks linguistic cohesion. Linguistically the two sentences are totally unrelated; communicatively they make perfect sense.

We see then that the choice of sentences depends largely on the linguistic context and the nonlinguistic situation. Part of the latter is the speaker's relationship to his interlocutor, the interlocutor's knowledge and the speaker's awareness of it, what each person wants, the physical surroundings, the time of day, and so on.

**VSLP 1.2.3:** *Language students need to be shown how to use different registers and styles.* Registers are different ways of speaking depending on the relationship to the interlocutors and to a lesser extent on the topic and other factors that affect the formality of the conversation. Joos [1967] proposed five registers: (1) oratorical or frozen, (2) deliberative or formal, (3) consultative, (4) casual, and (5) intimate. The word "styles" is usually reserved for different ways of writing, the study of which is the concern of stylistics.

**VSLP 1.2.4:** *Language students need to learn appropriate paralinguistic behavior.* Paralinguistic behavior includes all the nonverbal rules of conversation —how to get attention in a conversation, how to agree nonverbally, how to disagree nonverbally without offending, etc.— as well as all the other rules of "body language" such as those involving gestures, proxemics (accepted distances between speakers), eye contact, touching, and even clothing and appearance.

**VSLP 1.3:** *At the beginning and intermediate levels the emphasis of the language program should be on linguistic competence, at the advanced level on communicative competence, and at the very advanced level on cultural competence.* Many sociolinguistically oriented language teaching specialists would disagree with this principle, as they would prefer to emphasize communication from the start and make linguistic competence secondary or even subordinate to communicative competence. As we have seen in the case of the Immersion Approach, which emphasizes communication from the start and throughout the program, making linguistic competence secondary results, as could be expected, in linguistic incompetence. While there should be *some* communication from the start, it seems that best overall results will be obtained when communication does not receive primary emphasis until the advanced level. (At the intermediate level, linguistic and communicative competence would be stressed about equally.)

As there are many ways of performing most communication acts, it seems obvious that teaching them all as if they were linguistically unrelated would be very inefficient. Far more efficient is teaching the linguistic rules that allow the students to perform many different communication acts, and then slowly enabling them to perform each act in more and more sophisticated ways. *This calls for cyclical communicative teaching around a gradually expanding structural core.* The opposite, teaching at one time many grammatically heterogeneous ways of performing each communication act, is not only confusing to the students but doesn't lend itself to the teacher keeping tabs on what the students should know.

**VSLP 1.4:** *When teaching a second language for specific purposes, start by determining the communication needs of the learners.* When all the students in a two -week course are going to be airline stewardesses or border guards or customs inspectors, it makes sense to start by asking ourselves what it is they want to be able to understand and say, and organize the course accordingly. That is, specific purpose courses would be based on authentic situations and texts that the students are very likely to encounter. At the same time, note that such an approach would be totally unsuitable for general purpose courses where, as they will tell you, what the students want to learn is "the language."

**VSLP 1.5:** *When the purpose of a language teaching activity is communication, the teacher should not engage in "pseudocommunication."* Often language teachers are under the impression that they are communicating with their students when they really aren't. The sentence "This is a book," for example, is not a communication act unless your interlocutor has never seen a book. Similarly, "I'm opening the door" is not a communication act, as in normal communication one doesn't describe the obvious. If what one means is that in English a certain object which in, for example, Spanish is called "un libro" is called "a book" and a certain action described in Spanish with "abrir" is referred to with the verb "to open," then why not so indicate? The same artificiality applies to the noncommunicative act of the teacher asking questions for which he knows the answers. A further example is the presentation of sentences which, while linguistically correct in isolation, are not drawn from, or not shown to be related to, any particular communicative situation. These are examples not of communication acts but of putting language "on display" [Widdowson 1978:53]. There isn't anything wrong with such utterances if it is kept clearly in mind that they are *not* communication and that later they must be linked to real use of the language.

**VSLP 1.6**: *Communicative competence should be imparted on the basis of contrastive analysis.* In order to determine which communication skills must be taught and which are already known and may be transferred directly to the second language, it is essential to compare the ways in which the two languages are used. Of course, this may not be possible with heterogeneous classes.

# 8.2: Principles Regarding Evaluation

**VEP 2**: *Evaluation (E) is an indispensable adjunct to teaching.* Teaching is imparting knowledge, evaluation or testing is determining the extent to which learning has taken place. Much confusion has arisen from the erroneous notion that testing is a form of teaching, confusion that has led to the avoidance of certain quite valid testing techniques "because we are not supposed to teach that way."

That evaluation is indispensable can be demonstrated by the need to answer "None" to the following question: Other than evaluating what the student has actually learned, what way is there to decide whether he should go on to learn something else or should instead get further practice with previously taught material? Even in programs where there is no formal testing, such as those of commercial and government language schools, informal evaluation takes place and is the basis for deciding how to proceed. All language teachers evaluate their students, one way or another. Conscientious teachers evaluate every student response.[1]

**VEP 2.1**: *In formal teaching situations, formal testing is desirable.* Not only is formal testing (and some sort of grading) expected by school administrators, parents, and students, but it can help the latter (a) motivationally and (b) by providing them with detailed diagnostic feedback. Every test result should give the students specific information about their strengths and weaknesses, thereby allowing them to work on what they need to improve.

**VEP 2.2:** *In a formal situation, students study primarily what will be tested.* While the desire for good grades is a factor here, perhaps just as important is the students' perception that what is tested is what the teacher considers important in language learning.

**VEP 2.2.1:** *A program that claims to be audio-oral in emphasis* must *test listening and, especially, speaking.* It is hard to believe how many so - called "oral" programs fail to do this. With a language laboratory, mass oral testing is not difficult to arrange. There, the production of sounds, the use of selected grammatical rules and lexical items, and the ability to participate in a directed simulated conversation can all be tested in 20-25 minutes and scored at the rate of about three minutes per student. (See Appendix C for a sample laboratory speaking test of the type just described.)

If there are no laboratories available, then the students could be interviewed twice per semester. It takes about five minutes per student for a teacher to administer a progress interview. (Progress interviews differ from proficiency interviews in that they are not general but refer to specific material covered in a course.)

If for whatever reason —it is hard to think of any— progress interviews cannot be administered, the least the teacher can do is announce at the beginning of the course that a significant part of the grade will be based on spoken performance, and then proceed to evaluate, as objectively as possible, the oral performance of three or four students in each hour of class, keeping a detailed record in charts of various kinds.

**VEP 2.3:** *Progress language tests should make use of both discrete-point and global (integrative) testing techniques.* All language classes include the learning of specific second language elements, and most involve the learning of one or more specific rules, so every so often the language teacher (and the student) needs to determine which of these elements and rules have in effect been learned —the only way to do this is through discrete -point items. At the same time, it is true too that linguistic competence is not composed of isolated items but that all elements and rules must be integrated into a working whole. Since after just a few hours of language instruction some integration has taken place, even the *first* significant test in a language program should include one or more global sections in addition to the discrete-point sections. We see then that both types of approaches to testing are needed, for different but essential purposes, in the language program.

**VEP 2.4:** *Two testing techniques used in proficiency testing —cloze and interviews— can be adapted for use in progress tests.* Interviews have already been briefly discussed. The cloze technique can be used in progress testing by writing texts based on what has been covered, by blanking items rationally rather than at random (i.e., choosing spots where there are specific difficulties), and by providing multiple-choice answers for each blank, answers which should involve both discrete points and global comprehension. This is discussed in a little more detail in a recent article [Hammerly and Colhoun 1984].

**VEP 2.5:** *To establish initial grouping by ability, language aptitude tests should be used.* It should be kept in mind that such tests are not very precise tools, but they do allow placement into three roughly homogeneous groups —above average, average, and below average in aptitude. The predictive value of these tests is approximate; weakly motivated high-aptitude students may do poorly and strongly motivated students of below-average aptitude may do well if they work very hard. It follows that these tests are valid for initial placement but that low scores on them should never be a reason for excluding prospective students from the language program.

The language aptitude tests now available are especially suited to inductive audiolingual learning in the classroom and may be less suitable for other methods and situations. In terms of school levels, Carroll and Sapon's *Elementary Modern Language Aptitude Test* [1967] can be used in elementary schools, the *Pimsleur Language Aptitude Battery* [1966] is appropriate for high schools, and Carroll and Sapon's *Modern Language Aptitude Test* [1959] is best for college students and other adults. All three of these tests assume that the examinee is a native speaker of English. Aptitude tests, by the way, are one of the tools essential in experimental research in order to ensure the comparability of groups of subjects.

**VEP 2.6:** *Proficiency tests should be used to evaluate general proficiency, however arrived at,* not *to make curricular decisions or establish performance objectives.* Proficiency ratings, based usually on interviews, describe the rather faulty performance of second language speakers *despite* whatever exposure to the language, formal or informal, they may have had. This is performance that occurs when the examinee is pushed to speak beyond his competence. Thus, except for the highest rating, all proficiency ratings have linguistic inaccuracy built in. Surely it must be our policy to set accurate speech as the goal at all times (a goal that I believe is largely realizable when all important principles of language teaching are followed). If we establish imperfect performance as our goal, the results will be much worse than if we aim at what, for many students, will remain an ideal.

**VEP 2.7:** *In individualized programs, testing should be an ongoing process and grading will seldom result in failures.* As pace is individualized, students will be ready to be tested at different times, so there is a need for several versions of each test and for provisions to administer them at any time. As each student can have more than adequate time to prepare himself for each test, there is no reason for low marks other than for students who fail to do the work within the maximum time allowed.

**VEP 2.8:** *At reasonably frequent intervals, teachers, materials, courses, and programs should be evaluated, by relying mainly on (a) standardized tests, (b) student questionnaires, and (c) visits by supervisors and master teachers.*

**VEP 2.8.1:** *Standardized tests should be used fairly frequently, as they are the most objective means of teacher and program evaluation.* Of course, many teachers will "teach to the test" if they know its contents in advance —so they should not know it. (With a computerized bank of test items, it should be possible to produce many versions of each test.) Standardized tests are also extremely useful in research on language teaching.

**VEP 2.8.2:** *Rather subjective but valuable information about the teacher, teaching materials and activities, and the program can be obtained through student questionnaires.* Students are, after all, the "consumers" of our "product" —so why shouldn't we be interested in finding out what they have to say about it? The knowledge that their opinions are valued also increases the students' self-esteem and their feeling that this is "their" program. For these and other reasons I have included "the right to evaluate" the program, etc. as one of the rights in the language student's "Bill of Rights" (see Appendix B).

**VEP 2.8.3:** *Until a teacher masters the science and art of language teaching, he should be visited and evaluated, at reasonably frequent intervals, by supervisors and master teachers.* This may be the most subjective of these three techniques of teacher and program evaluation, as it is fraught with dangers of politics, personality conflicts, etc. At the same time, it is probably the most useful of the three techniques, as visitors who are very experienced language teachers are able to provide specific feedback and constructive suggestions. The success of this technique of evaluation depends largely on the spirit with which it is carried out.

# 8.3: Principles Regarding Technological Aids

**VTAP 3.1:** *The use of technological aids (TA) should be subordinated to the nature and goals of the program.* Clearly, if the emphasis of the program is audio-oral, recordings should play an important role and graphic aids like the computer should play a much smaller role, at least at the beginning level.

**VTAP 3.2:** *Emphasis should be on the use of technological aids that involve linguistic production and, if possible, interaction with the machine.* This means that, as desirable as radio and television may be for receptive purposes, they cannot be relied upon to build linguistic competence, which requires production with feedback.

**VTAP 3.3:** *Recordings with feedback should be the main medium in audio-oral programs, especially at the beginning level.* It should be obvious that, since language is primarily an audio-oral phenomenon, language students should benefit from the right kind of work with appropriate recordings. It is nothing short of a scandal the way language laboratories have been allowed to fall into disrepair and disuse in North America. Just because most people did not know how to use them in the sixties was no reason to abandon them wholesale —what was called for was finding better ways of using them.

Now that most language students have access to cassette machines, lending recordings out should be standard practice rather than the exception (some system of cassette machine rental and/or loan for students who do not have one should not be too difficult to establish). Clearly in an audio-oral program, practice outside of the classroom should be based on recordings, not written exercises.

Videotapes can have all the advantages of stereo master/student recordings plus the advantage of providing video stimuli; unfortunately, they are still beyond most school budgets. Videodiscs allow some interaction but no student recording, so they can only be a (very expensive) way to improve comprehension.

**VTAP 3.4:** At the intermediate level (and beyond) of an audio-oral language program, computers can aid the learning process by providing highly individualized practice, testing, and remediation. Of course, at the beginning level computers can also be valuable aids provided they are used in interface with tape recorders. Used by themselves, they would change the nature of the program from an oral emphasis to a graphic one. (Voice synthesizers in computers are still very far from producing "speech" that can serve as a model for language students.)

In the not too distant future we can expect microcomputers to have the power of the mainframes of the sixties and be able to do what Fernand Marty and others have done with PLATO at the University of Illinois, i.e., very sophisticated computer-aided instruction. But listening and speaking skills will continue to have to be imparted with the help of recordings. And, of course, any free speaking or free writing, and feedback about it, will continue to have to be done by live teachers, for computers are only extremely fast "dummies," unable to deal with anything unexpected which hasn't been programmed into their fast but dull "brains."

**VTAP 3.5:** *Technological aids should be designed especially for language teaching rather than adapted from other uses.* We should be able to tell manufacturers exactly what we want and be able to get it. Our requirements are for inexpensive aids that are simple to operate, not for gimmicky devices with expensive features. But we won't be able to get what we need until our profession is eager to use technological aids, thereby creating a large market for the machines we want.

# 8.4: Principles Regarding Self-Instruction

**VSIP 4.1:** *The receptive skills and the mechanical aspects of the productive skills can be learned through self-instruction (SI).* This applies to the development of listening and reading comprehension and to the mechanical manipulation and internalization of spoken and written vocabulary and grammar.

**VSIC 4.2:** *Any free production requires interaction and feedback, for which a live interlocutor is required.* This applies to the early introduction to the pronunciation of the language (although I don't think many teachers are sufficiently qualified to deal adequately with this), to all conversation, and to all recombinatory and free writing. Without immediate and specific human feedback, engaging in such activities may do the student more harm than good.

**VSIP 4.3: The conclusion, then, must be that** *for best results, self-instructional language programs cannot be totally self-instructional but must rely on human interaction for a small but significant part of the time.* While mature students can be trusted to be responsible for their own learning, they need to interact with a speaker of the language at least one of every four or five hours of study. When enrollments are so small or so erratic that regular teacher-led courses cannot be offered, then, a solution would be partial self-instruction in which the students are on their own most of the time but get together with native language assistants for conversation sessions every few hours of study.

**VSIP 4.4:** *Self-instructional materials must offer detailed, explicit guidance.* If students are to develop second language competence while being on their own almost all the time, all necessary instructions, explanations, and mechanical feedback must be available to them in an efficient and crystal-clear manner.

**VSIP 4.5:** *Only highly motivated, self-disciplined students should be admitted in self-instructional programs.* Without high motivation and the maturity and discipline needed to be responsible for his own learning, it is hard to see how a student could succeed in a self-instructional language program.

# 8.5: Principles Regarding Cultural Competence

**VCP 5:** *Language students cannot be considered fully trained unless they have been imparted cultural (C) competence.* It is not enough for second language speakers to be able to communicate messages with linguistically accurate sentences; they must also be able to exhibit the knowledge and behavior that the second culture demands.

**VCP 5.1:** *Imparting cultural competence means, first of all, teaching the cultural connotations of words and phrases and how to behave in different situations; secondly, teaching the important facts about the culture; thirdly, teaching about the culture's achievements; and finally, systematically contrasting the two cultures.* The traditional "civilization" courses, which concentrate on information about the culture, and the usual literature courses, which emphasize only one aspect of the achievements of a society, are insufficient for cultural instruction —such instruction, if it is going to enable a learner to function in the second culture, must stress attitudes and especially behavior. Note, by the way, that communicative competence, with its largely sociolinguistic basis, and cultural competence, which is largely based on anthropological concepts, overlap in the area of paralinguistic behavior (gestures, proxemics, etc.). But there are many aspects of cultural competence which lie outside the domain of communicative competence.

**VCP 5.2:** *Cultural instruction should not be divorced from the second language.* This principle in effect relates cultural instruction to linguistic instruction. Although it is true that most of the early *ad hoc* comments and asides may have to be in the native language, there is no reason why advanced cultural activities could not be conducted in the second language. Whatever cultural instruction there is should contribute to and expand language learning, not distract or even detract from it. The quality of systematic cultural study itself would benefit if the students have an advanced knowledge of the language.

**VCP 5.3:** *Cultural instruction should be based on contrastive cultural analysis.* Only through contrastive analysis can we decide what needs to be taught, what is already known, and the extent and nature of cultural transfer. The pioneering work in cultural contrastive analysis was Lado's *Linguistics Across Cultures* [1957]. **RS:** It is curious that since then no one has seen it fit to fill an important research gap: We need multicultural, or at least bicultural, dictionaries which one can consult to find out what other peoples' attitudes are and how they behave in a variety of situations.

**VCP 5.4:** *Cultural instruction should limit or moderate ethnocentrism.* Note that the goal should not be to eliminate ethnocentrism entirely, for a certain amount of ethnocentrism seems to be necessary to a sense of nationhood.

**VCP 5.5:** *Cultural instruction must show stereotypes for what they are.* Stereotypes are "convenient" overgeneralizations indulged in by lazy minds. Language teachers must make an effort to demonstrate to their students that stereotypes are from partially to totally wrong when applied to individual cases.

**VCP 5.6** *Cultural readings should emphasize the behavioral sciences, not literature.* Although some works of literature are culturally illuminating, most of them are not. One can learn far more about another culture, in much less time, by reading in the behavioral sciences than by reading literature. The argument that there should be an emphasis on literature within the second language program for the sake of cultural understanding seems therefore largely invalid. Literature is something one can read for enjoyment or study *after* having learned the second language through the advanced level; then one will be able to garner certain cultural insights from it.

# 8.6: For Discussion

1. *What would be the result of communicating without prior development of linguistic competence? What would be the result of producing linguistically correct sentences without awareness of their appropriateness?*

2. *Provide your own examples of differences in register and in paralinguistic behavior and compare them with the examples given by other students.*

3. *How would you ensure that communicative competence is developed without harm to linguistic competence, and vice versa?*

4. Does noncommunicative language such as "pseudocommunication" have any valid function in the language program?
5. Do you agree with the author that evaluation —whether formal or informal— is essential? Why or why not?
6. Why has the testing of the speaking skill been so widely neglected? What can be done about it?
7. Why shouldn't proficiency ratings be the "organizing principle" guiding curricular decisions in language teaching?
8. Discuss potential advantages and disadvantages in the use of standardized tests.
9. Are the misgivings many teachers have about anonymous student evaluation questionnaires justified? How can such evaluations be made more objective and reliable? Should they be used at all?
10. Which uses of recordings would facilitate audio-oral learning? Which might not help it or might even hinder it?
11. How can computers facilitate language learning? What are their limitations?
12. Are there any valid reasons for most universities not to offer numerous low-demand courses on a largely self-instructional basis? How could administrative and personnel hindrances to such programs be overcome?
13. Should the imparting of cultural competence wait until the advanced level? If not, how would you provide cultural information at the beginning and intermediate levels?
14. What do you think of the idea of a language program organized on the basis of a series of cultural topics rather than linguistic structures?
15. Can original literature, written for natives with large vocabularies, be profitably introduced within the second language program? Why or why not? Would editing it solve the problem?

### Footnote

[1]For general testing concepts and definitions of testing terms, see *Synthesis*, Chapter 21.

# Chapter 9: Integration —The Two-Cone Model Revisited

## Introduction and Summary

*The book* Synthesis in Second Language Teaching, *published in 1982, filled the need for a model of language teaching/learning as the latter should take place in the classroom, as opposed to various models that try to represent what seems to happen in natural linguistic environments like the nursery and the street. The Two-Cone Model represents in many respects the integrated theory proposed in the present book. After briefly reviewing the Two-Cone Model as originally presented, this chapter discusses further thoughts about it, including its centrifugal nature, its incorporation of basic principles of teaching, its account of interference and overgeneralization, the fact that it is both structural and communicative, how it compares with other models, and the relationship of the Two-Cone Model to learning theory, linguistics, and language teaching methodology.*

## 9.1: The Need for Integration

To develop a theory, it is not enough just to list a series of laws and principles. For propositions to constitute a theory, they should be integrated into a harmonious set in which each of the parts contributes to the functioning of the whole. A model —a theoretical representation— of such a body of propositions would be very useful in helping guide research, further theory development, and practice in our field. Unfortunately, the models advocated so far may adequately describe the process of natural language acquisition in nurseries and streets but seem quite inadequate, as we shall see, as representations of what does or should go on in language classrooms.

## 9.2: Integration: The Two-Cone Model

The Two-Cone Model, originally proposed in *Synthesis* in 1982, does provide an integrated representation for many of the principles proposed in the present book. It is furthermore a model specifically designed to represent second language teaching and learning in the classroom, not an attempt to represent processes that go on outside the classroom and cannot be reproduced within its walls. We shall therefore briefly review the Two-Cone Model and then discuss further thoughts about it.

## 9.3: Review of the Two-Cone Model

In the Two-Cone Model, the native language and the second language each appear represented as a cone, with pronunciation ("P") at the apex, morphology and syntax ("G" for "grammar") at the center of the cone, and vocabulary ("V") surrounding grammar and expanding especially at the open-ended base of the cone (see Figure 9.1).

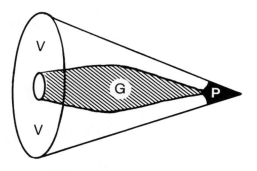

Figure 9.1

It is generally recognized that initial contact between the native language of the learner and the language he is learning is necessarily phonetic, as the learner must first of all learn to perceive and produce the sounds of the second language. This is represented, in Figure 9.2, as the contact between the apices of the two cones.

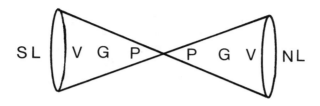

Figure 9.2

The two languages then start to interact. The two interacting cones are of course a representation of what happens in each language learner's mind, not of what happens in the class as a whole.

The second language emerges in the learner from interaction with the native language, one cone emerging from inside the other, first in the area of pronunciation, then mostly in that of morphology and syntax, finally mostly in the area of vocabulary. This is represented in Figure 9.3.

The reader is reminded that this is a representation of how a language should ideally be learned in the classroom, not of how languages may be actually "picked up" in the field. For example, a common practice of natural language acquirers is to concentrate from the start on learning a large vocabulary; it is claimed here that such an approach would have a negative effect on classroom language learning —it would encourage learners to communicate beyond their limited linguistic competence, thereby internalizing faulty rules.

With poor instruction —which is superficial, undemanding, and noncorrective— the second language that emerges (areas B and B-1 in Figure 9.4) from classroom instruction and interaction between the two languages (areas A-1 and B-1 in Figure 9.4) would contain fossilized faulty rules and elements, that is to say, bad linguistic habits (dots in area B in Figure 9.4).

Ideally, rules and elements would be learned one by one, linearly and additively, and would be integrated into transitional systems ("TS-1...-n" in Figure 9.5), the last of which represents the second language competence attainable within the program —which of course should be further developed through natural acquisition beyond the program.

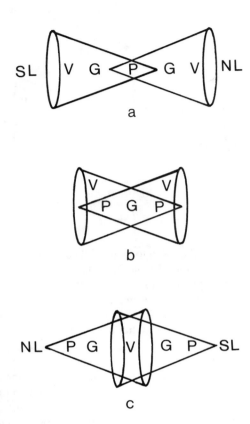

SL  V G ⟨P⟩ G V  NL

a

V V
⟨P G P⟩

b

NL⟨P G  V  G P⟩SL

c

Figure 9.3

Transitional systems are like partially built machines that can be used for limited functions. As more and more of the machine is built, more functions can be performed. But trying to use a partially built machine for the global functions which only the complete machine can perform will only result in faulty production. In language learning, using a limited competence for global purposes will result in faulty production that is soon internalized.

Each rule and element being learned should go through a series of instructional steps (shown in Figure 9.6), namely Presentation (involving Exemplification and Understanding), Manipulation (in terms of both

Mechanical Drills and Meaningful Exercises), and Communication (composed of, first, realistic Communicative Activities, and then, Real Communication).

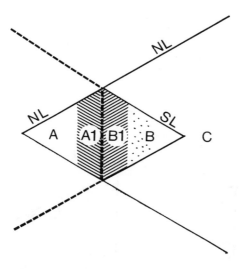

Figure 9.4

The linguistic environment is of course important. Where the second language is not spoken in the environment, i.e., when it is *remote* (this is usually called a "foreign language" situation), the language classroom is the only source of input. In the *environmental* situation, where the language is spoken in the environment (usually referred to as a "second language" situation), there is also input from the environment —which for beginners might do more harm than good. The two situations are represented in Figure 9.7.

As already seen earlier in this book, the Two-Cone Model represents second language competence —cognitive and especially performative knowledge of a second language— as a composite of three competences — linguistic, communicative, and cultural. Each of these is represented as a cone, with linguistic competence as the core. In other words, linguistic competence, the core cone, is used to communicate within a cultural context.

## 9.4: Further Thoughts on the Two-Cone Model

**9.4.1:** *The Two-Cone Model ("T-CM") is centrifugal.* The T-CM represents movement from the linguistic core to the communicative periphery.
This is very different from the natural language acquisition situation, in which movement goes in the opposite direction, that is, centripetally, by deriving knowledge of the structural core of the language *from* its use.

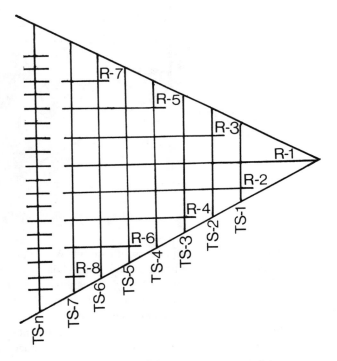

Figure 9.5

It seems only logical that, if in order to perform a function one needs to use a language structure, the structure should come under some degree of control before it is used. No technician, for example, would attempt a job before developing some dexterity with the tool or tools required to perform it.

For a centripetal or communicative approach to succeed in developing linguistic accuracy, the learner would need to interact almost constantly with natives, who would serve as "linguistic floaters" that keep him from "drowning" linguistically. Such conditions exist in the nursery and the street, but not in the language classroom.

Of course, anyone with a little imagination can produce language program graduates who chatter in something vaguely resembling a second language. All it takes is an emphasis on free communication from the start and a willingness to disregard accuracy. But such an outcome cannot be considered a valid instructional goal. Furthermore, why settle for barely "functional" bilingualism when, if sound principles are followed, excellent results are possible?

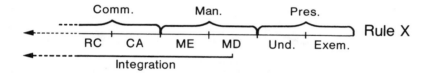

Figure 9.6

We have seen that under the best of circumstances —twelve to thirteen years of immersion— the centripetal, communicative approach produces speakers of a very faulty classroom pidgin. We are forced to conclude, then, that for best results classroom language teaching must be centrifugal, not centripetal —things should be learned first, then used, or, as Wilga Rivers [1976:23] put it, first "skill-getting," then "skill-using."

**9.4.2:** *The T-CM incorporates basic principles of teaching.* These include, among others, the following:

**9.4.2.1:** *Selection:* The last transitional system in the T-CM ("TS-n") represents a careful, principled selection of what should be learned within the second language program. Each non-terminal transitional system adds to the preceding one a specific structure carefully selected for that spot in the program on the basis of linguistic, psychological, and pedagogical principles.

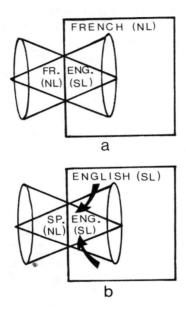

Figure 9.7

**9.4.2.2:** *Ordering of components:* Major components of the language are ordered in such a way as to teach each component after its prerequisite skills have been attained. For example, the learning of vocabulary should not be *emphasized* until there is a basic control of structure, and a considerable degree of mastery over the sounds of the language should be a prerequisite to all other activities.

**9.4.2.3:** *Gradation:* The T-CM requires detailed specification of the order in which rules and elements will be taught.

Together, the principles of selection, ordering of components, and gradation permit careful, continuous control of content and a precise definition of levels and sublevels of learning (which could be shown as planes cutting across the second language cone). This would seem much precise and objective than the "$i + 1$" input of Krashen's Monitor Model.

**9.4.2.4:** *Correction:* The T-CM assumes linguistic correction throughout, so that no errors will be allowed to become habitual or fossilized. Suggestions by some that linguistic errors need not be corrected are very ill-advised, as this will lead to the formation of bad linguistic habits, at least in the classroom situation. Furthermore, language students *want* to be corrected and feel lost without discriminative feedback. If errors are allowed to become habitual, it is virtually impossible to eliminate them entirely later, as students become complacent in their ability to communicate, however defectively.

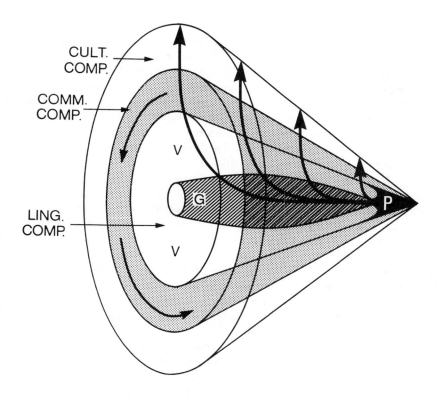

Figure 9.8

**9.4.2.5:** *Practice to the point of mastery:* The T-CM favors the idea of not proceeding to the next step in teaching until the preceding one has been mastered, if necessary going back to earlier steps to ensure or maintain mastery. This is very different from basing curricular decisions on definitions of proficiency which contain built-in linguistic incompetence —as ACTFL seems to be promoting now.

**9.4.2.6:** *Progressive integration:* As each new rule or element is learned, it should be integrated with everything else learned up to that point and used for communicative activities to the extent that the resulting transitional system will allow, but not beyond. Merely linear instruction is inadequate; but global use of a limited system also leads to a poor outcome, as communication beyond his competence causes the student — as we have seen— to internalize faulty rules —more errors occur than can be effectively corrected by the teacher or self-corrected by the student.

**9.4.3:** *The T-CM takes into account both interference and overgeneralization.* When a language student has not fully learned something in the second language or ventures beyond his limited competence, he will tend to fall back on the native language (especially at the beginning level) or to overgeneralize from whatever he does know of the second language (especially beyond the beginning level). These are by far the most frequent causes of errors. In the T-CM, interference could be represented, during initial learning of a rule, as an arrow going from area A-1 to area B-1 in Figure 9.4; overgeneralization would be represented as an arrow going from area B to area B-1 in the same figure.

**9.4.4:** *The T-CM is both structural and communicative.* The T-CM relies on the principle: *"Communication, yes, but accuracy first."* Communication without accuracy is not a valid educational goal. Communication *with* accuracy *is* possible in the classroom provided that accuracy is emphasized first and then gradually, very slowly, free communication comes to the fore.

**9.4.5:** *The T-CM seems more suitable for the classroom than other models proposed in recent years.* Krashen's Monitor Model and the unsuitability of its application to the classroom was discussed in Chapter 2 as part of the "Acquisitionist Theory." Four other models or hypotheses will be discussed briefly here:

**9.4.5.1:** *The Interlanguage Hypothesis [Selinker 1972]:* Unlike the T-CM, the Interlanguage Hypothesis represents the two languages, and even each of the intermediate interlanguages, as separate systems, which obscures the nature of their interaction. The name "-language" is a misnomer, as it confers on transitional systems a permanence and coherence that only a terminal linguistic system has. Note also that while interlanguages will inevitably develop in a natural language acquisition situation, the idea of the T-CM is that in the classroom we should aim at *preventing* the development of interlanguages; to a considerable degree this *can* be done.

**9.4.5.2:** *The Creative Construction Hypothesis [Dulay and Burt 1974; Bailey et al 1974]* holds that the learner "creates" or "constructs" the second language quite apart from the native language. This goes against much evidence that learners relate new knowledge to old knowledge and rely mostly on the latter when the former is very limited. Teachers of beginning language students in particular are especially struck by the degree to which the native language affects the learning process.

**9.4.5.3:** *The Pidginization Hypothesis [Schumann 1976]*, based on the observation that in many respects early interlanguages resemble pidgins, holds that such pidgin-like simplification and reduction is an inevitable early stage of second language acquisition. Although this hypothesis may very well fit the facts of natural language acquisition, where communication frequently occurs beyond the acquirer's competence, there is no reason for a pidgin-like stage to develop in classroom second language learning.

**9.4.5.4:** *The Acculturation Model [Schumann 1978]* holds that language acquisition is just one aspect of the process of integration in a society and that a second language will be acquired to the extent that the acquirer becomes part of the new culture. Again, this seems to apply quite well to immigrants and refugees but has no relevance for the language classroom, where a language can be learned quite well despite little or no contact with, or even hostility toward, the second culture.

**9.4.6:** *The T-CM is based on eclecticism in learning theory, linguistic theory, and teaching methodology.* It is unfortunate that eclecticism is a bad word for many. Perhaps a major reason for this —in addition to the usual North American neophilia— is that many eclecticists have practiced unthinking compromise. But it is also possible to have principled, "enlightened" eclecticism that combines the best from various sources into a harmonious and effective new whole. This is what the present integrated theory tries to accomplish and what the T-CM tries to represent.

**9.4.6.1:** *Learning theory:* The T-CM recognizes the value of both the behaviorist and the cognitive views of learning. Its basic learning formulation can be called *intelligent conditioning,* which combines the best of both theories into what could be called *cognitively mediated behaviorism.* Thus, one can use drills cognitively. For example, in a challenging grammatical drill cognition is active throughout, from attending to the stimulus, to deciding how to respond, to considering the feedback and its consequences.

**9.4.6.2:** *Linguistic theory:* The T-CM accepts the idea that many linguistic theories can contribute to language teaching. For example, while many valuable insights about syntax can be derived from transformational-generative grammar, the structuralists' approach to phonology and morphology seems more applicable to our purposes.

**9.4.6.3:** *Teaching methodology:* This is where the eclecticism of the T-CM is most clearly seen. The method that would emerge from all these considerations is discussed in some detail in the next chapter. Suffice it to say here that it would be cognitive (with habit formation), audio-oral (without neglecting the graphic skills), bilingual, and both structural and communicative.

# 9.5: For Discussion

1. *What characteristics should an* integrated *theory have?*

2. *What are the strong points and limitations of the Two-Cone Model as a visual representation of language teaching/learning according to the integrated theory proposed in this book?*

3. *Do you agree with the author that a given transitional system should be used to the extent it will function with linguistic accuracy and not beyond? Why or why not? How does this relate to the centrifugal/centripetal distinction?*

4. *Is "functional" bilingualism (managing to communicate in another language, no matter how inaccurately) defensible? Where would you draw the line?*

5. *Why must a sound theory of language teaching incorporate basic pedagogical principles such as selection, gradation, correction, mastery learning, and progressive integration? Is a linguistic theory that ignores one or more such principles likely to lead to the best results possible?*

6. *When and why should the native language be taken into account? Is the fact that this is usually not done in linguistically heterogeneous ESL classes a virtue to be praised or an unfortunate necessity due to the lack of multilingual ESL materials?*

7. *What is the relationship between structure and communication in the present theory, as discussed earlier and as represented in the T-CM?*

8. *Discuss the suitability for (a) natural language acquisition and (b) classroom language programs of the four other hypotheses or models referred to in this chapter. These are the Interlanguage Hypothesis, the Creative Construction Hypothesis, the Pidginization Hypothesis, and the Acculturation Model. Consider also the Monitor Theory/Model discussed earlier in this book. What does this tell you about the intensive language acquisition research that started in the late sixties?*

9. *Can eclecticism in learning theory, linguistic theory, and teaching methodology be "dignified"? How does eclecticism have to be in order to gain validity and "respectability"? What types of people object most strenuously to any form of eclecticism and why?*

# Practical
# Consequences

# Chapter 10: Consequences for Teaching

## Introduction and Summary

*In linguistics, theory is not very useful if it does not lead, more or less directly, to methodology. And methods not based on a sound comprehensive theory are likely to be extreme applications of one or a few assumptions of limited scope.*

There is no question that methods are very important. Although statistically they seem to account for less than twenty percent of variance, they relate in significant ways to all the other factors of success in second language learning. Methods are, moreover, the learning factor most amenable to control by the teacher. It follows that methodology is a crucial aspect of language teaching.

This doesn't mean that a method must be very good for language students to succeed. Some students are sufficiently intelligent and motivated to learn with any method —when the method is poor, such students would learn in spite of the method rather than because of it. The measure of success of a method should be how well the average and below-average students do with it. What students are willing to do seems almost irrelevant, as most seem quite willing to follow the teacher's guidance, even if he leads them into very unusual and unproductive activities.

The "ideal" method of language teaching would be one that would take all facts into account, borrow the best that existing and former methods have to offer, add innovations as needed, and combine all of this into a harmonious new whole in agreement with a sound comprehensive theory and adapted to the characteristics of the learners, to program goals, and to learning conditions.

Various existing methods violate important principles of language teaching. A new eclectic teaching method results from the application of the principles discussed in the main part of this book. It might be inappropriate, however, to call it "the Eclectic Method," as there could be many eclectic methods based on different combinations of existing and

165

*new features. Perhaps the best that can be done in terms of a name for this new method is to choose one that highlights certain of its most important characteristics. Then it would be hoped, rather overoptimistically, that the reader or hearer will not assume that what is in the name is all there is to the method and that he will take the trouble to read its complete description. A description of this eclectic method is contained in this chapter and, less directly, in* Synthesis.

*This method, to use the briefest "shorthand," can be called the "CA-OB Method" (or "CAB Method"), the initials representing three very important emphases of the method:* **C***ognitive (and behaviorist),* **A***udio-* **O***ral, and* **B***ilingual instruction. As noted, the CA-OB Method has many other characteristics not represented in its name; for example, it is structural, communicative, and cultural, it calls for a considerable use of recordings, etc.*

*After a brief discussion of certain shortcomings of other methods and an overview of the main features of the CA-OB Method, this chapter presents specific characteristics of this new method in terms of language components, skills, activities, and so on. Then the author presents, in a series of steps, what he considers the ideal language program, a program that can be offered, with appropriate modifications, beginning in Grade 5 or at age sixteen and beyond.*

# 10.1: Shortcomings of Certain Existing Methods

**10.1.1: The Grammar-Translation Method:** This and other methods that emphasize reading and/or writing are going, in this respect, against the nature of language, which is primarily audio-oral. By neglecting communication they also ignore the main *purpose* of language. The neglect of pronunciation or —worse yet— its teaching on the basis of the written language are misguided practices that lead to very poor results. The nearly exclusive use of deduction in the Grammar-Translation Method ignores the evidence that procedures that encourage discovery on the part of the student seem to be motivating and memory-enhancing and, if adequately guided, also efficient and effective. The teaching of vocabulary in isolation also goes against the nature of language, where all words occur in a linguistic and a nonlinguistic context; it's no wonder then that students don't know how to use the words. Constant use of the native language, especially in complex written translation exercises, ignores the nature of sentence generation, which naturally proceeds within the language being generated and does so by the modification and combination of thoroughly learned simple patterns; indiscriminately used translation inevitably results in a "pidgin" as second language sentences are based on the native language.

The Grammar-Translation Method has been called the "cookbook method" [Moulton 1966:18-9], one in which rules are the recipe, new vocabulary the ingredients, and written sentence translations the cake. Unfortunately, this results in culinary monstrosities. Generation after generation of language students have emerged from Grammar-Translation programs without the ability to carry on even a simple conversation.

**10.1.2: The Direct Method:** This method emerged as an extreme reaction to the Grammar-Translation Method, one that; initially, took the form of three negatives for its implementation in the classroom: (1) the native language should *never* be used, (2) explanations should *not* be given, and (3) there is *no* need for a very careful rule-by-rule order of presentation. Injunction (3) was soon abandoned; injunction (2) was abandoned by some Direct methodologists by the sixties; but all Direct methodologists still cling tenaciously to injunction (1) against any use of the native language.

By forbidding the use of the native language and discouraging the use of explanations (or allowing them only in the second language, which means that many won't be adequate or won't be understood by the students), Direct methodologists create for themselves a straightjacket of unnecessary limitations. They are forced, for example, to "teach" pronunciation strictly via imitation, a procedure that ignores native language interference or at least fails to deal with it in the most effective way, that is, overtly. Grammar is supposed to be learned entirely inductively, which means that this method forgoes overtly enlisting most of the cognitive ability of the students. This results in learning being much slower than it could be, with efficiency being sacrificed to the dubious claim that induction is preferable. In vocabulary learning, the Direct Method student faces numerous uncertainties, as the meaning of many words is never made quite clear and he is forced to make second language/native language equations in his mind (which all do) without any information as to their appropriateness. A result of this is that, despite the monolingual nature of the method, second language words are often used with native language meanings —the Direct Method does nothing (*cannot* do anything) to counteract this problem.

One can't help but feel a little sympathy for Direct methodologists. Their intentions are praiseworthy, but they have created a totally unnecessary set of limitations for themselves, limitations that drastically reduce the efficiency of their programs, so that they can teach much less than could be taught with a bilingual method in a given period of time. Their limitations also affect the effectiveness of their programs, as they cannot deal overtly with a large number of serious problems caused by native language interference. And yet, they have rationalized these matters to the point that they will defend these self-imposed limitations, as essential principles, with quasi-religious zeal. It is as if a prisoner were to sing the praises of his jail cell.

It seems to me that in the 1880s a reaction to the excesses and ineffectiveness of the Grammar-Translation Method was called for, but that the overreaction that followed should soon have been corrected. To keep on overreacting one century later is totally unjustified. The judicious use of the native language according to carefully set and observed guidelines is not only excusable but desirable if one wishes the language program to reach its maximum potential efficiency and effectiveness.

**10.1.3: The Audiolingual Method:** This method existed in several rather different versions. Only one variety of the Audiolingual Method followed fairly closely the Structural Method, which had been used with some success at such places as the Foreign Service Institute and Cornell University. Unfortunately the circumstances and attitudes in the schools and even in many colleges were such that, soon after it was introduced in them, the Audiolingual Method — in all its versions— became a very mechanical method that did not impart skill in communication. That, of course, defeated the entire purpose of language teaching. The fact that, where wisely used, the structural variety of Audiolingual Method produced very good results did not prevent the wholesale abandonment of the Audiolingual Method (or anything with that label) in the seventies. It should be noted, however, that there are still schools in North America successfully carrying out audiolingual teaching and that the Audiolingual Method (whether in an "enlightened" version or not) is still popular abroad.

**10.1.4: The Cognitive Approach:** One of the two reactions to the failure of much mechanical audiolingual teaching was in the direction of neotraditionalism, specifically in the form of an emphasis on deduction and more reading and writing practice. These were characteristics of the Cognitive Approach. Again, the reaction was extreme. While undoubtedly certain rules require a deductive approach, to follow such an approach with *all* rules denies learners the opportunity to discover much of the language by themselves, with help only as needed. While some audiolingual teaching neglected to give sufficient attention to reading and writing, the answer is not to give all four skills equal weight —in a general language program, listening and speaking should receive greater emphasis throughout.

**10.1.5: The Audio-Visual Method:** The other method that flourished for a while as a result of disenchantment with the Audiolingual Method was the Audio-Visual Method, a direct, monolingual method supported by visual aids that first came to be widely used in France. It was a type of direct method. Audio-visual students were supposed to grasp the meanings of words and phrases from the visual aids presented. No explanations were given except in the second language (thereby guaranteeing that many would not be understood). It is hard to see how Audio-Visual methodologists could not realize that only concrete objects and actions can be shown clearly via visuals, and that even these may frequently be misunderstood [Hammerly 1974-b]. Placing the visuals in sequences, as in filmstrips, does little to enhance comprehension; as recently shown [Hammerly 1984], the comprehension of dialogue sentences supported by filmstrips is about 50-60 percent (and the subjects in this study were experienced language teachers, not inexperienced students). We come to the conclusion that visuals can only make a modest contribution to solving the basic problems of the Direct Method.

**10.1.6: The Total Physical Response:** James Asher [1977] has clearly demonstrated that physical responses to commands and narrations result in enhanced comprehension. The problem with this method —and all other methods that delay speaking— is that they allow covert responses to go uncorrected for weeks or even months. Such subvocal responses are therefore internalized, and by the time the students finally start speaking ("when they are ready for it" is the usual slogan), they have already formed certain bad "speech" habits that are hard to eradicate. Two principles are being violated here: (1) that responses must be overt and (2) that correction must be immediate.

**10.1.7: The Silent Way:** While it is true that in some language classrooms the teacher talks too much, and that this needs to be corrected, the extremes to which the Silent Way will go to reduce teacher talk to the very minimum are unreasonable and the procedures resulting from this policy are largely contrary to the nature of language and language use. Above all, this method fails to provide sufficient modelling and guidance, as the learners are supposed to mostly fend for themselves, with production cues and indirect discriminative feedback as their only guide. Imitation, for example, is discouraged even though it is a normal part of the process of acquiring control over sounds or sentence patterns. Can we really accept that pronunciation is best learned by imitating other students and by reading sequences of letters the teacher points out on a "fidel"? Similarly, is reading words aloud following a pointer and producing silly sentences about colored rods really *speaking*, in any sense of the word? Furthermore, only lack of linguistic sophistication can lead to the idea that beginning language students should be reading so much.

Some students do quite well with this method. Some students seem to do quite well with just about any method. Given an enthusiastic teacher who is a firm *believer* in the method he is using, his enthusiasm will fire up at least some of his students, who will as a result be willing to put up with much methodological nonsense, work hard, and therefore learn a good deal of the language. But this, of course, is learning *in spite* of the method, not *because* of the method.

**10.1.8: Community Language Learning:** The idea of small-group conversation used in this method is, at the right time and in the right way, quite sound. But linguistically unsophisticated beginners are in no way capable of determining their own language curriculum. This method fails especially to provide structural gradation of any sort, as well as guidance. Most language learners need a considerable amount of both.

**10.1.9: Suggestopedia:** Like the Direct Method, Suggestopedia relies on induction, which no doubt works well for certain rules but not for others. The principle of correction is also violated, as the mistaken attitude is taken that accuracy will come in due course. Other than that, the main weakness of this method lies in its pseudoscientific pretensions. Even something as crucial to the method as the use of music for the purpose of relaxing the students and making them more susceptible to suggestion has not been carefully studied.

**10.1.10: The Natural Approach:** This method violates the principle of gradation by encouraging premature communication in the classroom that goes beyond the limited linguistic competence developed with drills and exercises done outside the classroom. To make matters worse, the principle of correction is also violated, as no errors are ever corrected in class, for this would presumably "interfere with the desire to communicate." It is reasonable to assume, therefore, that graduates of a program taught under this method would be able to communicate fluently, yes, but very inaccurately.

**10.1.11: The Communicative Approach:** What was just said about the Natural Approach can also be said of the Communicative Approach in its various versions: By emphasizing communicative competence at the expense of linguistic competence these methods are putting the cart before the horse and will inevitably produce graduates who communicate fairly fluently but very inaccurately.

**10.1.12: Conclusion on various methods:** While in this section we have discussed the shortcomings of a number of methods, it should be noted that each of these and other methods have one or more useful procedures or techniques that can be incorporated into an enlightened eclectic method. The rest of this chapter will discuss a new method which is eclectic and, if I may say so, "enlightened" in the sense that it takes all important factors into account and in many respects harmonizes extreme positions.

# 10.2: The New CA-OB Method: An Overview

In this section we shall discuss some of the most important characteristics of this new method. The CA-OB Method can be said to be:

**10.2.1: Cognitive With Habit Formation:** Cognition is used throughout, as the mental abilities of the students are enlisted to facilitate the learning process. An effort is made to ensure that everything is understood when it is presented or soon thereafter. Thus, at no time are uncertainties allowed to pile up on top of uncertainties, waiting for the magic moment when everything will finally make sense. But while cognition is valued, "habit" is not a dirty word. What may have started as an act of cognitive grasp needs to be practiced to the point where it can be used automatically whenever it is called for in communication (and this is all a linguistic habit is, however arrived at). This method stresses habit formation through intelligent conditioning, with the minds of the students active throughout the process. In this way, the apparently irreconcilable views of cognitive and behaviorist psychologists can be harmonized.

**10.2.2: Audio-Oral:** Listening and speaking are emphasized throughout. This corresponds to the nature and use of language and to the wishes of the great majority of our students (as shown repeatedly in surveys). Of course, this emphasis in no way means that reading and writing are neglected —at the right time, they too receive special attention. Incidentally, an audio-oral emphasis seems to have existed, intermittently, since ancient times. In the 19th century, we see it in the Natural Method, Gouin's Series Method, and the Reform Movement late in the century, which gave us the Direct Method. In recent decades, such an emphasis has been characteristic of linguistically oriented methods, especially the Structural Method.

**10.2.3: Bilingual:** It is undeniable that the native language, which facilitates second language learning in certain specific ways and interferes with it in others, is a very important factor in this process. Methods that ignore the native language fail to take full advantage of its facilitating effects and cannot counteract its interference effectively. The most efficient and effective method must necessarily take into account all the factors involved in language learning and manipulate them to best advantage. With respect to the native language, this means making judicious use of it in presentations, practice activities, correction techniques, and tests. One century is long enough as an overreaction to the excesses of the Grammar-Translation Method. The fact that at present linguistically heterogeneous classes such as most in ESL cannot reasonably take the native languages of the students into account is only an indication of the need to create multilingual ESL materials; in no way is it evidence that there is any virtue in monolingual instruction.

**10.2.4: Structural, Communicative, and Cultural:** In the CA-OB Method, the emphasis is on linguistic competence during the first half of the program. While some simple communication takes place from the start, communicative competence is not emphasized until the second half of the program. The cultural connotations of words and phrases are presented gradually from the beginning of the program, and so is appropriate cultural behavior, but cultural competence as such is not emphasized until the last level of the program (when the students can understand and use the second language quite well). This seems to place the three competences in a logical relationship: Students (1) use linguistic knowledge (2) to produce messages, (3) eventually within a culture they are studying.

# 10.3: Certain Specific Characteristics of the CA-OB Method

### 10.3.1: Teaching Language Components

**10.3.1.1: Teaching Pronunciation and Intonation:** Sounds and, to a lesser extent, intonation patterns will all occur repeatedly from the beginning of the language program, so one way or another the beginner will have to come to grips with them from the start. An unguided, unsystematic exposure to new sounds will inevitably result in faulty pronunciation habits —except perhaps for the occasional outstanding mimic— as mispronounced sounds are not corrected and attention shifts immediately to grammar and meaning. Although advanced remedial pronunciation courses can result in some improvement [Acton 1984], it should be clear that the most efficient and effective way to teach pronunciation would deny bad habits a foothold.

It is curious, in this regard, that scholars who would probably stake their reputation on the principle of gradation in grammar and vocabulary do not see the need for gradation when it comes to pronunciation and intonation. But phonological instruction too benefits from gradation, from mastering each of the problems one by one, and this at the beginning of the program, before faulty pronunciation habits have a chance to develop.

In the CA-OB Method, therefore, the first ten to fifteen hours of instruction consist of an Introductory Phonological Minicourse that emphasizes the mastery of the pronunciation (vowels and consonants) and the basic intonation patterns of the second language. Taking as a point of departure the sounds which are the same in the two languages, and need not therefore be taught, one or two pronunciation problems are taught in each hour of class, going, with each problem, through the steps of (1) Presentation, including (a) interlingual differentiation, if need be; (b) monolingual discrimination, for phonemes, or (c) distributional exemplification, for allophones; and (d) receptive tests; (2) Understanding, that is, cognitive awareness of what is involved in production; and (3) Production, first (a) mechanical (imitative), both with short and later with longer utterances, followed by (b) productive tests, and then (c) by meaningful practice, involving the learning of a pair of words or a short phrase with their meaning as well as, later, the learning of very short phonologically graded minidialogues, sayings, verse, etc. As more and more new pronunciation problems are mastered during the Introductory Phonological Minicourse, it becomes possible to have more and more meaningful language use.

In addition to class work, the students would spend considerable time in out-of-class study, preferably in a fully equipped language laboratory, but if this is not available they would study take-home cassettes. The objection that the students will not be able to hear their own errors can be largely remedied by providing them with adequate discrimination training, including, in particular, training in learning to distinguish between correct and incorrect pronunciations of words. Only by being able to tell correct sounds from incorrect ones in others (something that to some extent happens in the classroom) can students discriminate between correct and incorrect sounds in their own speech.

Materials for Introductory Phonological Minicourses such as the one described in this section are not yet available, and when they do become available, I am afraid that they would have to be largely self-instructional —many language teachers are not native speakers of the language they teach and could not therefore serve as good models; of those who are native speakers, few seem to have the knowledge of phonetics and phonemics needed to do an adequate job in such a minicourse. Until appropriate materials become available, the qualified teacher can find much help in pronunciation drillbooks such as the pioneering *Patterns of Spanish Pronunciation —A Drillbook*, by Bowen and Stockwell [1960] or others like it published in the sixties and early seventies. For English, Bowen's *Patterns of English Pronunciation* [1975] is a helpful aid. But pronunciation drillbooks, as helpful as they are, are just one aid among several and fall quite short of being adequate to the task.

It can be seen then that the CA-OB Method makes use of procedures from several methods for the teaching of pronunciation and intonation and that it introduces certain innovations of its own. From the Direct Method it takes the use of mimicry, from the Structural Method the use of drills and transcription, from the Phonetic Method the use of transcription and phonetic explanations, from structural linguistics the concepts of the phoneme and the allophone, from learning theory the idea of persistent and immediate correction so faulty habits will not be formed, and from transformational-generative grammar certain generative phonological rules that can be taught at the intermediate or advanced levels.

To these procedures borrowed from a variety of sources, the CA-OB Method adds an aid of its own, the Articulatory Pictorial Transcriptions (APTs) [Hammerly 1974]. These are strictly pedagogical transcriptions that (1) represent key articulatory features visually, (2) take into account the native language both in the choice of symbols and in the use of countermanding articulatory reminders, and (3) lead step by step from transcription to spelling. APT symbols would be used in introducing each new sound, in discrimination tests, during practice, in production tests, as a reminder of what is said in class, as an aid to home study during the "pre-reading" period, and especially as a help in bridging the gap between pronunciation and spelling.

The alternative to this is to introduce the students to reading from the start, with the inevitable result that they will base their pronunciation on spelling and thus form very poor pronunciation habits. Of course, if good pronunciation is *not* a serious goal of the program, everything in this section can be ignored. But I am convinced that very good pronunciation is possible for a majority of our students if we will only take the trouble to teach it properly, which means, among other things, not exposing the students simultaneously to the conflicting stimuli of speech and standard spelling but having them master one thing at a time —first the sounds, then how they are represented on paper.

Please note that during the Introductory Phonological Minicourse other activities in alternation with pronunciation practice are also engaged in. Having nothing but pronunciation practice would soon result in fatigue. The other activities would be meaningful (or at least *more* meaningful than pronunciation practice) and would include, as a mini-mum, (1) an orientation to the course, its goals, the nature of its tests, how to study, etc.; (2) a presentation of basic grammatical concepts and terminology; (3) a brief introduction to the second culture; and (4) the learning and performance of phonologically graded minidialogues, say-ings, verse, etc. Of these, clearly (1), (2), and (3) must be done in the native language, and (4) bilingually.

The Introductory Phonological Minicourse should end by introducing the students to the standard spellings that go with each sound as repre-sented in the APT. What should follow is not quick replacement of the transcription by standard spelling but a fairly long period during which the standard letters, however irregular spelling may be, are associated visually to the articulations they represent. This long period in which standard spellings are strongly associated in the learner's mind with the sound articulations they represent is crucial if the good pronunciation attained initially is to be maintained throughout the program. A premature shift from attention to sounds to attention to letters —without a long bridging period of attention to both— always seems to result in the fossilization of at least some native language spelling pronunciations.

**10.3.1.2: Teaching Grammar (Morphology and Syntax):** The teaching of morphology and syntax in the CA-OB Method includes fewer innovations than the teaching of pronunciation, as some existing methods have handled grammar rather well. From the Structural Method and the Bilingual Method two ideas are borrowed: (1) all grammatical explanations should be in the native language until there is strong reason to believe that they will be easily understood in the second language; and (2) some drills and exercises need to be bilingual, in terms of oral translation —this applies especially to those rules that are subject to strong interference, and the process is not unlike "desensitizing" in behavioral therapy (learning to respond to old stimuli in new ways).

The idea that most grammatical learning should be through guided discovery may be novel; but the view that some rules can be learned efficiently through induction is a reduction of the Direct Method position, and the concept of proceeding deductively for certain rules is a reduction in scope of the Grammar-Translation Method and Cognitive Approach philosophy.

Most drills and exercises can be done outside the classroom with the help of recordings and workbooks. This is an idea that the Natural Approach applies. Unlike the Natural Approach, however, the CA-OB Method (1) introduces a rule in class and drills it a little, (2) *then* asks the students to practice it intensively outside the class, and finally (3) engages in classroom conversation practice involving *only* that rule plus any other rules learned previously —students are actively discouraged from communicating beyond their limited linguistic competence, as to do so leads to the formation of faulty linguistic habits. Also, unlike what happens in the Natural Approach, classroom errors are corrected. Note that the amount of home study called for in the CA-OB Method may not be possible in elementary and secondary schools, where unfortunately "no homework" has become the usual practice. In the schools, therefore, it may be necessary to do everything in class, thereby drastically slowing down progress through the program.

The principle of "practice to the point of mastery" is also included in the CA-OB Method. This is largely borrowed from Individualized Instruction. A consequence of this principle is that pace should be to some extent individual-ized. What is meant by this "modified" individualization of pace is that, instead of having 100 students at 100 points in the program, minimum and maximum speeds would be controlled to the extent that there would be a small group of students working together at each extreme (as well as larger groups in the middle, which will naturally form). The alternative to pace individual-ization is having to restrain the progress of students with high aptitude and having a group of low aptitude students who are at a perpetual disadvantage and in constant fear of failing the course.

**10.3.1.3: Teaching Vocabulary; Presentations:** Vocabulary is not emphasized early in the CA-OB Method, as such an emphasis encourages students to communicate beyond their limited linguistic competence. This idea comes from the Structural Method.

Words and phrases are taught within both a linguistic and a nonlinguis-tic context, not in isolation. Thus a word would be taught within a sentence which would be within the larger context of several sentences which would in turn refer to a nonlinguistic situation of some sort. By teaching words in isolation, one-to-one matching with native language words is en-couraged, and the result is that very ungrammatical sentences are pro-duced. This concept of contextualized lexical instruction comes to some extent from the Direct Method, but primarily from the Structural Method.

An innovation in regard to vocabulary is the idea that the teacher should deal overtly with the likely misuses of words as they are taught. It is not enough, for example, to teach the French word *fenêtre* in context. Contrastive analysis, learning theory, and experience tell us that, unless warned not to do so, students will strongly tend to say *\*fenêtre de magasin* for "store window" instead of *vitrine* as required by the language. It makes sense, in such cases, to briefly point out what the second language word can and cannot be used for.

Until the late intermediate or early advanced levels, when most simple contexts can be understood with ease, the conveyance of meaning should be bilingual. This is very different from the use of translation in the Grammar-Translation Method. In our method, presentation devices such as dialogues and narrations place each new word or phrase within the context of a sentence and each sentence within the context of a conversa-tion, etc. that takes place in a given nonlinguistic situation. This helps the students to see the function and collocation of each word and to establish associations between that word and the linguistic and nonlinguistic con-texts in which it is used. The bilingual conveyance of meaning results in great efficiency and makes clear to the students the ways in which each word and sentence pattern *differs* from its closest native language equiva-lent. Sentence generation is *not* via translation, as in the Grammar-

Translation Method, but on the basis of word substitution and of combination of thoroughly learned *second* language sentences and sentence patterns. Thus, step by step, competence is developed in the second language without ignoring the facilitating and interfering effects of the native language. This idea is largely taken from the Structural Method.

**10.3.1.4: Teaching Discourse:** Recent years have seen the attention of the language teaching profession shift to discourse, under the influence of sociolinguistics and the resultant Communicative Approach. From this approach we would borrow the idea of the cyclical reintroduction of communication acts, so the students can learn more ways, and more sophisticated ways, of linguistic interaction. This, plus attention to speech registers and writing styles (such as, for example, in Marquez and Bowen's *English Usage* [1983] for ESL), would belong at the advanced and very advanced levels of the program. With beginners, we should be pleased if they can perform each communication act correctly in one or two simple ways and in one or two registers.

### 10.3.2: Teaching Language Skills

**10.3.2.1: Teaching Speaking Ability:** The emphasis of the CA-OB Method is on teaching the ability to speak the second language, plus of course the ability to understand it when spoken. As this whole book, and in particular this chapter, deal primarily with the teaching of speaking ability, there is no need to say very much in this subsection. Speaking, very simple and imitative at first, occurs from the start, an idea that goes back to the Direct Method. Among the speaking activities would be situations (most highly developed in the Situational Method); the variation and retelling of dialogues and other sample texts, as practiced in several methods; Silent Units (five-to-ten minute activities in which the teacher remains silent and encourages speech by means of various props) based on the Silent Way; and short student-initiated small group conversation sessions, which may be recorded and gone over, as is done in Community Language Learning. Of course, the number of possible communicative activities is much larger, as *Synthesis* and several other works will clearly show.

**10.3.2.2: Teaching Listening Comprehension:** Listening comprehension has to be taught per se; it cannot be assumed to result automatically from speaking activities. In fact, it is possible for a graduate of a language program to be able to express himself fairly fluently and correctly and yet be unable to understand fluent native speech. Among the activities that the teaching of listening comprehension should include are selective listening (listening for particular features in a passage), which can start quite early; five-to-ten minute Audio-Motor Units [Kalivoda *et al.* 1971], involving physical responses to commands and based on the Total Physical Response; listening a few minutes per class to short narrations, especially humorous anecdotes (without idiomatic punch lines!), something which, like the previously listed activities, can start in the beginning level; graded extensive listening, a type of intermediate listening activity for which materials are very much needed; and listening to radio and television programs, lectures, and films —these being activities for the advanced and very advanced levels.

**10.3.2.3: Teaching Reading Comprehension:** The idea that reading should not be started until a foundation has been established in the spoken language goes back to the Direct Method, at least in its early form, and more recently finds an echo in the Structural Method and in the structural variety of the Audiolingual Method. It is an idea that never lost its basic soundness, despite objections to it by neotraditionalists and others. The main objection, the claim that learners need visual support, is easily answered by providing them with a pedagogical transcription such as the APT as an aid to learning, recall, and review. If good pronunciation is considered important, this seems to be the only way to go.

The idea is to introduce the students to reading step by step, as everything should be done in the language program. In dealing with a new alphabet or a syllabary, which may pose few interference problems, a few hours of practice at this point should be enough. A logographic system (such as Chinese characters) is of course unrelated to pronunciation and in no way supportive (or disruptive) of it; it should be dealt with as a separate, advanced learning task.

Once the students start reading, reading activities can be either intensive (very short, containing a good number of new items, and to be studied thoroughly) or extensive (long, carefully graded so as to contain few new items, and to be read only once or twice). Long readings containing many new items —such as most of the usual literary readings— are not recommended, as this is not reading but laborious decoding, with the constant help of a dictionary, that leaves students tired and without much grasp of coherent meaning.

Before any reading, those items which should be part of the active vocabulary of the students should be practiced orally, not, of course, in isolation but within basic sentences. For the sake of efficiency and clarity, such preliminary presentations should be bilingual. At this time also prequestions can be asked. The text itself should have glosses, preferably at the foot of the page so that they cannot be consulted too easily; these glosses would normally be in the native language.

**10.3.2.4: Teaching Writing Ability:** The teaching of writing in the CA-OB Method includes several innovations. There are two serious problems with writing as it is usually practiced: (1) the students are allowed —even encouraged, by some— to write creatively far beyond their linguistic competence, and (2) feedback is not immediate but occurs several days later, by which time the students have forgotten the nature of the faulty decision-making that led them to make their errors.

In the CA-OB Method students are encouraged to write *what they can say*, rarely using a dictionary, and that to check some minor detail, not to select words with which to generate sentences. If a writing activity requires knowledge of certain new words or stylistic distinctions, these are to be taught, preferably audio-orally, before the writing task is carried out. To ensure immediate feedback, homework writing is avoided. Instead, classroom group writing with an overhead projector is emphasized. Thus it becomes possible to correct writing errors on the spot and to deal with the faulty criteria that led to the errors before these criteria fade from the learner's mind. Correction should be elicited from the student who made the error; but if hints fail in producing self-correction, peer correction can be used, provided that a friendly classroom atmosphere has been created. Students are more likely to remember "deep" corrections (corrections dealing with underlying criteria) that they arrive at, or that their peers provide than "surface" or even deep corrections issuing from the teacher.

**10.3.2.5: Multiskill Activities:** Initial activities would involve just listening or listening and speaking. Soon after reading activities start it would be desirable to have activities involving all three skills. Soon after writing activities start it should be possible to have four-skill activities. For example, students could listen to a narration, read it, discuss it, and then write a summary or adaptation of it.[1]

### 10.3.3: From Presentation to Testing

**10.3.3.1: Presentation:** Audio-oral presentations necessarily must emphasize real or realistic samples of the spoken language. This would mean short dialogues for intensive study at the beginning level, as in the Structural Method, and could include long dialogues for extensive study, such as those in Suggestopedia, at the intermediate level and beyond. The need for gradation means that beginning materials should be especially prepared for the program and can at best be realistic; real samples are seldom suitable for beginners.

Other audio-oral presentations can make use of short anecdotes, sayings, verse, etc. for beginners, and radio and television excerpts (the easiest of which are ads) for more advanced students. Efficiency and clarity require that audio-oral presentations be handled bilingually.[2]

The introduction of reading opens the door to a large variety of written presentations, from simple narrations and travelogues at the early intermediate level to short stories at the very advanced level, from the slice of culture provided by classified ads at the intermediate level to systematic cultural readings near the end of the program. All readings, of course, must follow the principle of gradation; their presentation should be preceded by preliminary audio-oral work, to teach key new items and go over difficult spots, and followed by discussion after the students have read it.

**10.3.3.2: The Use of the Native Language:** In the CA-OB Method the native language is used *as little as possible but as much as necessary to ensure efficiency and effectiveness.* Neither the Grammar-Translation Method extreme (constant translation and use of the native language to generate sentences) nor the Direct Method extreme (a total ban on the native language) is reasonable or acceptable. Much time can be saved and teaching effectiveness gained by using the native language for the orientation to the course, bilingual presentations, early cultural asides, early explanations, some of the drill and exercise practice, certain corrections, test instructions, and certain test items. At the same time, most communication can and should take place in the *second* language, without any need to use the native language, if the teacher is careful to keep the structures and vocabulary he uses within what the students know.

**10.3.3.3: Visual Aids:** As we have already seen, visual aids are not reliable as a way of conveying meaning, even with concrete nouns; furthermore, much in language cannot be represented visually. On the other hand, visual aids can be used in association with speech to help recall known (and understood) utterances. For example, having learned the sentences of a dialogue and their meanings, sentence recall will be facilitated by associating at that point each sentence with a picture (which need not even attempt to represent its entire meaning), these pictures to be used as cues during subsequent dialogue performance. Other advantageous uses of visual aids include their use as conversation stimuli (I have found certain posters and wordless cartoons very effective), to convey visual cultural differences, to make certain points of structure clear (i.e., with charts), and to create a second culture atmosphere in the classroom.[3]

**10.3.3.4: Practice:** Practice should continue until mastery of the rule at hand is attained, an idea emphasized in Individualized Instruction. Practice should follow a gradual progression from mechanical practice with attention to form only to conversation with attention to meaning only (control of form having previously been built in). At no time should practice exceed the students' competence, except in terms of the new item being studied. Practice should always include firm but gentle correction.

**10.3.3.5: The Correction of Errors:** The notion that errors need not be corrected because they will disappear by themselves —a notion dear to acquisitionists— does not correspond to the realities of the classroom. Errors should be corrected, in a kind and matter-of-fact way, yes, but consistently and persistently, for otherwise the students develop faulty habits. It is much better to deal with the criteria that led to the error (deep correction) than with the error itself (surface correction); what we need to change is the basis on which wrong decisions are made, not their surface manifestations. Whenever possible, correction should be elicited from the student, not just provided; it seems (this is a hypothesis) that students remember better what they discover or rediscover themselves. If the right atmosphere has been developed, correction can be turned into a group activity, with students not "criticizing" but "helping" each other.

**10.3.3.6: Technological Aids:** Since the CA-OB Method emphasizes listening and speaking, it follows that any practice outside class should also be primarily audio-oral in nature. This means mostly the use of language laboratories or loan-out cassettes, or both. Language laboratories were used very unwisely, very mechanically in the sixties, which may have been an important reason for their abandonment in the seventies. Where laboratories and loan-out recordings are used intelligently, they can be of tremendous help in the language program. After all, most of a language program can be on tape and in workbooks —only activities requiring personal interaction such as conversation and the evaluation of free production *require* a teacher.

Lately computer-aided language instruction has been coming to the fore. So far, computers have provided a graphic medium, so in a program that emphasizes listening and speaking their use should be delayed until the intermediate level. The kind of interactive practice that computers can provide is of course far superior in flexibility to the practice offered by sound recordings; but that shouldn't blind us to the fact that premature work with computers would have a negative effect on audio-oral skill. One doesn't learn to understand speech and to produce it by reading a screen or typing on a keyboard. When voice synthesizers match the audio quality of magnetic recordings, *then* work with computers would be suitable for beginners (although the high cost of such a use of computers may be prohibitive for the foreseeable future).

**10.3.3.7: Testing:** Perhaps the biggest shortcoming of many language testing programs is a failure to match the contents of tests to the stated goals of the program. It is not uncommon, for example, for a program to claim to be "oral" and yet give nothing but paper-and-pencil tests. Testing should evaluate knowledge of what was *taught*. In the CA-OB Method this would mean that early tests would be exclusively audio-oral and that in the rest of the program they would be mostly audio-oral, with some reading and, later, some writing.

Daily study can be evaluated through student performance in class or via quizzes. Other tests should be announced and their format described in advance. Whenever a new type of test or test question is to be used, practice items to familiarize the students with the new format should be presented beforehand to the class.

Tests should be as objective as possible. Laboratory speaking tests can be quite objective (see Appendix C). Even interviews can be made reasonably objective by quantifying the evaluation criteria. Most progress tests should include discrete-point items based on what was recently studied plus a global or integrative section to evaluate the overall proficiency attained to that point.

### 10.3.4: The Teacher and the Students

The teacher should be a strong and enthusiastic leader but empathetic, receptive to the needs of his students. It goes without saying that he should be highly qualified and should constantly aim to upgrade his qualifications.

The students should be encouraged to be self-reliant with what they know, not with what they don't know. Language students need guidance with the new, with the unknown. Again, as with so many other things, we have to beware of the extremes —in some methods, every little step is guided and students fail to develop self-reliance; in others, no guidance at all is offered and many students can spend months in a state of confusion.

Apparently the Suggestopedia practice of assigning to each beginner a second language name and fictitious life history is helpful. The students no longer feel that their real identities are in any way under attack and feel free, under the cover of their pseudoidentities, to take the risks necessary in learning another language.

The atmosphere in the classroom should be relaxed —and again Suggestopedia offers good ideas— but not so relaxed that laziness or carelessness takes hold of the students. In other words, the atmosphere should be *moderately* relaxed, with a low level of tension and anxiety. It seems that learning is better when there is a moderate level of anxiety present. Of course, high anxiety strongly interferes with learning.

# 10.4: The Ideal Language Program

### 10.4.1: Overview

The ideal language program would have an exploratory course (which could be called "Languages and Peoples of the World") required of all students. In elementary school this course would be offered over two consecutive grades, preferably Grades Three and Four. In high school it would last one year, and in college one semester.

(The study of any specific language should not be required, as unwilling students won't put in the necessary effort to meet successfully the demands of a language program. Large classes of unmotivated students can hardly be a desirable way of meeting the linguistic needs of a nation.)

Those who decide to study a specific language would go into a semi-intensive (two hours a day) or intensive (four or more hours a day) program. Given the other curricular demands, only semi-intensive instruction would seem feasible in most cases. This initial semi-intensive instruction would take four grades (Grades Five through Eight) in the elementary school, two years in high school, and one year (equivalent to four semesters of study) in college. Beyond that, the students who started the language in Grade Five would go into three years of further language study in terms of partial immersion (some subjects taught in the second language) and one year (Grade Twelve) of total immersion. The college equivalent of that would be the advanced level of the language program, plus partial immersion, and the very advanced level of the language program plus total immersion. As many program graduates as possible should be encouraged and helped to spend a few months of linguistic submersion in a second language community; this is especially important in those cases in which total immersion cannot be arranged as the last step in the program.

Note that while the possibility of starting in high school has been mentioned, it isn't desirable. During puberty many children are too self-conscious and too strongly influenced by their peers to be very good beginning language learners. The age to be avoided as a point of departure is twelve to sixteen. Age ten or eleven seems the ideal starting age, as such children are cognitively fairly mature (unlike younger children) and reasonably stable emotionally (unlike children during puberty). After having gotten to a good start at age ten, it seems that children may be better able to navigate the shoals of puberty, linguistically speaking. It is also possible to start after age sixteen —unaided acquisition of a perfect accent seems no longer possible, but careful, intelligent instruction in pronunciation can yield excellent results, in some cases accent-free speech.

### 10.4.2: The Ideal Progression

Ideally students should be *eased* into the second language, not forced to jump in, flounder about, and form, in the process, faulty linguistic habits.

**10.4.2.1: Introductory Phonological Minicourse:** The first challenge in the language program is to come to grips with a new sound system. This can be accomplished in about ten to fifteen hours of college instruction plus the study of recordings, preferably in a fully-equipped language laboratory (with individual record-compare facilities). This minicourse introduces and practices (drills and contextualizes) the new sounds one by one, with visual support as needed. During the minicourse, practice includes gradually more and more different sounds, until the entire sound system has been presented.

Teaching pronunciation is not all that should be done during the first few hours of the program. The students also need an orientation to the program and the course. This would include a background questionnaire to determine the linguistic background of the students and their motivation for studying the language, an introduction to basic terminology, tips on how to study, a description of the tests and the grading policy to be used, and an introduction to the second culture, especially in behavioral terms. Such activities, plus some exposure to ungraded speech to give a general idea of how the language sounds, plus a certain amount of meaningful (though phonologically graded) language practice are important in themselves and also serve to provide some relief from the phonological instruction —even the most highly motivated student would probably become bored and upset with relentless phonological instruction hour after hour.

**10.4.2.2: The early beginning level:** The rest of the early beginning level (about 75 hours of class plus study) would emphasize listening and speaking, exclusively if possible. Reading should be delayed as long as possible, something that *can* be done with the help of a modified pedagogical transcription. There would be no writing yet. Very basic grammar would be taught, such as basic sentence types, the present and present progressive tenses, pronouns, and very simple transformations. Only the most useful 400-450 words would be taught, avoiding true idioms for the time being; vocabulary would be introduced bilingually and in context and practiced in monolingual exchanges. Communicative activities would be very simple and largely imitative. There would be no cultural instruction as such but *ad hoc* cultural asides on the connotations of words and phrases plus perhaps occasional references to behavioral and informational culture.

**10.4.2.3: The late beginning level:** While in the late beginning level (about 90 hours of class plus study) emphasis would continue to be on listening and speaking, reading would be phased in (and transcription phased out). This period of transition to the written word has to be carefully monitored or faulty speech may result. There would still be no writing. Grammatical instruction would include, generally speaking, sentence coordination and simple subordination, past, perfect, and future tenses, reflexive, and additional, more complex transformations. About 550-600 additional words would be taught, and lexical instruction would include some idioms. Communicative activities would concentrate on variations of models within carefully set limits. Cultural instruction would emphasize behavior and could include the use of cultural assimilators in the native language.

**10.4.2.4: The early intermediate level:** This sublevel (about 70 hours of class plus study) would see expanded reading activities and the introduction of writing, in mechanical form at first. Reading would take place largely outside of class and class time would be devoted primarily to conversation and discussion of the readings, as well as additional grammatical and lexical instruction. The readings would be short and carefully graded in their linguistic content. Writing would involve just dictation at first, and then simple workbook exercises with immediate access to the answers for the purpose of self-correction. This sublevel includes the third and last part of basic grammatical instruction. Since the emphasis of this program is on mastery, students are not rushed through the grammar of the language in two semesters —at least three are needed for most languages. In this third part of the basic grammar, complex sentences would be introduced, as well as the subjunctive mood (if any), the conditional, and complex transformations. About 650 words and idioms would be taught. Communicative activities would concentrate on directed conversation without a model. Cultural instruction would continue to emphasize behavior but would include more references to informational culture.

**10.4.2.5: The late intermediate level:** In this level, which also covers about 70 hours of class plus study, all four skills are used, but emphasis remains, as throughout the program, on listening and speaking; as a result, a substantial amount of work continues to be done with recordings. Writing activities involve simple directed writing on very familiar topics, that is, essentially, variations of models. Grammar is de-emphasized and limited to infrequent, largely idiomatic rules. Vocabulary is emphasized to include about 800 new items. Communicative activities stress topically and linguistically delimited ("semifree") conversation. Achievement culture is introduced; the systematic study of the second culture is begun.

Note that all four sublevels (or four semesters of college in a standard program) discussed so far can be completed in two semesters if done on a semi-intensive basis.

**10.4.2.6: The early advanced level:** In this sublevel (which, like all the remaining sublevels, involves approximately 70 hours of class plus study) linguistically simple literature is introduced, if necessary editing it to fit the limited linguistic competence of the students. Writing is without a model but closely directed. Grammar is taught only remedially, if need be. Vocabulary continues to be emphasized, with another 950 items taught; idioms are stressed. Communicative activities concentrate on semifree conversation based on the cyclical reintroduction of communication acts (an idea first proposed in the Communicative Approach). All aspects of culture are attended to, and the systematic study of the second culture is continued.

**10.4.2.7: The late advanced level:** This continues the work of the early advanced level in every respect. Writing is now topically and linguistically delimited ("semifree"). Approximately 1,100 lexical items are added.

**10.4.2.8: The very advanced level:** This is composed, like the other levels, of two sublevels, that is, the equivalent of two semesters of college study at normal speed. As in all other levels, most of the work in class is audio-oral. Reading involves individual reading programs on a variety of topics, in the form of limited-credit units (what academics don't like to call "minicourses") to be carried out outside class and discussed in class. The topics may vary along the whole gamut of student interests, including the reading of literary works. Writing is free. The two semesters involve the learning of about 2,500 new vocabulary items. Cultural instruction is emphasized, in particular in terms of a systematic comparison of the two cultures in the early very advanced level and individual cultural research projects in the late very advanced level.

Note that the last four sublevels can also be done in one year if offered on a semi-intensive basis. This means that after two years the students would have mastered all the grammar and be in possession of a largely active vocabulary of about 7,000 words and idioms. This would allow them to proceed to advanced undergraduate courses *taught in the second language* —courses in literature, the arts, history or any other aspect of the second culture.

While the above progression has been described in terms of a college program, it should not be difficult to adapt it to other school levels and situations.

### 10.4.3: The Ideal Language Classroom

The ideal language classroom would (1) have all the necessary audiovisual devices; (2) be comfortable enough to allow moderate relaxation but not so comfortable that relaxation is total; (3) be culturally rich, with culturally authentic visuals and objects being changed every month or so (herein lies an interesting student project); (4) have a bulletin board; and, especially, (5) be equipped with chairs that can be snapped into place to face in several possible directions so as to form facing rows and lines, class halves, and small group circles for a variety of activities. Whether it should have windows is debatable. One school of thought is that windows are an invitation to distraction for many students. Another is that some students feel "trapped" in a windowless room. As both points of view are probably right, what is needed is a compromise —high windows near the ceiling, perhaps? The ideal classroom should be, if possible, close to a language lounge and a language laboratory. Finally, if the ideal classroom is going to be used for any teacher training or any research on language teaching, an observation room with one-way glass should be provided, fully equipped for audio and video recording. (Dreaming doesn't cost any money, only time.)

# 10.5: For Discussion

1. *What should be the relationship between theory and methodology?*
2. *If it is true that some students can learn with any method, how important can methods be?*
3. *Would "the ideal method" (given certain students, goals, and conditions) likely be a completely new departure or would it necessarily have to make certain choices among existing alternatives?*
4. *Discuss the strong and weak points of currently popular methods. How do their strengths and weaknesses relate to the nature of language, of learning, and of teaching? To the characteristics and goals of learners? To the competence of language teachers? To the availability of technological aids?*
5. *In practice, how can linguistic habits be formed with the help of cognition?*
6. *Is it valid to emphasize the audio-oral skills throughout the language program?*
7. *Can harm come from using the native language to convey and clarify meaning? As a basis for sentence generation? For early explanations? For frequent written translation?*
8. *What does learning theory have to say about late instruction in pronunciation?*
9. *Is a pedagogical transcription necessary at the beginning level of the language program? Why or why not? (Hint: Consider intralingual inconsistency and interlingual transfer.)*
10. *What are the conditions for success of an Introductory Phonological Minicourse? What factors could cause it to fail?*
11. *If most grammatical drills and exercises could be done outside the classroom, what should be done in class? How should class work relate to outside practice?*
12. *Would you emphasize lexical learning immediately if a learner were to leave for a foreign country in two weeks? Would the same early emphasis on vocabulary be justified if he will be in a second*

*language classroom for four years?*

13. *Why doesn't the ability to understand fluent speech result almost automatically from the ability to speak the language?*

14. *Discuss the transfer from speaking to reading and vice versa. In which direction is the transfer greater, given a good fit between sounds and letters of the alphabet? What does this say about the order in which language skills should be introduced?*

15. *Is creative writing in a second language a useful skill for our students to have? Why or why not?*

16. *As an informal "experiment" on the ability of visual aids to convey sentence meaning, draw a visual representation of a sentence and see if your classmates can guess what the sentence is.*

17. *Is there any reason not to make recordings available to all students in a language program? Why are so few language programs doing that?*

18. *Why do most language teachers prefer paper-and-pencil tests that defeat the very purpose of the "oral" instruction they claim to engage in?*

19. *How much should the student rely on his own abilities? How much should he depend on the teacher? How much help and support should he seek from the other students?*

20. *What is your concept of the ideal language program? How does it compare with the program proposed in this chapter?*

21. *Do you agree with the author's suggestions regarding the ideal progression in the teaching of competences, language components, and language skills? Why or why not?*

22. *What advantages or disadvantages are there in studying a second language on a semi-intensive basis? On an intensive basis? Slowly? What consequences would different speeds of learning have on the rest of the curriculum?*

23. *What would you consider to be ideal language learning conditions and facilities? Which of these can realistically be expected to become possible or available in the near future?*

## Footnotes

[1]Much of *Synthesis* deals with the speaking skill; Chapter 19 in that book discusses listening comprehension, reading, and writing in some detail.

[2]How to teach a dialogue bilingually was demonstrated in Chapter 16 of *Synthesis*.

[3]Chapter 14 of *Synthesis* discusses the uses of the native language and visual aids.

# Chapter 11: Consequences for Research

## Introduction and Summary

*Experimental research is essential to theory validation. Only by testing theories and the hypotheses that make them up can we determine the relative validity of different theories. From this process better theories emerge.*

*Research in languistics has suffered from the lack of sufficiently explicit, comprehensive, testable theories. Research has to answer specific theoretical questions, although many such questions can be initially posed by practitioners.*

*Of the various types of research possible, the most useful, the most conducive to the development of languistics as a science would be experimental classroom language teaching research. Although there are certain difficulties with such behavioral research, it will yield far more reliable information than more subjective studies.*

*What to investigate is also an important question. We have spent too much time studying isolated bits and pieces of the field of language teaching. Comprehensive, integrated theories should allow us to seek answers to the most important questions in a systematic, productive way.*

## 11.1: Research and Its Importance

**Research** can be defined as *the systematic search for answers to questions.* To be systematic, the search must follow a careful methodology. The questions must be posed in explicit terms and be answerable, preferably, quantitatively rather than qualitatively. All research is problem-solving of one kind or another.

Much writing in many disciplines —and language teaching may be an extreme example of this— is singularly unscholarly, being made up of

190

unsubstantiated personal opinions. Add to that the tendency of behavioral fields to follow fads and trends —a tendency largely due to North American neophilia— and the result is a situation where an accepted body of knowledge cannot emerge —theories are proposed, and before they have had a chance to be properly tested, new theories replace them.

A research-based body of knowledge would protect our field against fads. Through the conduct of solid and substantial research our field could really become a profession and, maybe, a science.

# 11.2: Theories Have to Be Tested

It isn't enough for a theory to seem to make sense. Each theory should be carefully tested, especially in those areas in which it contradicts other theories.   All theories are tentative; none is final. As Hebb [1969:27] put it, "A good theory is one that holds together long enough to get you to a better theory." All theories are tentative hypotheses and, as Popper [1972:261] said, "...growth of our knowledge is the result of... *the natural selection of hypotheses*...; a competitive struggle... eliminates those hypotheses which are unfit."

To be testable, a theory must be stated, if possible, in terms of explicit hypotheses of a quantitative nature. That is, it must be subject to corroboration or rejection, preferably by methods similar to those of the physical sciences.

The requirements for theory validation are such that many corroborations do not establish the "truth" of a theory but a single careful falsification is enough to reject it. Of course, if a theory has passed many tests it can be said to have proven its mettle and can be used as a reliable guide to action, even though some day a better theory may emerge.

Although no theory can be considered 100 percent verified, we *can* ask which theory is better corroborated, and act accordingly. A theory may be partially falsified, in which case only some of its hypotheses will require revision. A few stray contradictions to a theory should not lead us to reject it as a whole; such general rejection is justified only when general reproducible effects refute the theory.

Statements about personal experience are unsuitable for validation of a theory. Personal experience can help us decide between statements but cannot corroborate any statement. Theories must be tested severely in an attempt to determine what their shortcomings are. Then substantial corroboration would lead to acceptance (for the time being, until a better theory replaces it) and substantial falsification immediately would open the way for new theories.

Certain theories or hypotheses have been "immunized" against criticism by being worded in such a way that they are not subject to empirical refutation. A common way of doing this is to define what may contradict the theory or hypothesis as "meaningless" and "trivial" matters not worthy of consideration. Thus certain theoreticians manage, cheaply, to attain "unassailability." No scientific statement should thus be protected against falsification. Theoreticians who resort to such trickery do not deserve to be taken seriously.

What results from the testing of theories and hypotheses should be more successful theories. A better successor theory "will be in most cases (1) of at least as high a degree of generality or universality as the predecessor theory.... In addition, it will either (2) apply to situations about which the predecessor theory had nothing to say; or it will (3) correct some of the mistakes of the predecessor theory; or it will, preferably, do... all these things...." [Popper 1972:369]

# 11.3: Experimental Research Requires Theory

Research in languistics has suffered from a theoretical vacuum. It has been carried out in the absence of theories or on the basis of inadequate, partial theories which have seldom been explicit. Even a major study like the Pennsylvania Project [Smith 1970] was plagued by the lack of complete agreement on methodology, much less theory.

Experimental research should be guided by theory from beginning to end. It is for the theoretician to formulate the research questions and to do so as clearly and objectively as possible. Then the researcher carries out the experiment and interprets its results in the light of theoretical considerations.

Theories should underlie all research. Any theory is better than no theory at all, for it provides us with statements to test. A comprehensive, explicit theory amenable to quantitative testing is the most useful basis for research that will increase our systematic knowledge.

# 11.4: Research in Languistics

In order to elevate languistics to the level of a science we must scientifically test our theories and hypotheses; we can no longer defend unscientific beliefs and procedures on the basis that ours is a service profession, an art or a technology. This means that rather than spending most of our time and energy frantically searching for patch-up solutions to current problems, we should emphasize the careful testing of comprehensive theories. As an applied science, we *must* place the emphasis on the development and experimental validation of theories. A sound theory will take care of most of our practical problems.

As practitioners, we cannot of course wait until the best theory has been corroborated; we have to choose now between more or less valid theories, a choice that theoreticians can stay aloof from. As practitioners, our choice should be the best-tested theory that is relevant to our needs; but we must remain flexible enough to change our choice as new evidence may demand.

There was considerable research on language teaching in the sixties. Unfortunately, from the early seventies on research shifted to natural language acquisition, which is largely irrelevant for the very different classroom situation. Disillusionment with the results of the Pennsylvania Project may have led many applied linguists to abandon classroom language teaching research. It is a pity that such a defective study should have had such a negative effect on research in our field.[1]

Virtually none of the innovations in language teaching since the early seventies has been tested experimentally. In fact, some of the innovators have expressed outright contempt for experimental research. Experimental research is needed more than ever before, as a fifteen-year-old tangle of contradictory claims needs to be sorted out and evaluated.

If we are going to continue to invest great effort and expense in offering second language training, we must find out which principles are valid and which procedures work best, so that we may improve the efficiency and effectiveness of the learning process. This involves the open-minded evaluation of established practices and of new practices as they are proposed.

Unfortunately many people —even some scholars in our field— think that language teaching, unlike linguistics or literature, is not amenable to a research approach. At the other extreme, some language specialists seem too ready to apply any and all research findings, however tentative and dubious. Neither extreme is desirable. The best attitude toward research in our field seems to be to recognize its limitations but also admit that it is our only key to the advancement of knowledge.

Research in languistics, like any other research involving human behavior, suffers from difficulty in controlling variables. In addition to that, there is a dearth of researchers, due largely to the fact that second language specialists are typically rejected in both departments of linguistics and modern language departments dominated by literature specialists. The fact that very few researchers are being trained may account for the low quality of language teaching in North America.

A further problem is that linguistic findings must compete with "common sense" —every language teacher and most language students think they "know" how languages should be taught and learned. But if it is to become a science, linguistics must go beyond "common sense" and provide careful empirically based answers to our questions.

Making research in linguistics even more difficult is the constant demand that it should "pay off" in terms of immediate applications to practical problems. It is true that eventually a sound theory would have positive consequences for the development of materials, for teaching procedures, for testing, for program evaluation —in a word, for all aspects of language teaching. But it may take a number of years for a comprehensive theory to be corroborated and modified as needed. In the meantime, the practitioner should be an intelligent consumer of research results, could pose many research questions, and could even help answer some of them.

Research on language teaching is challenging and is very much needed. It is hoped that the present chapter will serve to encourage many young professionals at the beginning of their careers to devote most of their efforts to such research.

# 11.5: Types of Research

We can distinguish between three types of research in linguistics: (1) historical, (2) descriptive, and (3) experimental. In addition to these, some people use the name "action research" to refer to the preparation of teaching materials, program development, and other practically oriented activities; but these are not really research as such (no new knowledge is being created) — they should consist in the application of research findings.

Historical research involves tracing methods or procedures through decades or centuries, studying the lives and contributions of well-known language teachers from the past, and so forth. The most comprehensive historical studies present the history of language teaching since ancient times [e.g., Kelly 1969] or with emphasis on recent times [e.g., Titone 1968]. It is regrettable that the two major historical studies just mentioned, which are the only comprehensive histories of language teaching available in English, suffer from a marked pro-Direct Method bias. Historical research on many aspects of language teaching is needed; but it should be research that does not start from a basis of *a priori* assumptions.

While historical research attempts to determine what happened in earlier times, descriptive research tries to specify what is happening now in our classrooms under typical conditions. It does not involve, as experimental research does, control groups and the manipulation of independent variables. One subtype of descriptive research is what has been called "ethnographic" research. This is taken from anthropology and sociology and consists in observation, in-depth interviews, surveys, and case studies of subjects. In such research, hypotheses are formulated inductively as the data is obtained, not in advance (as in experimental research); the idea is to develop a theory as work progresses, not to test an existing theory. Included in ethnographic research is subject self-reporting, which has yielded valuable information in several studies in our field [e.g., Hammerly 1974-b, Hosenfeld 1979]. Much more research of this nature is needed.

The emphasis in our field should be, however, on experimental research, which allows us to test the validity of existing hypotheses and theories. It would be preferable, for the time being, to concentrate on small-scale studies that manipulate only one or two variables; while keeping scale small does not reduce the number of variables to be controlled, it makes such control more manageable. By small scale I mean two or at most a few classes. Once a theory has been fairly well corroborated on the basis of small-scale studies it would be time to engage in large-scale comparisons. The same principle applies to the scope of experimental research studies —numerous small-scope studies involving only one or two independent variables should precede any attempt at overall methodological comparison.

# 11.6: Conducting Research

A serious difficulty in conducting linguistic research is a problem common to all the social or behavioral sciences —the methods of the physical sciences cannot be strictly adhered to. The neatness of the laboratory is rarely possible. Conditions change frequently. Predictions cannot be precise and may affect outcomes. It is very difficult to be perfectly objective. One inherent problem is that human behavior is largely dependent on context, but context is what the experimental situation often needs to be stripped of if the results are to be generalizeable. Further complicating matters is the fact that linguistic problems tend to have relevant variables that cannot be fully controlled.

But just because there are difficulties with linguistic research is no reason to give up. Much can be learned from experimental research that attempts to control variables as thoroughly as possible, even if perfect control remains elusive. Posing important questions, carefully and consistently carrying out specific teaching procedures, collecting and analyzing empirical data, and reporting the results to the profession in such an explicit, objective and unambiguous way that replication is possible is an activity that will yield much useful new knowledge. There is no alternative —this is the only way in which our field can establish a body of knowledge and become a science rather than a subjective "art."

At the same time, we should have learned very important lessons from the methodological comparisons of the sixties. One is that, as the Colorado Study showed [Scherer and Wertheimer 1964], only while methods are kept quite distinct and separate will there be major differences in the results.[2] Another lesson, shown by several studies, is that what is emphasized in the program is largely what the students will excel at (as if this weren't obvious). Another important conclusion based on these comparisons, especially the very large-scale Pennsylvania Project, is that under normal teaching conditions and when many teachers participate it is very difficult to keep methods distinct and thus few differences will show. This doesn't mean that methodological comparisons should not be conducted. Under the right conditions, small-scale comparisons held at one or two centers, schools or universities could be sufficiently controlled to yield valuable results. But this should follow considerable research with single independent variables.

Thus what very large-scale studies can show is only what happens under typical conditions when methodological differences are minimized by numerous largely uncontrolled (and uncontrollable) variables. For example, the Pennsylvania Project showed what typically happened to the Audiolingual Method and with language laboratories under circumstances adverse to the Audiolingual Method and favorable to the Grammar-Translation Method; it did not show what the Audiolingual Method could accomplish under favorable circumstances. The false conclusion reached from a superficial look at that study is that no method is better than any other method. No wonder confusion followed. No wonder language teachers now feel they are on their own, to manage as best they can in the present confusion. No wonder few scholars are choosing research in language teaching as their career emphasis.

Small-scale experimental research limited to testing single hypotheses is our best hope for increasing our knowledge. But note that a single hypothesis should not be tested apart from others to which it is closely related or even dependent on. For example, order-of-teaching hypotheses that depend on cognitive activity on the part of the students should not be tested mechanically. Another example: The value of a procedure recommended for initial learning is not being tested fairly if the procedure is used for remedial instruction. Still another: What is supposed to work longitudinally should not be evaluated on a short-term basis.

It is hoped that despite the difficulties and *caveats* discussed in this section many readers will feel encouraged to do experimental research in languistics and to report their findings not only to other scholars but also to language teachers and even, when warranted, to the general public.

# 11.7: What to Research

Research in language teaching has lacked direction because until recently there had been no comprehensive theories of classroom language teaching and because of disillusionment with the limitations and results of classroom research. Perhaps it is because of these same two reasons that many researchers turned, in the seventies, to the study of natural language acquisition. But such research has little or no relevance to language teaching, as the sociolinguistic environment of natural language acquisition cannot be reproduced within the second language classroom.

Cooper *et al.* [1980] have suggested that research should concentrate on (1) linguistic and psycholinguistic considerations; (2) the teaching/learning process, that is, what works in the classroom; and (3) the role of foreign language study in the total educational process. These seem very broad aims indeed.

It seems to me that the most useful results will be obtained when researchers test the specific hypotheses of the various theories of language teaching discussed in this book. In particular, they should concentrate on testing theoretical predictions that contradict current theories, for example my prediction that the Communicative Approach will result in very inaccurate speech vs. the communicationists' prediction that errors will naturally disappear, and the associated prediction that once a pidgin is allowed to develop it becomes terminal. Also, when two or more theories explain the same facts, their contradictory predictions must be tested experimentally.

Much new knowledge would be gained and much confusion would be cleared away if the hypotheses of the various competing theories were systematically tested. But there is also much need for research that simply describes what happens under typical language teaching conditions —this certainly *is* serious research, even though it doesn't fit any of the traditional research designs (it involves no new treatment). Descriptions of behavioral culture are badly needed; contrastive cultural analyses would provide a far better basis for cultural instruction than the usual haphazard collection of anecdotes and casual observations.

In terms of so-called "action research," several types of new language teaching materials need to be developed. Chief among these are materials for Introductory Phonological Minicourses as well as —most important— materials that bridge the gap between attention to form and attention to meaning, that is, between an emphasis on accuracy and an emphasis on fluency with built-in accuracy. But more than that, whole curricula need to be developed that do not center around textbooks —which are hardly appropriate for a primarily audio-oral activity— but around (1) recordings from the beginning level on, plus (2) computers from the intermediate level on.

If a few research centers scattered throughout North America would undertake programs of systematic research such as the one suggested in this chapter, it would not take many years before most of our questions would be answered. Then linguistics would truly become a profession and would be on its way to becoming a science.

# 11.8: For Discussion

1. *Why is research the only way to establish an acceptable (and, it is hoped, accepted) body of knowledge in languistics?*
2. *Can a theory be considered valid if its statements have not been tested against competing statements of other plausible theories? Can it be considered to "make sense"?*
3. *How much can we rely on personal experience in the absence of empirical evidence? When empirical evidence seems to contradict it?*
4. *Give an example or two of theories or hypotheses that have been "immunized" against criticism.*
5. *What has been the result of conducting experimental languistic research in the absence of comprehensive, explicit theories?*
6. *In what sense is a good theory practical?*
7. *Why are some leaders in our field contemptuous of experimental research? What does this say about them and their views? What does it say about our field?*
8. *What is your attitude toward research? How did you arrive at that attitude?*
9. *Can the difficulties inherent to research with human subjects be largely overcome? Are the variables more likely to be controllable under typical field conditions or in small-scale studies at research centers?*
10. *Do you agree with the author that overall methodological comparisons should follow years of research in which single variables are tested? Why or why not? Have methodological comparisons carried*

*out so far served any useful purpose?*

**11.** *Prepare a list of what you see as the languistic questions that most urgently need empirically based answers. Rank them in order of priority. How would you go about obtaining answers to your questions?*

**12.** *Do you have any ideas for "action research" that needs to be done?*

## Footnotes

[1]Some of the most serious shortcomings of the Pennsylvania Project have been discussed briefly in *Synthesis*, pp. 636-8.

[2]At the end of one year, during which the methods were distinct, there were marked differences; after all students were taught the same way during the second year, the differences largely disappeared.

T.G.B.T.G.

# Appendices

# Appendix A: Prematurities in Language Teaching

*The theory presented in this book emphasizes the principle of grada-tion. Unfortunately, there are many ways in which the principle of gradation is violated in our classrooms. Many carts are being put before many horses in language teaching —perhaps this, more than a myriad other reasons frequently adduced, accounts for the limited success of many of our language programs.*

*At least eleven "prematurities" can be recognized in our teaching practices. All of these prematurities can be detrimental to the language learning process, although some more so than others.*

# 1. Premature Instruction

As some would have it, no time is too early to start learning a second language. Adult fascination with the apparent speed and ease with which young children pick up languages has led to the proposition "The earlier the better."

But as we have seen, this is a myth based on faulty observations. Given the same amount of linguistic interaction, adults should do as well or better than children (except in the area of pronunciation) in picking up the language of a foreign country. That adults are better overall learners than children has been known for a long time.

It is only in the area of motor memory that young children have an advantage over adults; but *if* sufficiently motivated and properly taught, most adults seem capable of developing excellent pronunciation.[1]

While another language can be acquired with ease by a child in a natural sociolinguistic environment, the same cannot be said of classroom instruction. In the classroom, young children develop a very faulty pidgin, older children do a little better, and adults do best (except, again, for untutored pronunciation). It seems, therefore, that language instruction should not start before the child has developed some cognitive maturity and is responsive to linguistic correction.

The ideal point to begin classroom language study would therefore be at about the age of ten or eleven, when children have more cognitive maturity but have not yet lost their motor memory advantage. Then, after about three or four years of systematic, semi-intensive study (about two hours a day), several years of partial immersion (some subjects taught in the second language) should follow, this in turn followed, if possible, by a year of total exposure to the language.

It is premature, then, to offer classroom second language exposure or instruction to young children who are cognitively immature and incapable of responding to specifically linguistic feedback.

Another aspect of prematurity of instruction refers to our attempts to teach languages to students who are not motivated to learn them. Language learning involves a long-term commitment which isn't possible without a high level of motivation. While it is true that motivation can be enhanced through successful teaching, I think that language teaching would be much more successful if we made an effort to create some motivation first.

Motivation to learn other languages can be generated through exploratory courses. Perhaps an introductory exploratory course on the peoples and languages of the world should be the first or even the only required course in our field. It would be followed by courses in specific languages for those who have developed the motivation needed to put in the long-term effort required to learn them.

*The remaining ten prematurities all refer to teaching/learning activities or stages that are desirable as eventual activities or goals of language instruction. The problem is that many have considered these goals and have simply turned them into procedures for reaching them. It is important to recognize that the best way to attain many pedagogical goals is through procedures that are* indirectly *related to the goals. Nothing is gained and much is lost by neglecting preliminary procedures and rushing students into the performance of activities that resemble the final goals. Or rather something is "gained": a false feeling of confidence and creativity, false because it is a castle hastily built on the sand.*

# 2. Premature Ungraded Input

While a good argument can be made for some use of ungraded listening materials for "selective listening" exercises [Nida 1957, Minn 1976, Gomes de Matos 1980, Taylor 1981] designed to abstract specific linguistic features from the stream of speech, and while the same argument could be made for "selective reading," extensive early exposure to ungraded input for comprehension and competence development purposes seems to be quite harmful.

Such exposure is, first of all, frustrating. No one likes to listen to or read material of which he understands only ten or twenty percent. It is quite discouraging to have to decode texts laboriously by looking up every second or third word in the dictionary —this can hardly be called "reading," even if it satisfies the (by now fortunately mostly abandoned) unrealistic dictum "First-year students must read literature."

Early ungraded input is inefficient. Little or nothing is learned thoroughly, for the learner is exposed from one to a few times to much data that he can't possibly absorb —a waste of time— and very little data recurs often enough to be internalized.

Finally, premature ungraded input often seems to result in inaccurate rule internalization. Why this happens is not difficult to explain: When we hear or read something, even something we understand reasonably well, we restructure it for storage in memory, and we do that by reorganizing it and eliminating all redundancies —discarded are all fine points of phonology, almost all endings, etc. Lack of gradation makes this worse —most of the time restructuring isn't even possible— but the problem is present in any comprehension approach that emphasizes extensive early input. Internal representations, which at the beginning are very faulty, cannot be corrected if they are not expressed (this explains why after many hours of listening and/or reading, when Comprehension Approach students start speaking they make many, largely ingrained, errors).

Krashen's [1981] definition of "comprehensible input" as "$i + 1$" — input that is slightly beyond the language acquirer's current competence— may be adequate for natural language acquisition situations and is the kind of input that mothers and helpful foreigners naturally produce; but it is not precise enough for the language classroom. In the language classroom, input must be very precisely graded to include only what has been taught before plus the new item or items just taught —in other words, classroom instruction seems to be more successful when the principles of gradation and integration are narrowly interpreted, i.e., followed one point at a time.

Ungraded linguistic input belongs at the end of the second language program, at the very advanced level, after the learners' competence has been systematically developed to the point where they can largely understand such input.

# 3. Premature Free Communication --Speaking

When linguistic adventurism —communicating beyond one's competence— is encouraged, many errors will occur. A student can only rely on what he knows, and if he doesn't know enough of the second language to say something, he will rely either on his native language (and thereby make interlingual errors) or on the little he knows of the second language (and thereby make intralingual errors) —usually it's a combination of both. Since such errors cannot be dealt with effectively in the language classroom —for they aren't "distortions" of what has been learned but "faults" about what hasn't been learned [Hammerly 1982]— they tend to quickly fossilize in the form of inaccurate linguistic habits (or "faulty internalized rules"). The fact that some practitioners in our field would reward students for what they say and ignore how they say it only serves to speed up the process of fossilization of a classroom pidgin.

The present emphasis on communication in our field tends to obscure the above facts. Our students should, by all means, communicate in the language, but only within the limits of their growing competence, that is, by putting to communicative use everything they learn after they learn it. Even staunch advocates of the Communicative (Functional) Approach [Widdowson 1978, Widdowson and Brumfit 1981] have come to recognize that communication acts in the second language should turn around a structural core. What is hardly predictable (communication) must be based on what is highly systematic and predictable (language structure), not the other way around.

The terminal classroom pidgin developed by early French Immersion students by Grade 5 or 6 is definitive evidence that when communication is emphasized early, accuracy suffers greatly. Students will no doubt learn to communicate if allowed to do it any way they want. But the resultant very defective interlanguage can hardly be considered a worthwhile outcome of language study.

# 4. Premature Coordinate Bilingualism

The production of coordinate bilinguals capable of functioning separately in the two languages is perhaps the most important *ultimate* goal of our programs. But again, some have tried to turn an ultimate goal into a procedure for reaching it. Thus, those who want to imitate bilingual acquisition as a method of second language learning urge the building of a wall of separation between the two languages which is never to be crossed, not even in the early stages of language instruction.

Paradoxically, that is not the way in which natural bilinguals develop. Bilingual development from infancy shows considerable linguistic interaction, even when specific persons and environments are associated with each language. At one time, I followed the development of a Spanish/ English bilingual child from infancy. This was a child exposed to distinct environments, and yet he showed phonological interference until the age of four, syntactic interference until the age of ten (and occasionally into adulthood), and lexicosemantic interaction throughout (and still today) [Hammerly 1964]. Numerous studies of language switching have shown that the two languages continue to interact lexically in adult bilinguals who, furthermore, can readily engage in natural translation [Harris 1978]. What these various studies show is that a coordinate bilingual seems to emerge slowly from an at least partially compound system and never keeps the two languages totally apart.

Our ultimate goal of coordinate bilingualism is not, therefore, a valid reason for ignoring the native language of the learner. Ignoring it means, moreover, being unable to deal effectively with both "intrusive" and "preclusive" interference errors [Hammerly 1982] —errors that result from mental interlingual associations which monolingual instruction in no way prevents. For example, the majority of errors by children after years of monolingual immersion instruction are interference errors of one sort or another. Nor can one, by ignoring the native language, take full advantage of the potential positive transfer from the known language to the new language.

Our profession is sharply divided on the question of the use of the native language, with about half the methods favoring it and half rejecting it. This polarization resulted from an extreme reaction to the misuse and overuse of the native language in the Grammar-Translation Method, a method that produced generations of language program graduates who could only generate pidginized written sentences. But a century is long enough for an overreaction.

The view that the *judicious and limited* use of the native language can increase the efficiency and effectiveness of language teaching has a respectable history, going back to Henry Sweet [1899] and Harold Palmer [1917]. According to this view, a monolingual second language classroom is desirable and possible at the advanced level but unnecessary, premature, and counterproductive at the beginning level.

# 5. Premature Graphemization

Spoken and written language refer to the same underlying competence but differ in many important ways. Writing is based on speech and is a usually faulty representation of it. While the written language can serve as a rough reminder of the general content of speech, it also pulls the attention of the learner away from the facts of speech in numerous significant ways.

Graphemic stimuli that contradict the spoken language can result in serious deterioration of second language pronunciation even when the sounds involved exist in the native language [Hammerly 1970]. In addition to this intralingual problem there is the interlingual one of the learner misinterpreting second language graphemes according to the phonemic-graphemic correlations of the native language. Pimsleur [1980] was quite right when he said, in reference to French and English, that beginning learners should "[n]ever look at the letter *r*," a piece of advice that can be extended to much of the alphabets of most languages.

The prereading period first advocated by Pestalozzi (1746-1827), a Swiss educational reformer, and more recently proposed by Delattre [1947] after World War II, has never ceased being a sound idea, despite the fall from grace of the Audiolingual Method, some of whose advocates used it. Prereading did run into practical problems of implementation, especially because no adequate visual support for it was developed, thus making review of old material and a gradual and orderly transition to reading very difficult. But there are now special pedagogical transcriptions for use during the prereading period which allow for a step-by-step progression between transcription -supported spoken language and standard spelling [Hammerly 1974].

A significant delay in the presentation of the standard written language has also been made easy by the ubiquitous cassette. There no longer is any reason —if there ever was one— why a second language should be learned from a textbook, with the numerous negative effects early access to one has.

# 6. Premature Grammatical Formulation

A cognitive grasp of grammatical rules no doubt facilitates performance, provided it is followed by an adequate amount of practice in the form of "intelligent conditioning" [Hammerly 1982] and graded communicative activities. This does not mean, however, that intellectual awareness through deduction should be the point of departure in dealing with *all* grammatical rules. On the contrary, it seems that, while a certain number of complex rules can best be handled deductively, many simple rules can be learned inductively with efficiency, and the majority of rules are best learned via "guided discovery," a process that combines induction and deduction and that was already proposed by Jespersen [1904] under the name "inventional grammar."

What is lost by starting every grammatical presentation with a predigested formula? First of all, gone is the challenge of dealing with language learning as a series of little problems to be solved, an activity that casts the students in the interesting, motivating role of minilinguists. Secondly, lost is the memory-enhancing advantage, which may be considerable, of the students discovering facts about the language by themselves, helped as needed by the teacher. Thirdly, missed is the opportunity to develop the powers of linguistic observation and the grammatical sensitivity of the students, both skills that would stand them in good stead as they try to acquire intuitively the many rules that are not overtly taught in the language program.

# 7. Premature Grammatical Integration

Another current tendency is to rush the students into the global use of the language rather than ensure its mastery one point at a time. A complex system such as a language cannot come efficiently or effectively under control if it is approached holistically. The result of trying prematurely to use the whole system is that many of its parts will not be adequately mastered, thus contributing to the early fossilization of a very defective, terminal interlanguage.

The systematic learning of a language in the classroom should be a process of additive mastery and progressive integration. It is like building a language "machine" part by part (additive mastery) while frequently using the growing, partially assembled machine for whatever it can do (progressive integration). Most machines cannot be used that way, of course, but the second language competence "machine" *can* be built and operated that way, with much better results than can be obtained by the premature, incompetent use of the whole system.

# 8. Premature Lexicalization

There is a widespread belief that learning a second language is mostly a matter of learning words. It is true, of course, that without vocabulary nothing can be said. So if a beginner is put in a situation where he must communicate beyond his linguistic competence, he will find vocabulary more useful than structure. But we *mustn't* put beginners in such situations nor ever aim at linguistically incompetent communication, for that results in terminal linguistic incompetence.

The view of many in the fifties and sixties that only the vocabulary necessary to illustrate phonological and grammatical rules needed to be taught was extreme —our students want very much to communicate in the classroom, so we must teach them enough vocabulary to make controlled communication possible. But this doesn't mean that vocabulary should be *emphasized* early in the language program.

An early emphasis on vocabulary has serious negative effects. It leads to a corresponding neglect of structure, which should be the primary concern at the beginning and intermediate levels —structure is, after all, the skeleton of language around which everything else is built. Students whose vocabulary is proportionately much more developed than their control of structure are constantly tempted —a temptation they seldom resist— to communicate beyond their linguistic competence, which as we have seen results in the early establishment of a very defective classroom pidgin.

# 9. Premature Cognatization

Some would "facilitate" the lexical learning task by introducing numerous cognates at the start of the program. But the presentation of cognates should be delayed, for at least two reasons. Their introduction *en masse* early in the program (1) contributes to difficulties in pronunciation, as they tend to be pronounced with native language sounds, and (2) creates the false impression that the two languages have a general vocabulary similarity, when in fact the similarity may apply only to infrequent and learned words. Thus the use of many cognates early in the program leads to erroneous cognatization —e.g., such "words" as *"péncilo" and *"huila" for, repectively, Spanish *lápiz* (pencil) and *rueda* (wheel). In fact, this false assumption of interlingual similarity seems to affect not only vocabulary but also morphology and syntax. Generally, better results in language teaching seem to follow a policy of emphasizing differences, not similarities between the two languages.

# 10. Premature Semantization

In teaching lexical items, whether contextualized words, phrases or sentences, we have to impart to our students, initially, two things: form and basic meaning (and later, usually over a period of time, connotations and usage).

Of these two things, form and meaning, the practice of many is to concentrate the students' attention, from the start, on the meaning of the new utterances, apparently in the belief that form will take care of itself. But if insufficient attention is paid to form, it will not be adequately learned.

Listening and reading activities would naturally lend themselves to almost exclusive concern with meaning; but when our students have to learn to *say* something new, both *how* it is said and *what* it means should receive adequate emphasis. Since the human mind cannot pay full conscious attention to more than one thing at a time, it follows that we are limited to a choice between the sequences *what, then how* or *how, then what*.

The fact that students are primarily interested in the meaning of the new utterance suggests a solution. Psychologists [e.g., Premack 1962] have shown the effectiveness of conditioning a pleasant reward on the previous performance of a less pleasant activity —in our case, attention to form. The solution to our *what/how* or *how/what* dilemma is therefore to withhold the reward —the ascertainment of the meaning of the utterance— until the utterance has been reproduced with acceptable accuracy. When the students know that they won't be given, or allowed to overtly guess, the meaning of a word or sentence until they have produced it accurately, accurate production becomes much more important to them, as a way of obtaining their "reward" (the meaning) from the teacher.

I have found that conditioning the conveyance (or elicitation) of meaning on the accurate rendition of form is very effective, especially with dialogues, and results in a high standard of speech being attained and maintained.

# 11. Premature Creativity --Writing

Before or as we write something, we say it subvocally to ourselves; so writing, when properly understood, is based on speech. Language students who "write" texts with the constant help of dictionaries and grammar books are not really writing, then, but putting down on paper misunderstood and misshapen pieces of a puzzle —with the disastrous result that what they end up doing is practicing the production of errors.

Most native speakers cannot write creatively very well at all. For us to expect second language learners to do what very few native speakers can do is totally unrealistic and counterproductive.

(Incidentally, note that when it comes to linguistic practice, spoken practice is far more efficient and effective than written practice. In a given period of time, an item can be practiced orally many more times than it can be written. Furthermore, oral practice allows immediate feedback, which is much more effective than the long delayed corrections of written assignments.)

To be able to write freely with adequate accuracy (with only an occasional error), language students need (1) a thorough foundation in the listening and speaking skills, during which they internalize all important rules, and (2) extensive experience in listening and reading, which gives them models of expression and allows them to acquire at least a passive control over many of the minor syntactic rules that are not formally taught in the program. Thus free writing (free composition), if done at all in the language program, should be an activity for the very advanced level.

It isn't the objective of our language programs to produce Joseph Conrads. And even if that were a defensible objective, the way to reach it would *not* be to ask our students to write freely and creatively before they have developed an advanced control over the tool of language.

## 12. Conclusion

*We have discussed premature language teaching as well as ten teaching procedures which from some to most members of our profession use prematurely. Such prematurities in language teaching seem to be largely responsible for the poor results obtained in many programs. The avoidance of these and other prematurities in language teaching should result in a significant improvement in the percentage of fluent and accurate bilinguals that our classrooms can produce.*

### Footnote

[1]A few of my English-speaking students in their late teens, 20s, and 30s have developed perfect Spanish pronunciation.

# Appendix B: A Bill of Rights for Language Students

## 1. Introduction

In our concern for methods and procedures, teachers and their preferences, being up-to-date regarding professional trends, etc. sometimes some of us seem to forget that language students should have certain rights and that by consistently respecting these rights we might not only enhance their attitudes and gain their allegiance but also increase the efficiency and effectiveness of the language teaching process. What follows is an attempt to express what those rights should be. I realize that a permanent document on language student rights should maybe be elaborated by a committee in which all elements of our discipline would be represented; but there is no such committee nor much likelihood that a representative profession-wide committee on anything will soon be formed. This "Bill of Rights" should therefore be considered a very tentative personal proposal made in the hope of stimulating discussion. Unfortunately, there seems to be no way to propose a largely axiomatic "Bill of Rights" without using a more-or-less aphoristic style, sounding a little sententious, and thereby producing what looks like a quasi-legal document. It is hoped that the reader will forgive this, as the author himself is the first to recognize that these rights are not quite "carved in stone"...

## 2. A Bill of Rights for Language Students

*Language students should have the following rigths:*
**I.** *The right to a fully qualified teacher who is committed to excellence.*
This right (as do several others) represents an ideal. This is also the most axiomatic of all the rights to be discussed.

Although there is considerable disagreement and a variety of jurisdictional definitions about what should constitute minimum qualification standards for language teachers, a set of suggestions regarding "full" (or ideal) qualifications seems in order. To be fully qualified, it would seem that a language teacher should have:

(1) Proficiency in the second language of at least $3+/4$ on the F.S.I. scale [Wilds 1975] (5 is for natives). Since very advanced students in very good language programs can reach the $3/3+$ level, at least *their* teachers should have equal or superior linguistic competence. Teachers of beginners, who will be serving as models of pronunciation and intonation (unless they use recordings for that purpose), need to have a native or near-native control of the phonology of the second language or their students will probably adopt their bad pronunciation habits. (On the other hand, note that teachers of beginners need not have a very advanced control of vocabulary.)

(2) Proficiency in the native language of the students —assuming they have a homogeneous linguistic background— adequate to enable the teacher to provide guidance in that language as needed. A great deal of time may be saved, without apparent loss in effectiveness, by the occasional use of directions, equivalences, and explanations in the native language.

(3) Knowledge of the structures of the two languages adequate for contrasting them in order to understand the students' problems and help them solve them. Many, in some studies a majority,[1] of the errors of beginners and most of the errors of very advanced learners[2] are traceable to interference from the native language. A knowledge of the structure of the native language would enable the teacher to understand such errors and be in a better position to deal with them, both preventively and remedially.

(4) Good knowledge of the psychology of second language teaching and learning. Such knowledge would tend to lead the teacher away from extreme behaviorism and extreme cognitivism into a synthesis that admits valid roles for a variety of procedures, including imitation, intelligent conditioning [Hammerly 1982: 49, 53-4], and more cognitively oriented creative activities.

(5) Good knowledge of second language methodology, testing, and the use of technological aids. This would seem an axiomatic requirement for any professionally competent language teacher.

(6) Good knowledge of the second culture and the native culture, especially in terms of the cultural connotations of words and phrases and of appropriate sociolinguistic behavior. After pronunciation, behavioral culture seems to be the most neglected aspect of language teaching. If prospective language teachers enrolled in courses in sociolinguistics and area studies instead of taking so many literature courses (which give limited direct insights about a culture), they would be better able to deal with the cultural aspects of language teaching.

(7) Some facility in consecutive interpretation and written translation. Language teachers do not need, of course, to be trained as professional translators, but they could benefit from some training in *natural* translation [Harris 1978], the kind of translation that most bilinguals are capable of. Sometimes occasions arise in the language classroom in which such a skill is very useful.

(8) Good understanding of communicative needs and functions, as analyzed and discussed in recent years by the leaders of the Communicative (Functional/Notional) Approach. This understanding can help the teacher in the choice and conduct of progressive communicative activities.

Regarding commitment to excellence, which is of course impossible to measure objectively, this would seem to involve two aspects — commitment of teachers to their own excellence, and commitment to foster excellence in the students. Teachers committed to excellence would continually try to upgrade their qualifications, including, where needed, spending time abroad. The teacher's desire for excellence in the students would lead him to be a fairly demanding teacher, which is, incidentally, the kind of teacher most students seem to prefer.

**II.** *The right to be given an orientation to the course or program and its objectives, and the rationale for its procedures.*

Probably no one in our profession would disagree with this principle, but few seem to be applying it.

When the learners understand the nature of their course or program and are aware of its objectives, they can better direct their efforts toward both long-term goals and the short- and intermediate-term goals to be attained.

An orientation seems so important for the students that it would seem desirable that the teacher, instead of submerging the students in the language from the start, should spend portions of the first few hours of the course or program in providing them with such an orientation. The orientation could, in addition to discussing general objectives, obtain questionnaire information about the students' backgrounds, motivation, and interests, teach basic linguistic terminology, explain how to study for the course and how to use the teaching materials and facilities, make clear the nature of the testing and grading procedures, and introduce, if possible, a few interesting facts about the second culture. (With beginners, all of this would have to be done in the native language, of course.)

Throughout the course or program, whenever a new type of procedure or activity is introduced, it would be desirable to explain its rationale. For example, few beginners appear ready to spend the time and effort required to memorize sentences or dialogues or to internalize rules through systematic, intensive exercise practice without an explanation of the purposes of such activities and of the benefits that can be derived from them in terms of fluency and accuracy in the use of the language.

**III.** *The right to be informed in advance of the performance objectives of learning activities and tests.*

Again, not a very controversial principle and one that is often included in methods courses. But for many teachers, it seems to remain in the realm of nice theory.

It is eminently desirable that language students should know at all crucial points, and if possible at all times, what is expected of them, i.e., what they should learn to do, under what conditions, and at what level of performance. General guidelines are adequate for much of the time, but specific performance objectives [Steiner 1975] are particularly important when a certain knowledge or behavior will be measured for a significant percentage of the course grade. This principle is built into individualized programs; but a program doesn't have to be individualized in order to observe it.

**IV.** *The right to be taught systematically, according to such principles as selection, gradation, and progressive integration.*

Certain second language methods do not follow this principle and seem to extoll the virtues of picking up a language in "sink-or-swim" fashion, as if a language were not a complex, integrated system of systems. Extreme advocates of the Communicative Approach, for example, condemn any course or program organization based on the structure of the language and want to base the curriculum, instead, on the various communication acts possible [e.g., Wilkins 1976]. But what is hardly systematic (communication) should be based on what is highly systematic (language structure) rather than the other way around. Fortunately more moderate leaders of the Communicative Approach have recognized this problem and have proposed that communication acts should turn cyclically around a structural core [Widdowson and Brumfit 1981].

Another current trend is to assume that language teaching should be modeled after what is known about natural first and second language acquisition —Krashen and his associates have strongly promoted this view. But as we have seen in Chapter 3, given its best chance ever such an approach produces speakers of a very faulty pidgin. It would seem that we would do well to recognize without any apologies that language teaching in a classroom is unavoidably "artificial" —there is nothing natural about speaking a strange language within four classroom walls— and gear our teaching to those specific learning conditions, which in some ways are better than those of natural language acquisition.

One of the advantages of the classroom over the nursery, the street, and the playground is that it allows for controlled, systematic input, manipulation, and internalization of linguistic data. This is an important advantage that should not be relinquished, as it is generally accepted in psychology that an organized body of data is easier to learn than a disorganized one.

The principles of selection, gradation, and progressive integration have already been discussed in this book. Suffice it to say that any method of language teaching which ignores one or more of these basic principles does a disservice to language students. Students find it much easier to learn a language when the course or program is based on a principled choice of what will be taught, a careful plan of step-by-step presentation, and sufficient use of everything learned up to any particular point in the program.

V. *The right to the balanced development of their linguistic, communicative, and cultural competence.*

At various times each of these three types of competence has been emphasized almost to the exclusion of the others. As distorted by many into dialogue memorization, mindless drilling, and not much else, at least one version of the Audiolingual Method concentrated almost exclusively on linguistic competence; it is no wonder that many audiolingually trained students did not learn to communicate with any fluency in their target languages. Some have proposed a Cultural Approach [Strasheim 1981], but again this seems to overemphasize one of the three competences at the expense of the other two. The Communicative Approach, taken to its extreme, would sacrifice linguistic competence for the sake of fluent communication, however faulty.

Balanced development of the three types of competence does not mean equal emphasis on all three at all times. To reach the goal of fluent *and accurate* communication in the second language, it would seem necessary to emphasize accuracy —basically, linguistic competence— first, and very gradually shift to an emphasis on communicative competence. While denying the opportunity for graded communicative activities is demoralizing to the students and therefore self-defeating, premature emphasis on free communication always seems to result in the early development of a terminal pidgin.

Regarding cultural competence, those cultural aspects —connotations and behavior— that are closely tied to linguistic and communicative considerations should be taught as needed from the start; a systematic study of the two cultures would seem more appropriate at the advanced or very advanced level.

VI. *The right to an emphasis on the language skills that each student would like to develop.*

In practice this would mean primarily that those students who want to develop their listening and speaking skills should not be denied that right.

Such a denial is far more common than the denial of the students' right to learn to read a language, something which, incidentally, they can learn to do independently with relative ease (if provided with explicit printed materials or computer software).

All surveys that I know of[3] have shown that a great majority —about 80 percent— of language students would like to learn to *speak* the second language. Yet a very small minority of language programs seem to emphasize listening and speaking throughout the program; most so-called "oral" programs shift in emphasis, by the intermediate level, from speaking to reading, with the result that the early proficiency developed in listening and speaking often deteriorates.

Any student who wants primarily to learn to speak a language should have the right to an emphasis on listening and speaking throughout the program, even at its most advanced level (and it should be possible for him to obtain such instruction right in our schools and universities, without having to go to Berlitz!). Of course, anyone who just wants to learn to read should also have the right to such instruction, although he should be forewarned that any later attempts to speak the language would probably be fraught with problems.

**VII.** *The right to have their native language used to facilitate the teaching/learning process.*

Our profession is about evenly divided on this the most controversial of all issues, with about half the methods making use of the native language and the other half forbidding it altogether. On the one hand, there are (there *still* are) those who misuse and overuse the native language in the form of constant translation, with the result that their students seem to develop not much else than the ability to read, and that haltingly. On the other hand, there are those who have understandably reacted to such an abuse of the native language by eliminating it totally from their classrooms, beginning in the 1880s.

But one century seems to be long enough for an overreaction. There is also a moderate tradition, going back to Henry Sweet [1899] and Harold Palmer [1917] that claims that the *limited and judicious* use of the native language can contribute greatly to the efficiency and effectiveness of language teaching. Perhaps we should ask ourselves if there is virtue in extremism, of either kind, and if it isn't likely that the best answer would lie in the moderate, reasonable middle ground.

Since the native language is the most frequent source of error for beginners as well as very advanced students, it makes no sense to ignore it in the classroom. So contrastive analysis —which is seeing a resurgence in North America and has been very much alive in Europe— should be an important basis for drills, exercises, graded communicative activities, and tests. All learning, after all, is based on some kind of awareness of differences and similarities, so it is hard to believe that interlingual awareness, and activities based on it, would not be helpful in second language learning.

**VIII.** *The right to have their errors corrected —kindly, promptly, and persistently.*

Students *want* to be corrected, often more so than teachers want to correct them —evidently students find feedback essential to learning [Cathcart and Olsen 1976].

If done kindly, in a matter-of-fact way, error correction does not seem to be either offensive or inhibiting. The key would be to accompany negative linguistic feedback with, whenever possible, positive communicative and affective feedback. Correction should be prompt, as psychologists have long known that delayed correction is largely ineffective (this argues against doing written homework, which is usually corrected with a considerable delay). Persistence in correction is also very important; it is hardly enough to correct an error once or twice —errors should be corrected as long as they occur. If an error persists despite numerous corrections, it would seem that the thing to do would be to direct the student to remedial work.

How errors are corrected is also very important. Students should be treated in this regard like the intelligent persons they are, not like parrots. Providing the corrected utterance for repetition is a very passive technique, perhaps justifiable only in the case of certain pronunciation errors. For most errors, it would seem better to elicit correction from the student himself, or from his classmates, and to deal with the cause of the error rather than with its surface manifestation.

Implied in the right to correction is the need to have someone present to correct errors —at least the important errors— during communicative activities. For example, small-group communicative activities should not be engaged in by the students without a qualified corrector. If the teacher or his assistants (if any) cannot be there, it would be desirable to have a competent advanced student in charge of each group.

Not correcting errors may make some students comfortable —it seems to give them a sense of confidence, that is *false* confidence— but the mild discomfort of being corrected is nothing compared to their terminal discouragement at discovering that after many years of instruction they have internalized a very faulty interlanguage upon which they cannot improve.

**IX.** *The right to have adequate access to native speakers, technological aids, and language teaching materials.*

Where native speakers are not available to interact live with the students, at least their voices should be available via recordings. It would seem that language programs that claim to emphasize the spoken language should make considerable use of language laboratories or individual cassette machines —these provide the only means for useful graded oral practice outside the classroom. Spoken language cannot be learned well from textbooks, the beliefs of many publishers notwithstanding. Ideally, each language student should have access to a cassette machine most of the time, something that the reduction in the cost of cassette equipment has made quite possible.

The use of computers in language teaching would seem desirable — throughout for a reading program, from the intermediate level on for an oral program— but not essential. In fact, there is the danger that the use of computers in our field will strengthen the already misplaced emphasis on graphic skills in many programs. Already computers are being misused, for example, to translate words in isolation, in a kind of Computer Age one -to-one bilingual word list game.

Among the language teaching materials that all students should have ready access to —but many don't— are good reference materials (large bilingual and monolingual dictionaries, etc.) and "general materials," i.e., materials designed for remediation and review within any program.

**X.** *The right to fair evaluation based on what is taught.*

Fair evaluation demands that second language tests be as objective as possible; but of course a certain amount of subjective evaluation seems unavoidable in reference to the free or even semifree use of the language. Subjective evaluation of the speaking and writing skills can be made more objective by controlling content, using numerical evaluation scales, and relying on more than one judge. For the subjective evaluation of written output, it seems that the rights of students would be better protected if test papers are identified by student number only, not by name, thereby minimizing the possibility of conscious or unconscious discrimination.

Fair evaluation means also fair grading practices. The common practice of assigning grades according to fixed percentages of correct answers is quite indefensible except for those tests for which norms have been established. Without norms, whether 80 percent should be a C- or an A+ would depend entirely on whether the test is easy or difficult.

While daily quizzes with very small weight in the final course grade would require neither advance notice nor a preview of their content, the interests of the students would seem to demand that no significant test should hold surprises for them either in content or time of administration. The practice of testing, for example, what has not been emphasized in teaching seems unconscionable.

The contents of tests should correspond to the stated goals of the course and the program. It seems deplorable, for instance, that many programs claiming to be "oral" have mostly, or even exclusively, written tests. In oral programs, listening and speaking should be the basis for most of the course grade.

**XI.** *The right for each to proceed at his/her own best pace or, if that isn't possible, the right to supplementary remediation and enrichment activities as needed.*

As language students differ greatly in aptitude, ideally they should be allowed to proceed through the program at their own pace. This would eliminate boredom for the best students, which in lockstep instruction have to proceed much more slowly than they could, and discouragement for the weak students, who find themselves always falling behind.

Individualized programs, however, are not easy to establish and maintain, which means that, until computer-assisted instruction becomes widespread, all that most language programs will be able to offer to the students, in terms of their different abilities, is remediation or enrichment. This has of course been the informal practice of many teachers; but apparently there are still many programs were no formal effort is made to provide for individual student differences.

Since slow students would not benefit much from going over and over the main materials (they would tend to learn to answer from memory, not from manipulation of the crucial point), there should be supplementary remediation materials available to them, largely for individual study, which go over the same points but with a different selection of familiar vocabulary.

For the better students, individualized enrichment materials would be the answer; however, such materials should concentrate on cultural as opposed to linguistic enrichment, for if they result in the further improvement of the linguistic competence of these students the disparity in the classroom would be aggravated rather than reduced.

**XII.** *The right to have their views considered through periodic anonymous evaluations of teachers, courses, teaching methods and procedures, teaching materials, and the program as a whole.*

Central to this right is the view of the language student as a fairly informed *consumer* having certain legitimate preferences and capable of evaluating a "product," as opposed to the view of the student as an ignorant and inexperienced *child* who must blindly follow the lead of the teacher *qua* parent and superior.

Of course, children before the age of about twelve would lack the necessary maturity and cognitive ability to evaluate teachers, courses, etc. objectively. Furthermore, even mature college students and adults seem unable to be totally objective in these matters. However, most older students —especially college students— seem quite capable of producing *useful* evaluations. If nothing else, such student feedback helps to spot problems before they become serious and to take the necessary corrective measures. Seeking student views also helps to convey the idea that the teacher cares about them as thinking individuals.

Nevertheless, if teachers are going to be evaluated for salaries, promotions, etc. partly on the basis of student questionnaires, it seems that in order to protect the *teachers'* rights (they, too, have rights) the evaluation should be based on years of feedback, not just on one or a few courses. Moreover, perhaps more important than student feedback would be the *results* of the teachers' efforts, i.e., the degree of progress in performative knowledge attained by their students *over the years* as measured by standardized tests. Evaluation based on student feedback and performance, if properly used, could greatly help improve the effectiveness of language teaching.

# 3. Conclusion

It is hoped that the above discussion has not sounded too dogmatic —a danger when proposing something as legal-sounding as "rights." Underlying this proposal is my bias —by now well-known to the reader— in favor of enlightened eclecticism in language teaching.

Several of the rights in this "Bill of Rights" —namely I, II, III, X, XI, and XII, and to a lesser extent IV and VIII— apply to teaching in general or at least to certain school subjects other than second languages. I thought, however, that they should be included in "A Bill of Rights for Language Students," precisely because they are often violated in language programs.

My hope is that these language student "rights" will be considered for what they may be worth as postulates, i.e., as reasoned hypotheses, partly supported by research, on which useful discussion and further research can be based.

### Footnotes

[1]Politzer 1965:131, Duškova 1969, Buteau 1970, Tran-Thi-Chau 1975, Powell 1975, many more; Richards 1974:172-88 shows that even when a "noncontrastive" approach to error analysis is used, the majority of errors may turn out to be interlingual.
[2]Hocking 1973, Sheen 1980
[3]Politzer 1953, Hammerly 1971; there have been several others, some fairly recent.

# Appendix C: Sample Laboratory Oral Test

*The speaking skill can be tested even after only a few lessons by means of laboratory oral tests. (Of course, listening would also be emphasized from the start, so it should also be tested.) In the sample oral test given below, which was used successfully after four units of Bolinger's* Modern Spanish *[third edition, 1973], the students don't read anything —they just listen to instructions and cues and record their answers.*

*The Pronunciation Section asks the students to record their imitation (without pauses to think) of five very short sentences. Each of these sentences contains two pronunciation problems which have been practiced in class, but of course the students don't know which sounds are being scored in each sentence. Each sound in question is scored on a 0/1 basis, that is, either it is pronounced the way a native —any native— would pronounce it, or it is not. I have found that trying to give partial credit for partially correct pronunciations doesn't work —it makes the scoring very subjective and very difficult.*

*In this test, the Grammar Section consists of three drills designed to measure control over noun-adjective agreement, the choice between* ser/estar, *and the form and position of direct object pronouns. Other grammatical points could have been chosen, but it seems that more than three or four drills would be too much in a test of this kind. Between the cue and the response the students should be given a pause to think of the answer — about 7-10 seconds depending on the difficulty of the operation involved. The easiest way to score these drills is by assigning 1 point for the key part of each frame, although here partial deductions or partial credit would seem to make sense and to be more manageable.*

*By the end of the first semester of the program, if pronunciation has been properly taught, corrected, and tested, there shouldn't be any need to test it any further. On the other hand, the testing of the growing vocabulary becomes important. Among other ways, vocabulary can be tested by means of laboratory oral tests. It seems that the best way of doing this —best because it doesn't give the answers away and because it elicits specific answers— is to present short second language sentences for repetition and then cue lexical substitu-*

*tions in the native language. In other words, it is oral translation based on a second language model and native language cues. A second language sentence is the point of departure, so this is not translation in the old, traditional sense. Here also there should be a pause to think of the answer. Scoring is 1 point per correct lexical item used.*

*So far we have dealt only with discrete-point items. These tests contain also an integrative or global part, in the form of a Directed Dialogue Section. I believe that the ability to put sentences together in an accurate and meaningful way should be tested from quite early in the program. The Directed Dialogue Section presents a situation, describes the interlocutors, and gives directions on what to say in the simulated conversation. The directions are in the native language, but direct translation is impossible, as the directions are indirect and the required speech is direct. The pauses needed here by the students in order to put the sentence together in their minds would have to be about 10-12 seconds in duration. As here there can be several errors per sentence, scoring is based on the number of errors: 3 points for each sentence in which there are no errors or omissions, 2 points if the sentence contains one or two errors or omissions, 1 point if it contains three or four errors or omissions, and 0 point if it is worse or if there is no answer.*

*Together with a listening test, tests like the laboratory oral test presented below can give a very good idea of student progress in the early part of a program. Later reading sections, and finally writing sections can be added; but if these are used very early (not to speak of using them exclusively!) the students get the idea that the audio-oral skills are not too important in the program, and therefore will tend to neglect them.*

*Although an oral test like this one may take 20-25 minutes to administer, each student's responses can be scored in about three minutes. This is accomplished by excluding all instructions, pauses, etc., from the student recordings —the students are directed to record only their answers, all together, and to stop the tape recorders as soon as they have recorded their answers. Of course, with remote control at the laboratory console, this is a "cinch," but it can also be done quite well without it.*

*Note that all instructions and cues should be given twice. The possibility that a student might miss an item or even a whole section because he didn't quite hear an instruction or cue must be minimized.*

*Of course, giving tests like this one presupposes that the students have been working with recordings all along. It would be quite improper to give it to students who haven't done so, as they would be quite unfamiliar with the equipment and procedures. Even when students have been working with recordings, it is a good idea to give them a sample laboratory oral test before they take the first official one.*

# TEST AFTER UNIT 4

*(What the student hears appears between quotation marks. The crucial part of his answer —what is scored— appears in bold type.)*

## 1. PRONUNCIATION

"Record your imitation of the following phrases; there won't be a pause for you to think of the answer."

1. "¿Cuándo vamos?"
   ¿Cuándo **vamos?**............................... 0 1 2
2. "La clase de español."
   La clase **de** español........................... 0 1 2
3. "Es el señor López."
   Es el señor López............................. 0 1 2
4. "Tengo una hermana."
   Teng**o una h**ermana ........................... 0 1 2
5. "Me gusta la rubia."
   Me gust**a la** rubia ............................. 0 1 2

_____

/10

## 2. GRAMMAR

"Here you will have to provide answers to three drills. There will be a pause for you to think of each answer before you record it. Please don't speak during the pause to think. Record your answer immediately when you are instructed to."

"Drill No. 1. This is a correlation drill. Substitute the words given to you and produce the complete sentence, making all necessary changes."

"Repeat: La pluma es nueva."
La pluma es nueva.
"Now substitute: Los libros.........."
Los libros **son nuevos** ........................... 0 1
"Los libros son nuevos."
"Substitute: El cónsul...."
El cónsul **es nuevo**............................. 0 1
"El cónsul es nuevo."
"Substitute: Las alumnas...."
Las alumnas **son nuevas** ........................ 0 1
"Las alumnas son nuevas."

"Substitute: El tocadiscos...."
El tocadiscos **es nuevo**. . . . . . . . . . . . . . . . . . . . . . . . . . .    0 1
"El tocadiscos es nuevo."
"Substitute: La calle...."
La calle **es nueva**. . . . . . . . . . . . . . . . . . . . . . . . . . . . . . .    0 1
"La calle es nueva."

_____
/5

"Drill No. 2. This is a translation drill, but most of the Spanish words will be provided. Pay particular attention to the choice between _ser_ and _estar._"

"1. Olga is sick (now). Translate: Olga...enferma."
　　Olga **está** enferma. . . . . . . . . . . . . . . . . . . . . . . . . . . .    0 1
"2. The records are here: ...discos... aquí."
　　Los discos **están** aquí . . . . . . . . . . . . . . . . . . . . . . . . . .    0 1
"3. Julio is intelligent: ...inteligente."
　　Julio **es** inteligente  . . . . . . . . . . . . . . . . . . . . . . . . . . .    0 1
"4. María is my wife: ...mi esposa."
　　María **es** mi esposa . . . . . . . . . . . . . . . . . . . . . . . . . . . .    0 1
"5. The party is at the university: La fiesta... en la universidad."
　　La fiesta **es** en la universidad . . . . . . . . . . . . . . . . . . . . .    0 1

_____
/5

"Drill No. 3. Replace the nouns in the following sentences with direct object pronouns. Two examples from English: If you hear _I see the car_, you replace it with _I see it_; if you hear _We bought the apples_, you replace it with _We bought them_. Now the test continues:"

"1. Abrimos los libros."
**Los abrimos** . . . . . . . . . . . . . . . . . . . . . . . . . . . . . . . . . .    0 1
"Los abrimos."
"2. Quiero las tazas."
**Las quiero**. . . . . . . . . . . . . . . . . . . . . . . . . . . . . . . . . . . .    0 1
"Las quiero."
"3. Escuchas la música."
**La escuchas**. . . . . . . . . . . . . . . . . . . . . . . . . . . . . . . . . . .    0 1
"La escuchas."
"4. Pueden dejar el número."
**Pueden dejarlo** _or_ **Lo pueden dejar** . . . . . . . . . . . . . . . . . .    0 1
"Pueden dejarlo" _or_ "Lo pueden dejar."

"5. Ella deja el disco."
Ella **lo deja** .................................... 0 1
"Ella lo deja."

_____
/5

_____
/15

## 3. DIRECTED DIALOGUE

"In this part of the test you are to imagine that you are at a party and that Mr. Huerta is introducing you to his wife. You will be given instructions as to what to say in the ensuing conversation."
(Mr. Huerta:) "Quiero presentarle a mi esposa Luisa."
"Tell her that you're pleased to meet her."
Mucho gusto (Encantado/a) de (en) conocerla ........... 0 1 2 3
(Mrs. Huerta:) "Igualmente. ¿Usted es de aquí?"
"Reply that you are from Vancouver but live in Burnaby."
Soy de Vancouver, pero vivo en Burnaby ............... 0 1 2 3
(Mrs. Huerta:) "¿Conoce usted a la familia López?"
"Reply that you do, and that you're friends. Add that they live near your home."
Sí, somos amigos. Viven cerca de mi casa .............. 0 1 2 3
"Add that they have a very large and beautiful house."
Tienen una casa muy grande y (muy) bonita............. 0 1 2 3
"Add that you're planning to see them tomorrow."
Pienso verlos mañana .............................. 0 1 2 3

_____
/15

# Bibliography

# Bibliography

(Items preceded by an asterisk did not appear in the bibliography of *Synthesis in Second Language Teaching*)

*Acton, William. 1984. Changing Fossilized Pronunciation. *TESOL Quarterly* 18:71-84.

Asher, James J. 1977. *Learning Another Language Through Actions: The Complete Teacher's Guidebook* (Los Gatos, California: Sky Oaks Productions).

Bailey, Nathalie, Carolyn Madden, and Stephen D. Krashen. 1974. Is There a "Natural Sequence" of Adult Second Language Learning? *Language Learning* 24:235-43.

Bolinger, Dwight, et al. 1960. *Modern Spanish*, a project of the Modern Language Association of America; third edition, 1973 (New York: Harcourt Brace Jovanovich).

Bourque, Jane M. and Linda Chehy. 1976. Exploratory Language and Culture: A Unique Program. *Foreign Language Annals* 9:10-6.

Bowen, J. Donald. 1975. *Patterns of English Pronunciation* (Rowley, Mass.: Newbury House).

Bowen, J. Donald and Robert P. Stockwell. 1960. *Patterns of Spanish Pronunciation: A Drillbook* (Chicago: University of Chicago Press).

Brown, H. Douglas. 1980. *Principles of Language Learning and Teaching* (Englewood Cliffs, N.J.: Prentice-Hall).

Burstall, Clare, Monika Jamieson, Susan Cohen, and Margaret Hargreaves. 1974. *Primary French in the Balance* (Windsor, England: National Foundation for Educational Research).

Buteau, Magdelhayne F. 1970. Students' Errors and the Learning of French as a Second Language: A Pilot Study. *International Review of Applied Linguistics* 8:133-45.

Butzkamm, Wolfgang. 1973. *Aufgeklärte Einsprachigkeit: zur Entdogmatisierung der Methode im Fremdsprachenunterricht* (Heidelberg: Quelle und Mayer).

Carroll, John B. 1975. *The Teaching of French as a Foreign Language in Eight Countries* (New York: Wiley).

**Carroll, John B. and Stanley Sapon. 1959.** *Modern Language Aptitude Test* (New York: The Psychological Corporation).

**Carroll, John B. and Stanley Sapon. 1967.** *Elementary Modern Language Aptitude Test* (New York: The Psychological Corporation).

**Cathcart, Ruth L. and Judy E.W.B. Olsen. 1976.** Teachers' and Students' Preferences for Correction of Classroom Conversation Errors. In John F. Fanselow and Ruth H. Crymes, eds., *On TESOL '76* (Washington, D.C.: Teachers of English to Speakers of Other Languages), 41-53.

**Chastain, Kenneth D. 1980.** Native Speaker Reaction to Instructor-Identified Student Second Language Errors. *Modern Language Journal* 64:210-6.

**\*Chomsky, Noam. 1957.** *Syntactic Structures* (The Hague: Mouton).

**\*Cooper, Thomas, Gilbert Jarvis, and Stephen Krashen. 1980.** Priorities: Research. In *Proceedings of the National Conference on Professional Priorities* (Hastings-on-Hudson, N.Y.: ACTFL), 70-1.

**Corder, S. Pit. 1973.** *Introducing Applied Linguistics* (Hammondsworth, England: Penguin Books).

**Curran, Charles A. 1976.** *Counseling-Learning in Second Languages* (Apple River, Ill.: Apple River Press).

**Delattre, Pierre. 1947.** A Technique of Aural-Oral Approach. *French Review* 20:238-50 and 311-24.

**\*Delisle, Helga. 1982.** Native Speaker Judgement and the Evaluation of Errors in German. *Modern Language Journal* 66:39-48.

**Dulay, Heidi C. and Marina K. Burt. 1974.** Errors and Strategies in Child Second Language Acquisition. *TESOL Quarterly* 8:129-36.

**\*Dulay, Heidi C., Marina Burt, and Stephen Krashen. 1982.** *Language Two* (New York: Oxford University Press).

**Dušková, Libuše. 1969.** On Sources of Errors in Foreign Language Learning. *International Review of Applied Linguistics* 7:11-36.

**\*Ensz, Kathleen Y. 1982.** French Attitudes Toward Speech Errors. *Modern Language Journal* 66:133-9.

**Fries, Charles C. 1945.** *Teaching and Learning English as a Foreign Language* (Ann Arbor, Mich.: University of Michigan Press).

**Gagné, Robert M. 1977.** *The Conditions of Learning*, third edition (New York: Holt, Rinehart and Winston).

**Galloway, Vicki B. 1980.** Perceptions of the Communicative Efforts of American Students of Spanish. *Modern Language Journal* 64:428-40.

**Gattegno, Caleb. 1972.** *Teaching Foreign Languages in Schools: The Silent Way*, second edition (New York: Educational Solutions).

**\*Genesee, Fred. 1982.** French Immersion Programs. In Stan M. Shapson et al. 1982:25-38.

**Gomes de Matos, Francisco. 1980.** A Case for Selective Listening. *Linguistic Reporter 23,1:14.*

**Guntermann, Gail. 1978.** A Study of the Frequency and Communicative Effects of Errors in Spanish. *Modern Language Journal* 62:249-53.

**Hammerly, Hector. 1964.** A Study of the Spanish Spoken by a Bilingual Child. Unpublished manuscript, University of Texas at Austin.

**Hammerly, Hector. 1970.** And Then They Disbelieved Their Ears. *Hispania* 53:72-5.

**Hammerly, Hector. 1971.** Student Preference Between a Traditional and an Oral Approach to the Teaching of Spanish. *Hispania* 54:100-2.

**Hammerly, Hector. 1974.** *The Articulatory Pictorial Transcriptions: New Aids to Second Language Pronunciation* (Blaine, Wash.: Second Language Publications).

**Hammerly, Hector. 1974-b.** Primary and Secondary Associations with Visual Aids as Semantic Conveyors. *International Review of Applied Linguistics* 12:119-25.

**\*Hammerly, Hector. 1982.** *Synthesis in Second Language Teaching: An Introduction to Linguistics* (Blaine, Wash.: Second Language Publications).

**\*Hammerly, Hector, 1984.** Contextualized Visual Aids (Filmstrips) as Conveyors of Sentence Meaning. *International Review of Applied Linguistics* 22:87-94.

**\*Hammerly, Hector and Edward R. Colhoun. 1984.** Rational Multiple-Choice Cloze and Progress Testing. *Hispania* 67:411-5.

**Harley, Birgit and Merrill Swain. 1977.** An Analysis of the Spoken French of Five French Immersion Pupils. *Working Papers on Bilingualism* 14:31-46.

**Harley, Birgit and Merrill Swain. 1978.** An Analysis of the Verb System Used by Young Learners of French. *Interlanguage Studies Bulletin* 3:35-79.

**Harris, Brian. 1978.** The Difference Between Natural and Professional Translation. *Canadian Modern Language Review* 34:417-27.

**\*Higgs, Theodore V. and Ray Clifford. 1982.** The Push Toward Communication. In Theodore V. Higgs, ed., *Curriculum, Competence, and the Foreign Language Teacher*, ACTFL Foreign Language Education Series (Lincolnwood, Ill.: National Textbook Company), 57-79.

**Hocking, B.D.W. 1973.** Types of Interference. In John W. Oller, Jr. and Jack C. Richards, eds., *Focus on the Learner: Pragmatic Perspectives for the Language Teacher* (Rowley, Mass.: Newbury House), 88-95.

\*Hosenfeld, Carol. 1979. Cora's View of Learning Grammar. *Canadian Modern Language Review* 35:602-7.

Jakobovits, Leon A. 1970. *Foreign Language Learning: A Psycholinguistic Analysis of the Issues* (Rowley, Mass.: Newbury House).

James, Carl. 1980. *Contrastive Analysis* (London: Longman).

Jespersen, Otto. 1904. *How to Teach a Foreign Language* (London: Allen and Unwin).

\*Joos, Martin. 1967. *The Five Clocks* (New York: Harcourt Brace and World).

Kalivoda, Theodore B., Genelle Morain, and Robert J. Elkins. 1971. The Audio-Motor Unit: A Listening Comprehension Strategy that Works. *Foreign Language Annals* 4: 392-400.

Kelly, Louis G. 1969. *25 Centuries of Language Teaching* (Rowley, Mass.: Newbury House).

Krashen, Stephen D. 1981. *Second Language Acquisition and Second Language Learning* (Oxford: Pergamon Press).

\*Krashen, Stephen D. 1982. *Principles and Practice in Second Language Acquisition* (Oxford: Pergamon Press).

\*Krashen, Stephen D. 1984. Immersion: Why It Works and What It Has Taught Us. In H.H. Stern, ed. 1984:61-4.

\*Krashen, Stephen D. and Tracy C. Terrell. 1983. *The Natural Approach: Language Acquisition in the Classroom* (Oxford: Pergamon Press/Alemany Press).

\*Kuhn, Thomas S. 1962. *The Structure of Scientific Revolutions* (Chicago: University of Chicago Press).

Lado, Robert. 1957. *Linguistics Across Cultures: Applied Linguistics for Language Teachers* (Ann Arbor, Mich.: University of Michigan Press).

Lado, Robert. 1964. *Language Teaching: A Scientific Approach* (New York: McGraw-Hill).

Lado, Robert. 1970. Language, Thought, and Memory in Language Teaching: A Thought View. *Modern Language Journal* 54:580-5.

Lambert, Wallace E. and G. Richard Tucker. 1972. *Bilingual Education of Children: The St. Lambert Experiment* (Rowley, Mass.: Newbury House).

Lozanov, Georgi. 1978. *Suggestology and Outlines of Suggestopedy* (New York: Gordon and Breach Science Publishers).

\*Ludwig, Jeannette. 1982. Native Speaker Judgements of Second-Language Learners' Efforts at Communication: A Review. *Modern Language Journal* 66:274-83.

Mackey, William F. 1965. *Language Teaching Analysis* (London: Longmans).

*Marquez, Ely J. and J. Donald Bowen. 1983. *English Usage* (Rowley, Mass.: Newbury House).

Minn, Jay P. 1976. Clue-Searching: An Aid to Comprehension. In Renate A. Schulz, ed., *Teaching for Communication in the Foreign Language Classroom* (Skokie, Ill.: National Textbook Company), 93-100.

Moulton, William G. 1966. *A Linguistic Guide to Language Learning* (New York: Modern Language Association).

Nida, Eugene. 1957. *Learning a Foreign Language* (New York: Friendship Press).

Oller, John W., Jr. and Dean H. Obrecht. 1968. Pattern Drill and Communicative Activity: A Psycholinguistic Experiment. *International Review of Applied Linguistics* 6:165-74.

Palmer, Harold E. 1917. *The Scientific Study and Teaching of Languages* (London: Harrap). Reprinted in 1968 (London: Oxford University Press).

Pei, Mario. 1973. *How to Learn Languages and What Languages to Learn* (New York: Harper and Row).

*Pellerin, Micheline. 1984. Une évaluation de l'enseignement immersif: L'expression orale après 13 ans d'immersion francaise. Unpublished manuscript, Simon Fraser University.

Piazza, Linda G. 1980. French Tolerance for Grammatical Errors Made by Americans. *Modern Language Journal* 64:422-7.

Pimsleur, Paul. 1966. *Pimsleur Language Aptitude Battery* (New York: Harcourt Brace Jovanovich).

Pimsleur, Paul. 1980. *How to Learn a Foreign Language* (Boston: Heinle and Heinle).

Politzer, Robert L. 1953. Student Motivation and Interest in Elementary Language Courses. *Language Learning* 5:15-21.

Politzer, Robert L. 1965. *Teaching French: An Introduction to Applied Linguistics*, second edition (New York: Blaisdell).

Politzer, Robert L. 1978. Errors of English Speakers of German as Perceived and Evaluated by German Natives. *Modern Language Journal* 62:253-61.

Politzer, Robert L. 1980. Foreign Language Teaching and Bilingual Education: Research Implications. *Foreign Language Annals* 13:291-7.

*Popper, Karl. 1959. *The Logic of Scientific Discovery* (New York: Basic Books).

*Popper, Karl. 1972. *Objective Knowledge; an Evolutionary Approach* (Oxford: Clarendon Press).

Powell, Patricia B. 1975. Moi Tarzan, vous Jane? A Study of Communicative Competence. *Foreign Language Annals* 8:38-42.

**\*Premack, D. 1962.** Reversibility of the Reinforcement Relation. *Science* 136:255-7.

**Richards, Jack C. 1974.** *Error Analysis: Perspectives on Second Language Learning* (London: Longman).

**Rivers, Wilga M. 1976.** *Speaking in Many Tongues: Essays in Foreign-Language Teaching,* expanded second edition (Rowley, Mass.: Newbury House).

**\*Rivers, Wilga M. 1981.** *Teaching Foreign-Language Skills,* second edition (Chicago: University of Chicago Press).

**Scherer, George A. C. and Michael A. Wertheimer. 1964.** *A Psycholinguistic Experiment in Foreign-Language Teaching* (New York: McGraw-Hill).

**Schumann, John H. 1976.** Second Language Acquisition: The Pidginization Hypothesis. *Language Learning* 26:391-408.

**Schumann, John H. 1978.** The Acculturation Model for Second-Language Acquisition. In Rosario C. Gingras, ed., *Second Language Acquisition and Foreign Language Teaching* (Arlington, Va.: Center for Applied Linguistics), 27-50.

**Selinker, Larry. 1972.** Interlanguage. *International Review of Applied Linguistics* 10:209-31.

**Selinker, Larry, Merrill Swain, and Guy Dumas. 1975.** The Interlanguage Hypothesis Extended to Children. *Language Learning* 25:139-52.

**\*Shapson, Stan M., Vincent D'Oyley, and Ann Lloyd, eds. 1982.** *Bilingualism and Multiculturalism in Canadian Education* (Vancouver, B.C.: University of British Columbia).

**Sheen, Ronald. 1980.** The Importance of Negative Transfer in the Speech of Near-Bilinguals. *International Review of Applied Linguistics* 18:105-19.

**Smith, Philip D., Jr. 1970.** *A Comparison of the Cognitive and Audiolingual Approaches to Foreign Language Instruction: The Pennsylvania Foreign Language Project* (Philadelphia: Center for Curriculum Development).

**\*Snelbecker, Glenn E. 1974.** *Learning Theory, Instructional Theory, and Psychoeducational Design* (New York: McGraw-Hill).

**Spilka, Irène V. 1976.** Assessment of Second-Language Performance in Immersion Programs. *Canadian Modern Language Review* 32:543-61.

**Steiner, Florence. 1975.** *Performing with Objectives* (Rowley, Mass.: Newbury House).

**\*Stern, H.H. 1983.** *Fundamental Concepts of Language Teaching* (New York: Oxford University Press).

*Stern, H.H., ed. 1984. *The French Immersion Phenomenon*, Special Issue (No. 12) of *Language and Society*.

Strasheim, Lorraine A. 1981. Establishing a Professional Agenda for Integrating Culture into K-12 Foreign Languages: An Editorial. *Modern Language Journal* 65:67-9.

Swain, Merrill. 1978. Home-School Language Switching. In Jack C. Richards, ed., *Understanding Second and Foreign Language Learning: Issues and Approaches* (Rowley, Mass.: Newbury House), 238-50.

Sweet, Henry. 1899. *The Practical Study of Languages* (London: J.M. Dent and Sons). Reprinted in 1964 (London: Oxford University Press).

*Tatto, Mabel A. 1983. A Comparative Analysis of Grammatical Errors in the Written Code Between Grade Eleven Immersion French and Grade Eleven Core French. Unpublished M.A.T.F. Project, Simon Fraser University.

Taylor, Harvey M. 1981. Learning to Listen in English. *TESOL Quarterly* 15:41-50.

Terrell, Tracy C. 1977. A Natural Approach to Second Language Acquisition and Learning. *Modern Language Journal* 61:325-7.

Thorndike, Edward L., Elsie O. Bregman, J. Warren Tilton, and Ella Woodyard. 1928. *Adult Learning* (New York: Macmillan).

Titone, Renzo. 1968. *Teaching Foreign Languages: An Historical Sketch* (Washington, D.C.: Georgetown University Press).

Tran-Thi-Chau. 1975. Error Analysis, Contrastive Analysis, and Students' Perception: A Study of Difficulty in Second Language Learning. *International Review of Applied Linguistics* 13:119-43.

Tucker, G. Richard and Alison d'Anglejan. 1972. An Approach to Bilingual Education: The St. Lambert Experiment. In Merrill Swain, ed., *Bilingual Schooling: Some Experiences in Canada and the United States* (Toronto, Ontario: The Ontario Institute for Studies in Education), 15-21.

*Widdowson, Henry G. 1978. *Teaching Language as Communication* (London: Oxford University Press).

*Widdowson, Henry G. and Christopher J. Brumfit. 1981. Issues in Second Language Syllabus Design. In James E. Alatis, Howard B. Altman, and Penelope M. Alatis, eds., *The Second Language Classroom: Directions for the 1980's* (New York: Oxford University Press), 197-210.

Wilds, Claudia P. 1975. The Oral Interview Test. In Randall L. Jones and Bernard Spolsky, eds., *Testing Language Proficiency* (Arlington, Va.: Center for Applied Linguistics), 29-38.

Wilkins, David A. 1976. *Notional Syllabuses* (London: Oxford University Press).

Winitz, Harry, ed. 1981. *The Comprehension Approach to Foreign Language Instruction* (Rowley, Mass.: Newbury House).

# Index

# Index

**Accuracy:** 26, 36, 37, 38, 39, 57, 61, 63, 64, 66, 67, 68, 69, 71, 72, 77, 95, 96, 103, 105, 116, 120, 124, 127, 130, 141, 155, 158, 170, 196, 197, 203, 204, 209, 210, 214, 215.

**Acquisitionist Theory:** 15, 21-3, 26, 40-1, 42, 181.

**Age:** 34-5, 40, 106-7, 116, 128, 183, 201-2.

**Analogy:** 88, 120.

**Analysis:** 88, 120.

**Anxiety:** 106, 182.

**Approach:** 112.

**Aptitude:** 104, 114, 117, 123, 141, 176, 219.

**Army Method:** 16.

**Associations:** 86-7, 89, 90, 94, 99, 103, 106, 123, 175, 176, 180, 205.

**Attention:** 91-2.

**Attitudes:** 104.

**Audiolingual Method:** 15, 16, 19, 65, 113, 168, 178, 195, 206, 215.

**Audio-oral skills:** 65-6, 73, 74.

**Audio-Visual Method:** 15, 168-9.

**Axiom:** 5.

**Behaviorist psychology:** 16-7, 159, 212.

**Bilingual(ism):** 34, 36, 37, 41, 52, 66, 76, 91, 100, 124-5, 129, 155, 171-2, 174, 175, 176, 178, 179, 180, 184, 204-5, 212.

**CA-OB Method:** 171-82.

**Centrifugal learning:** 25-6, 39, 60, 61, 130, 154-5.

**Centripetal learning:** 25-6, 36-7, 39, 154-5.

**Classroom:** 186-7, 214-5.

**Classroom "pidgins":** 19, 25, 31, 33, 34, 36, 37, 41, 42, 155, 159, 167, 196, 201, 204, 205, 208, 214, 215.

**Cloze tests:** 141.

**Cognition:** 81-2, 83, 84, 89, 103, 120, 123, 160, 167, 171, 201-2, 212.

**Cognitive Approach:** 17-8, 168, 175.

**Cognitive psychology:** 17-8, 159, 212.

**Cohesiveness and coherence:** 136, 137.

**Communication:** 14, 19, 20, 21, 22, 23, 25, 36, 37, 39, 54, 55, 60, 61,